T0323016

KINSHIP, STATE FORMATION AND GOVERNANCE IN THE ARAB GULF STATES

Scott J. Weiner

EDINBURGH
University Press

Edinburgh University Press is one of the leading university presses in the UK. We publish academic books and journals in our selected subject areas across the humanities and social sciences, combining cutting-edge scholarship with high editorial and production values to produce academic works of lasting importance. For more information visit our website: edinburghuniversitypress.com

Edinburgh University Press Ltd
The Tun – Holyrood Road
12(2f) Jackson's Entry
Edinburgh EH8 8PJ

Typeset in 11/13 Adobe Garamond by
IDSUK (DataConnection) Ltd, and
printed and bound by CPI Group (UK) Ltd,
Croydon, CR0 4YY

A CIP record for this book is available from the British Library

ISBN 978 1 4744 8816 7 (hardback)
ISBN 978 1 4744 8818 1 (webready PDF)
ISBN 978 1 4744 8819 8 (epub)

CONTENTS

ILLUSTRATIONS

ACKNOWLEDGEMENTS

I wish to thank several individuals and institutions without which this book would not have been written. Without the consistent support of Ronnie Olesker and Richard Eichenberg at Tufts University I would not have completed an undergraduate thesis or pursued a doctorate in political science. Jamal al-Kirnawi introduced me to the world of Bedouin tribal politics. Kimberly Kagan provided invaluable advice on completing graduate studies that prepared me for the marathon of doctoral study. Along with Marisa Sullivan, she introduced me to the 'aggressive pursuit of knowledge' that defines rigorous scholarly research.

I am grateful to Marc Lynch and Mary Casey at the Project on Middle East Political Science for a Travel-Research-Engagement grant that convinced me of the importance of archival and interview fieldwork in political science. In preparation for my fieldwork, they offered advice, support and edits at a moment's notice for fellowship applications. Because of the support of Geri Rypkema and Eileen Lavelle at the Office of Graduate Student Assistantships and Fellowships at The George Washington University, I secured a David L. Boren Fellowship, which Michael Saffle at the Institute of International Education worked with me to complete. Ambassador Edward 'Skip' Gnehm graciously extended his kindness, advice and consistent support of my project on my behalf. I also thank Wendy Pearlman and Kanchan Chandra for their guidance in the early stages of the project. I received invaluable advice about fieldwork in the Arab Gulf region from Lama al-Humaidan, Samyah al-Foory and Zaid Darwish. Madeleine Wells Goldburt, whose friendship pre-dated my graduate study, provided advice and constant intellectual, logistical and emotional support before, during and long after my time in the region.

In Kuwait, I completed fieldwork with the support of the Center for Gulf Studies at the American University of Kuwait (AUK). Farah al-Nakib was a supervisor who quickly became a personal mentor. Noura Qasem provided invaluable support throughout my first semester at AUK. I was granted the opportunity to present my preliminary findings to AUK students through Pellegrino Luciano and Hesham al-Awadhi, both of whom also offered research support and mentorship during my time in Kuwait and thereafter. Emanuela Buscemi played a fundamental role in shaping my research agenda as a scholar interested in the politics of identity. Both she and Roberto Fabbri were wonderful colleagues. I am also grateful for my brief overlap with Shea Garrison and Susan Kennedy at the Center for Gulf Studies.

The students of AUK who supported this project are too numerous to name. They were generous, selfless, patient, and often courageous to sit with me for hours at a time discussing their lives, experiences, families, and hopes for the future. Some opened their homes to me or provided invaluable research support. Others were supportive of my efforts to improve my Arabic speaking. Their enthusiasm and passion are an asset to Kuwait and speak well of its future leaders.

Several individuals in Kuwait provided invaluable access to written materials on Kuwait's history. I am deeply thankful for access to the library at the Center for Research and Studies of Kuwait (CRSK). Abdullah al-Ghuneim took time from his busy schedule to meet with me and provided important direction for my studies at CRSK. Amal Salah Berekaa's extensive knowledge of the Center's holdings made doing research there a pleasure. I am also grateful to Talaal al-Rameedhi of the Kuwait Writers Association, Hamza Alayan at the al-Qabas Archives, the staff of the Gulf and Arabian Peninsula Studies Archives at Kuwait University, and Thomas Cherian Kutty and the library staff at AUK.

Several people opened their homes and families to me during my stay in Kuwait. This hospitality was not only an important part of my research, but the basis of personal relationships and a sense of belonging despite being thousands of miles from home. Mishary al-Fares brought me to weddings, funeral observances, and many other family gatherings. The al-Barrack family were deeply supportive of my work and provided critical evidence for my findings. Dhari al-Wazzan, Ahmed Issa, Hamed al-Saeed, Siham Nuseibeh and Ahmed Arafat all showed me a level of hospitality and kindness to which I was by no means entitled. I am particularly grateful to Ahmed Bin Barjas for his willingness to share his deep knowledge of Kuwaiti tribal politics and help connect me with his extensive network of tribal sheikhs and influential leaders. His books on Kuwait tribal history were an important guide for my research and an invaluable asset for any scholar of Kuwaiti tribal politics. I also wish to thank his nephew Fares Ali Barjas who provided helpful translation support during interviews.

Dana al-Otaibi, formerly of the British Embassy in Kuwait, blew me away with her knowledge of Kuwait and its politics. I was also fortunate in Kuwait to have the unrelenting support of Rivka Azoulay, who has since become a dear friend.

The development of my project in Kuwait was advanced by conversations with experts and scholars who generously shared with me their intricate knowledge of the country. These included Talal al-Saeed, Saleh al-Nafisi, Saud al-Enizi, Rania Maktabi, Ghanem al-Najjar, Lubna Alkazi Yagoub al-Kandari, Mohammed al-Bogaili, Dhari al-Jutaili and Kristen Kao. I was also deeply privileged to discuss my work with John Peterson, who provided important comparative perspectives between Kuwait and Oman.

In Oman, my research benefitted immensely from academic conversations with Marike Botenbal, Heba Aziz, Corien Hoek, Crystal Ennis and Raid al-Jamali. I also benefitted greatly from discussions with Mohammed al-Muqadam, Ahmed al-Mukheini and Abdullah al-Ghafri. Said al Rahbi at the Oman Studies Center at Sultan Qaboos University was beyond hospitable, as were the staff of the library at the University of Nizwa. Julia al-Zadjali of the Centre for Omani Dress also provided important cultural context to my work.

I am grateful for the support of Khalfan Al-Abri'e at the Omani Ministry of Heritage and Culture, as well as Nasser al-Rawashie and Nabil al-Khanjeri of the Ministry of Regional Municipalities and Water Resources. I also wish to thank Al-Shaima Al-Raisi of the Muscat Municipal Council and Batul al-Lawati of the Embassy of the United States in Oman.

I am grateful to the staff of Hala FM for their friendship and kindness. The students of Sultan Qaboos University, The University of Nizwa, German University of Technology and the Higher College of Technology in al-Khuweir took time from their studies to speak with me about their lives, experiences and impressions. I am grateful for their willingness to help and inspired by their dedication to the betterment of Oman. Finally, I wish to thank Rafiah al-Talei whose guidance and advice at multiple points throughout the project has been instrumental in my understanding of contemporary Oman.

I recognise a deep debt of gratitude to all of my interviewees, who graciously performed the labour of explaining the society and politics in which they live to an outsider. While their names are protected by confidentiality, I have tried to write a book that encapsulates the breadth and depth of their insights about their expertise, knowledge and experience. I have tried to honour their hospitality, kindness and generosity by representing their statements with an awareness of my positionality and in a way that furthers scholarly understandings of the Arabian peninsula.

Early drafts of this project were improved thanks to feedback from the Comparative Politics Workshop at The George Washington University Political Science Department and the Dissertation Workshop at the Institute for Middle East Studies at the Elliott School of International Affairs. Harris Mylonas, Evgeny Finkel and Eric Kramon provided important feedback, and I am also grateful to Stephen Hanson for his highly informed Weberian theoretical perspective. I also thank Keith Darden of American University for his useful comments and feedback. Finally, Dina Bishara, Jessica Anderson and Dillon Stone Tatum were patient, insightful and encouraging in numerous conversations.

Kristin Smith Diwan was and remains an invaluable source of insight on Arab Gulf politics, and I am forever indebted to her for the mentorship she has provided me and other junior scholars in the field. Her assistance was critical for facilitating my attendance at the 2017 Gulf Research Meeting and I deeply appreciated the opportunity to attend.

While many panelists, discussants and chairs provided important feedback for this project at conferences, I am particularly grateful to Mary Ann Tetrault for her guidance and support. Professor Tetrault's foundational work on the Gulf and mentorship as a scholar will long endure among scholars studying the Gulf region and her loss is felt deeply in the field. I am also grateful to Amaney Jamal for helping me improve the methodological robustness of this book. Finally, I thank Jessie Moritz for her friendship and willingness to share her expertise on Oman, and Andrew Leber for his engagement on politics in the broader Gulf context.

During my doctoral studies I benefitted immensely from the guidance of Nathan Brown, a true scholar whose advice, support and guidance sets the standard for mentorship in political science. Marc Lynch consistently pushed me toward greater methodological rigour and taught me to analyse with an eye toward the bigger picture. Henry Hale responded to any research obstacle I presented with a host of solutions and a relentless sense of optimism.

Countless friends, including many members of the Middle East Discussion Group of Young Professionals in Foreign Policy, have supported me throughout the process of writing this book.

I would like to thank Emma Rees, Louise Hutton and Eddie Clark at Edinburgh University Press for their thoughtful feedback, and for their care and attention to the manuscript. I am grateful for their patience navigating a first-time author through publishing across five time zones and during a global pandemic.

Most importantly, my family has also been a consistent source of support. All four of my grandparents have, in unique ways, inspired my interest in kinship and family and my dedication to completing a doctorate. I am thankful for their love and support. My uncle, Professor Herbert Golden of Boston University, inspired me with his love of language and commitment to the academic profession. My two sisters have kept me grounded during the writing process as only siblings can, but continue to be inspiring in their own fields of work and study. I thank my parents for the educational opportunities, support and encouragement they have given me throughout my life. Finally, I am forever grateful to my wife Allie for her patience the many days and nights book writing took me away from activities more enjoyable during a pandemic lockdown. Her boundless curiosity, unrelenting humour and deep personal strength have kept me grounded.

1

INTRODUCTION:
A SYSTEMATIC INQUIRY INTO
KINSHIP POLITICS

State formation ends with the state but begins with the society. In the colonised Middle East, Western states shaped the mediation of power, choosing leaders and creating the bureaucratic blueprints for states. The mixed success of these projects – from the colonial perspective – has been highly instructive for scholars of state formation, political economy, and authoritarianism. In some cases, it has led some to question whether these polities are states at all. Egyptian diplomat Tahseen Bashir famously quipped that they were nothing more than 'tribes with flags'. Though the concept is quickly dismissed by many contemporary scholars of the region, there is no clear counter-concept. If these states are not tribes with flags, what are they? How do tribes interact with state bureaucracies, and why does this interaction vary across states?

The inability to answer these questions satisfactorily is a result of research which has centred the politics of colonial actors rather than those of the societies they colonised. Scholars explain the strong role of tribes in the Arab Gulf states as a function of the state capacity of national governments and their ability to co-opt these groups, often following a surge in revenue from the sale of oil. Such an explanation is not entirely misguided, as states themselves are clearly a key element in state formation. However, our focus on the state has elided the complex and sophisticated power dynamics that pre-date it. The discovery of oil in the region was a critical juncture of Gulf politics but not a clean break from the ways societies in the region managed their affairs in the past. In order to understand the states that emerged from this period, we must first stop writing the societies of the Arab Gulf states out of their own politics.

Tribes, clans, bands and other kinship hierarchies affect the distribution of access to power and resources in states. Whether in the Middle East, Africa, Latin America, or elsewhere, these hierarchies play an integral role in state–society relations. Despite their prevalence, however, few analyses in political science take on the question of where kinship hierarchies fit into the ecosystem of state–society relations. Further complicating things, the placement of kinship hierarchies differs in meaningful ways from case to case.

This book addresses why the political salience of kinship authority varies in contemporary states. The term 'kinship' refers to the genuine belief between individuals in descent from a common ancestor. Kinship is an identity. It is the basis upon which people in certain societies associate to gain access to power and resources. These kinship groups are hierarchical, which makes them inherently useful for politics.[1] Hierarchies generate a certain authority. Because of this authority, kinship hierarchies have political salience, albeit to varying degrees. This book explains the variation in the political salience of these hierarchies.

Kinship politics are not the relic of a pre-colonial past. Despite structural differences between them, hierarchical kinship groups exist on every continent that humans inhabit. From South America to Africa to Central Asia to the Middle East, these hierarchies are political institutions that shape people's lives in important ways. Additionally, kinship hierarchies play an active role in state governance at all levels of power. Kinship politics can even impact who is appointed head of state. Uzbekistan's clans, for example, have a major effect on determining who sits in a leadership position in the country. Kinship politics can also determine who is elected to parliament. Venezuela has reserved parliamentary seats for indigenous tribal members and has a tribal political party – the National Council of Venezuelan Indians. Eight members of Botswana's House of Chiefs are appointed from the country's major tribes. Kinship in these states also can determine who runs regional councils, which constituencies are favoured by the government, and who has the ear of these various power holders. While there may be region-specific features of kinship hierarchies, the existence of such hierarchies is not itself regionally specific. Rather, kinship hierarchies actively shape the politics of states and societies the world over.

While it is a common element of state governance, social science still tends to treat kinship as unworthy or incapable of being understood through rigorous systematic analysis. There is some scholarly consensus over the idea that kinship politics is based on constructed identities that provide some sort of material gain. However, few accounts have rigorously studied how kinship politics work and how these dynamics shape state-level political outcomes.

Scholars have instead tended to think of kinship groups in terms of other constructs more common in contemporary Western states, ignoring the pervasiveness of kinship groups elsewhere. Some treat these groups as patronage networks to show how states maintain loyalty through payoffs. Others describe kinship groups as functionally equivalent to ethnic groups to explain intra-state conflict or cooperation. Still others model tribes as electoral constituencies to explain election outcomes and patterns of parliamentary control.

Despite the casual leverage many of these models offer, kinship groups differ from patronage networks, ethnic groups, and electoral constituencies in important ways. Patronage networks are based, ultimately, on material gain. Yet kinship groups combine material incentives with a politics of identity that a functional approach does not fully explain. Kinship groups resemble ethnic groups in certain respects – for example, in their role as descent-based identity groups. However, the intimately personal nature of kinship differs starkly from the bonds of co-ethnicity. Kinship groups are certainly important to electoral outcomes.[2] However, the effects of kinship politics in states go beyond who is elected to a national parliament.

Kinship groups share commonalities with other kinds of groups. However, studying kinship groups in *terms* of these other constructs essentialises kinship and leaves its conceptual core unexplored. It allows scholars to deploy kinship as a variable without truly accounting for the full extent of its explanatory leverage. What is it about kinship that allows it to behave sometimes like a patronage network, sometimes like an ethnic group, and sometimes like an electoral constituency? Given the pervasiveness of kinship groups across states, and the broad effects they have on state governance, better defining the conceptual core of kinship and linking it to causal outcomes is an important scholarly endeavour.

A lack of rigorous attention to kinship politics is more than just a conceptual blind spot. It prevents the understanding of fundamental questions about how states work. Max Weber contends in *Politics as a Vocation* that 'the state is a relation of men dominating men . . . If the state is to exist, the dominated must obey the authority claimed by the powers that be.'[3] While social scientists have qualified this somewhat stark claim for decades, we have much to gain from better theorising how authority works when it is shared within the state. A better conceptualising of kinship sets the groundwork for a stronger understanding of this concept in the many states where kinship groups exist and matter in politics. It may also allow scholars to better predict when bureaucratic authority will control a certain aspect of governance, and when kinship authority will control that same aspect. These predictions can improve our understanding of how the state maintains authority within its borders.

The lack of sufficient attention to kinship politics also leaves puzzling questions unanswered. We would expect that states prefer their own bureaucratic means of authority, yet in practice states seem to preserve kinship authority even when it is not in their evident interest to do so. Some states bring kinship hierarchies within the formal governing apparatus, but others use them informally to distribute patronage. Our existing accounts cannot explain why these differences emerge. They treat these differences as uninteresting even though they drive at fundamental issues of governance and the state's control of power within its borders. They also indicate that important processes are occurring during state building that merit further interrogation. What are these processes and how do they constrain state building to produce different outcomes? *What explains variation in the political salience of kinship authority?*

Overview of the Theory

The political salience of kinship authority varies based on the historic ways in which sets of kinship groups in non-urban areas accessed vital limited resources. States are the main actors during state building, but their actions are constrained by conditions before state building in non-urban areas of the state.

Access to vital limited resources can be either competitive or cooperative. In some cases, a set of kinship groups are in competition for access to and control of these resources. The most typical case where competitive access exists is when a set of migratory kinship groups seek access to resources dispersed throughout a territory. This set of kinship groups may have ad hoc institutions that settle disputes as they arise, and they may also have certain norms that shape relations between groups. However, there is no permanent institution that holds authority above all these groups. Since each group acts more or less independently, the state must engage each group individually during state building. As the state engages these groups as kinship groups, it enshrines the importance of kinship identity in the relationship between members of that group and the state. Group members have an incentive to continue using kinship as a means of obtaining resources and access. The state benefits from pre-existing durable institutions of authority. At the end of state building where these conditions are present, kinship authority will have governing political salience, determining access to resources and power in the state.

In other cases, access to vital limited resources is cooperative; this means that a set of kinship groups coordinate in order to gain access to vital limited resources. The most typical case where cooperative access exists is when a set of settled kinship groups seek access to a resource concentrated within a territory. Given the repeated interactions these settled groups have, conditions exist for cooperation between them and the establishment of institutions that have power beyond the individual tribe. These institutions, which we can refer to as *proto-bureaucracies*, are not as extensive as full ministries, but they are bureaucratic in the sense that their staff includes individuals with expertise on how the proto-bureaucracy itself operates. They also have expertise on the management of access itself. Because states are incentivised to reach out to proto-bureaucracies during state building, they can use proto-bureaucracies as the basis for local branches of national ministries. Since bureaucratic governance is now an effective means of resource access, members of kinship groups are more likely to use it to obtain these resources. As a result, kinship authority in such cases will have instrumentalised salience, allocating resources and power within the parameters set by the bureaucratic state.

Governing and instrumentalised salience each describe a set of outcomes, but they speak as categories to meaningful and observable differences in statecraft and the provision of resources. Governance occurs in fundamentally different ways when kinship authority has governing versus instrumentalised political salience. In the former, the independent power of kinship authority represents an institution that the state must constantly manage and negotiate. In the latter, kinship authority is embedded into the state apparatus and requires less management and negotiation. Questions of kinship authority, therefore, drive at the fundamental nature of state governance and the relationship between the state and its population.

This book examines states that pursue a certain kind of state building. These states share a common experience, but not one that is universal to every case of state building where kinship groups held authority beforehand. This common experience is characterised by the imposition of impersonal governance. Following this imposition, the state uses three elements in sequence to build up the state: infrastructure, bureaucracy and nationalism. First, the state creates infrastructure in order to gain control over the provision of resources. It then uses this infrastructure not only as a means to distribute resources but as a means of extending bureaucratic governance. Electric lines provide electricity to homes, for example, but that provision can then be taxed and regulated by the bureaucratic state. To further incentivise buy-in to the state-building project, the state creates a nationalist idiom. Nationalism acts as a force multiplier for state building, creating incentives for people to buy into the state-building project on top of the incentive of better infrastructure. This pattern of state building reflects a particular analytical scope but is common to states in the Middle East as well as Central Asia. The basis of the model, furthermore, draws upon scholarly accounts of state building from around the world. The empirical analysis of this book draws upon cases from the Arab Gulf states, using Kuwait, Qatar and Oman as a most common case comparison of kinship authority. While kinship authority was important in all three states prior to state building, differences between them emerged such that after state building, kinship authority had governing salience in Kuwait and Qatar and instrumentalised salience in Oman. Given similar starting conditions, this difference in salience after state building is puzzling.

Alternative Explanations

Patterns of access to vital limited resources is the most important factor constraining the political salience of kinship authority. State building is a process involving the convergence of many variables in a particular way. However, other variables play a role as well. Considering the explanatory power of these variables is useful for defining exactly what resource access patterns can and cannot explain. It also creates a benchmark for judging whether the theory presented here is an improvement over existing models.

Culture

Some anthropological accounts investigate kinship through the lens of culture. These accounts would contend that kinship is an ideological construct or idiom that shifts over time. The history, traditions and customs surrounding kinship are therefore what shape its salience in states.[4] While such approaches have greatly informed constructivist approaches to kinship, they exhibit shortcomings for variable-driven political science research for three reasons. Firstly, culture is often an ill-defined variable that means different things in different accounts. This variation makes comparative analysis difficult, hampering research agendas in both political science and anthropology.[5] As used by scholars, culture is often an amalgamation of several variables that sometimes give theoretical models less analytical leverage than more specific variables. This specificity carries extra importance in a Middle Eastern context where scholars have used cultural explanations in orientalist ways, suggesting that corruption, low mobilisation, or a preponderance of violent conflict are inherent to Arab or Middle Eastern culture. Second, culture as an explanation can create endogeneity in a causal argument. Kinship has governing or instrumentalised salience because of culture, but culture is often defined in terms that relate closely to the salience of kinship. This conceptual closeness increases the risk of circular argumentation. Finally, even when examining cases with a similar 'culture' of kinship, differences in the political salience of kinship authority still emerge. As such, culture as a variable cannot sufficiently explain variation in the political salience of kinship authority.

Critical Approaches

Arguments grounded in critical approaches identify the role of colonialism and the imperial desires of Western colonial states to subjugate non-Western populations. The interaction between kinship and bureaucratic authority in such accounts is framed as one of domination. Colonial states imposed bureaucratic governance onto kinship groups that were ultimately powerless to prevent it. Where the domination of states over kinship groups was successful, kinship authority has instrumentalised salience. Where it was not successful, kinship authority has governing salience. Critical perspectives construct important counter-narratives to Western accounts of colonialism. However, the details of many of these narratives are not borne out in reality. Colonial powers shaped the politics of many states, but empirical evidence suggests that kinship groups were not passive actors in the process. In addition, the argument that kinship groups themselves lacked political agency plays into the same narratives that served to oppress them in the first place, feeding orientalist narratives that focus solely on the agency of colonising states while ignoring the agency of those colonised. While there is substantial evidence that colonial states oppressed kinship groups, there is also copious evidence that these kinship groups retained political agency. Accurate models of the salience of kinship must take this agency into account.

Patrimonialism

Patrimonialist arguments describe a linkage between state and tribal distribution networks. Studies of the concept encompass considerations of kin ties, patron–client relations, personal allegiances, and combinations of all three.[6] Patrimonialism is a system in which 'the prince organizes his political power over extrapatrimonial areas and political subjects . . . just like the exercise of his patriarchal power'.[7] States use patrimonial ties to support the economic development of clientelist and corporatist groups within the state through business, welfare and social services.[8]

The basis of patrimonialism is the father–son relationship. Scholars argue that in patrimonial societies, leaders frame themselves as the 'father' of the national 'family'.[9] This template provides the basis for access to resources, but also inspires loyalty to the 'father' for reasons that go beyond purely rational considerations. In Kuwait, for example, citizens sometimes referred to Emir Sabah bin Ahmad al-Sabah as '*Baba Sabah*' or 'Papa Sabah'. Papa is an informal term of endearment that constructs the relationship between Kuwait's leadership and its citizens as patrimonial. Not all citizens use this title (others such as 'His Highness the Emir' connote no less respect), but practically all Kuwaitis understand to whom it refers.

Studies of patrimonialism often trace the concept from its origins in traditional rule into the bureaucratic state. Such systems exist throughout the Middle East, having been used historically in the Ottoman empire as well as Morocco and Iran.[10] However, patrimonialist accounts often contradict each other in describing its origins and effects. Some accounts argue that patrimonialism endures where the state fails to penetrate, but others contend that state penetration engineered by colonial powers made patrimonialism stronger.[11] This disagreement makes it difficult to evaluate hypotheses about the effects of patrimonialism on kinship endurance specifically. In addition, studies of patrimonialism do not delve into variations in the patrimonial relationship, or variations within kinship groups themselves. Patrimonialism is helpful in theorising the causal role of identity, but it is too broad an identity category to explain variation in kinship endurance. There are elements of the father–son relationship in kinship identity, but that is only one aspect of kinship. Neither patrimonialism nor the broader literature of state capacity account sufficiently for the full causal role of identity in the political salience of kinship authority.

In addition, African cases speak to a specific kind of patrimonial relationship. Colonial powers in Africa sought to exploit natural resources. This process, however, required a massive labour force that could work in mines or fields. Control of populations was key to the success of African colonial projects. These states, however, had different goals in other regions. In the Gulf, the primary objective was control of territory rather than control of people. While the possibility of exploiting oil resources became a larger motivation over time, this industry required an educated workforce in addition to able bodies. Since the role of populations differs across these cases, accounts of African patrimonialism and state capacity speak only partially to the experience of regions like the Gulf.

State Capacity

As opposed to cultural and the critical perspectives, state capacity arguments offer significant causal leverage, and are a viable alternative argument. State capacity refers to a state's ability to generate its preferred political outcomes. Scholars tend to measure this ability in terms of a state's military strength, bureaucratic strength, and quality of its political institutions.[12] Capacity itself is a function of physical resources and political authority. States with the resources and bureaucratic authority to enact their will within the state have high state capacity, while those that do not have low state capacity. State capacity arguments – and arguments closely related to them – are well grounded in the comparative politics literature. They have the potential to explain many interactions between states and societies. However, they cannot account fully for variation in the salience of kinship.

State capacity arguments focus on the limited capacity of the state to extend its bureaucratic means of governance to all areas within its borders. States operate under bureaucratic authority rather than traditional kinship authority. During state building, states penetrate from the centre into non-urban areas of the state. For example, in many African cases, 'the penetration of colonial powers into the interior of Africa brought in its train the forces of the market and the state'. This penetration created a 'means whereby the members of a group [could] coerce themselves; and . . . attain the capacity for collusive behavior'.[13] The linkages between state and countryside explain the autonomy, strength and coherence of African states.[14] In Northern Rhodesia, for example, British colonial authorities distributed resources via 'tribal' chiefs, incentivising affiliation with these leaders. The result was that such an affiliation became politically salient.[15] Along with infrastructure, they bring bureaucratic forms of governance. The ability to penetrate into these areas, however, requires the capacity to obtain and organise resources, transport them, install them, and incentivise people to use them. This process is not always successful. State building in Africa, for example, often suffered from the state's lack of capacity to extend into the periphery.[16] It could thus be the case that states with strong capacity would be ones in which kinship hierarchies are embedded into the state apparatus. In contrast, weaker states lacking the capacity to embed kinship hierarchies would see these groups endure independently of the state apparatus. Essentially, the state must negotiate in such cases with – or around – these actors to gain authority in a given area.

Since it is the state that conducts state building, its role as a causal agent is critical. As the name of the concept implies, states design, execute, and allocate revenue for the process of state building. Existing accounts, furthermore, have shown that states have the ability to shape identities. Schools give states the capacity to inculcate nationalist values. Urban planning gives states the ability to impact the salience of geographic identities in the state. The state's agency is thus a crucial component of the state-building process. The shortcoming of state capacity as an explanation however, is that it does not account for the power of kinship hierarchies, nor how the state invests the capacity it has in state building. State capacity is a necessary component of the state-building process, but as recent literature on the rentier state points out, capacity itself does not guarantee state building success or assent to rule from a population.[17]

Why Kinship Matters

Kinship hierarchies, all of which pre-date the state in the Arab Gulf context, were existing forms of authority with which states needed to contend. States did not merely penetrate into a vacuum of power. Rather, they encountered non-bureaucratic forms of authority whose means of assigning power differed from that of the state. Empirically, there exists evidence that states with sufficient strength to embed kinship hierarchies within the state bureaucracy did not do so. While kinship authority and its idioms may change over time, elements of the conceptual core of kinship were a major factor in this variation. State capacity arguments, by virtue of being state-centric, cannot account for this important part of the state-building equation.

Accounting for variation in kinship salience can help scholars to better understand the different ways in which tribes – or similar kinship groups – and states engage each other. This line of inquiry is important for four reasons. First, variation in the political salience of kinship identity indicates that different state bureaucracies administer their populations in different ways. Political science tends to treat these societies as virtually analogous but this is not the case. Some governments provide certain goods and access while others do not. These debates over state resource provision and interaction with sub-state groups are central in comparative politics, particularly in the literature of state formation.

Second, explanations of variation in kinship salience speak to contemporary debates over patronage politics and ethnic identity. Recent work on patronal politics and patronage networks highlights the importance of understanding resource access below the state level of analysis.[18] Kinship groups are one entity which engaged historically in this distribution. Furthermore, recent work on ethnic identity has opened new avenues for explaining the conditions under which such identities are politicised. The study of kinship salience compliments and adds to these research agendas by better theorising these conditions and the mechanisms by which kinship is the basis for patronage distribution.

Third, studying variation in the salience of kinship identity showcases the importance of society-level variables in a literature focused heavily on state actors. Existing accounts of kinship politics in bureaucratic states highlight colonial powers and state decision-making bodies as relevant variables. Yet other variables at the sub-state level may explain variation where such explanations fall short. The causal power of such variables ought to be explored if scholars seek a full understanding of state–society dynamics in such cases.

Finally, variation in the salience of kinship is not obviously explained by existing theories. This lack of explanation is not merely a conceptual gap to be filled. Rather, it indicates that a different conception of kinship altogether may be warranted. Existing theories either do not tackle kinship directly, or do so in a specific historical context (for example, African colonialism or the post-Soviet period). Theories that examine kinship and state formation tend to overgeneralise state–tribe relations, treating different cases as functionally the same. While all these explanations lay important groundwork, they do not explain why similar states see variation in the endurance of kinship after state building. Theories explaining variation in the success of nation building also lay important groundwork but speak to slightly different aspects of the state formation process. Political variables important to state building are under-theorized in the literature, and would improve our analytical leverage if better exposed.

Plan of the Book

Theories of state building are complex because they account for many elements over a long period of time. In order to present a parsimonious account of the state-building process, this book proceeds in stages. Each element of the theory is paired with an explanation of the empirical phenomena that demonstrate its validity.

Chapter 2 lays the foundation for the book by analysing the concept of kinship. It synthesises conceptual debates across academic disciplines to provide a useful working definition of the term. It argues that kinship is both a personal identity and a source of group durability. Both of these elements are critical for understanding how kinship groups gain access to resources. An overview of kinship in the Arab Gulf states anchors these theoretical concepts in empirical phenomena.

Chapter 3 introduces a theoretical model of kinship hierarchies' effects on state formation. It considers the underlying factors incentivising cooperative and competitive access to vital limited resources. It then shows how these differences in access shape the state's establishment of infrastructure, bureaucratic authority, and a national idiom. Referencing existing work on modernisation, state formation and nationalism, it offers a causal argument linking different patterns of resource access to different outcomes of kinship salience after state building.

Chapter 4 provides an empirical look at access to vital limited resources in Kuwait. Using archival evidence, government documents and interviews, it shows how Kuwait's kinship groups instrumentalised bureaucratic authority despite the government's creation of infrastructure, moving of non-urban populations onto that infrastructure, imposition of bureaucratic authority, and creation of buy-in for this authority through a nationalist idiom based on time.

Chapter 5 supplements the empirical analysis of Kuwait with an examination of kinship authority in Qatar. It shows that, like Kuwait, Qatar's kinship groups instrumentalised bureaucratic authority during state building despite the government's building up of public administration and engineering of settlement patterns. Similar to Kuwait, Qatar's nationalist idiom is temporal and kinship authority has governing salience.

Chapter 6 contrasts Kuwait to the case of Oman. In Oman, access to vital limited resources was cooperative rather than competitive. Omanis had already established proto-bureaucratic authority prior to state formation. The chapter uses similar archival, government and interview sources to show how Oman extended infrastructure and national networks to non-urban populations, subsumed existing bureaucratic infrastructure within the national state, and created buy-in for this project through a different nationalist idiom than Kuwait had used.

Chapter 7 introduces formally the concept of kinship salience and describes systematically how it is observable. Introducing systematic inquiry to the study of kinship salience, it provides a means of determining the difference between cases of governing and instrumentalised kinship salience. Applying this framework, it then assesses the salience of kinship in Kuwait's government and among its people. It leverages extensive interviews with academics, government officials, tribal leaders and students to provide a rich and detailed account of kinship politics in contemporary Kuwait. The chapter then contrasts Kuwait with Oman, where kinship authority has instrumentalised political salience after state building. Presenting a parallel comparison of government and society in Oman, the chapter draws on interviews with Omani academics, national and local government officials, policy experts, students and NGO leaders to provide an account of contemporary kinship politics in the Sultanate with an eye toward identifying similarities and differences with Kuwait. It concludes with an epilogue of kinship relations in contemporary Kuwait, Qatar and Oman, explaining the importance of historic patterns of resource access and the political salience of kinship authority to politics in the contemporary Arab Gulf. In particular, the chapter focuses on the role of kinship during protests that occurred in Kuwait and Oman in 2011. It sets out guidelines for analysts to identify significant trends in regional politics when and where they occur.

Chapter 8 considers the generalisability of its conclusions beyond the Arabian Peninsula with the cases of Somaliland and Iran. It then concludes the book by considering the broader implications of kinship salience for comparative politics, arguing that authoritative kinship must be understood in its own right to truly elucidate state–society relations in states where kinship groups play a political role.

The question of what defines kinship could motivate an entire research project itself. For our purposes, however, the question can be crystallised in terms of how political science specifically should conceptualise kinship such that it lends itself to cracking political science puzzles. The following chapter takes on this question of what kinship is as a precursor to understanding what kinship does.

Notes

1. Politics refers to the allocation of resources or access. This definition follows Al-Naqeeb, who highlights political tribalism as an organising mechanism for resource distribution: Khaldoun al-Naqeeb, 'Political Tribalism and Legitimacy in the Arab Peninsula', presentation at the Council on Foreign Relations, New York, NY, January 1992.
2. See, for example, Courtney Freer and Andrew Leber, 'Defining the "Tribal Advantage" in Kuwaiti Politics', *Middle East Law and Governance* (forthcoming).
3. Max Weber, *Politics as a Vocation*, trans. H. H. Gerth and C. Wright Mills (Philadelphia, PA: Fortress Press, 1972).
4. See, for example, Francis L. K. Hsu, *Kinship and Culture* (New Brunswick, NJ: Aldine Transaction, 1971); Janet Carsten, *The Heart of the Hearth: The Process of Kinship in a Malay Fishing Community* (Oxford, UK: Clarendon Press, 1997).
5. Janet Carsten, *After Kinship* (Cambridge, UK: Cambridge University Press, 2004): 9.
6. Mounira M. Charrad and Julia Adams, 'Introduction: Patrimonialism Part and Present', *Annals of the American Academy of Political and Social Science* 636 (July 2011): 7. Such wide breadth has led some scholars to question the utility of the term altogether. See Henry E. Hale, *Patronal Politics: Eurasian Regime Dynamics in Comparative Perspective* (Cambridge, UK: Cambridge University Press, 2014): 24.
7. Max Weber, *Economy and Society: An Outline of Interpretive Sociology*, ed. Guenther Roth and Claus Wittich (Berkeley, CA: University of California Press, 1978): 1012–13.
8. Joseph Kostiner, 'The Nation in Tribal Societies: Reflections on K. H. al-Naqib's Studies on the Gulf', in *Tribes and States in a Changing Middle East*, ed. Uzi Rabi (Oxford, UK: Oxford University Press, 2016): 224.
9. Mounira Charrad, 'Central and Local Patrimonialism: State-Building in Kin-Based Societies', *Annals of the American Academy of Political and Social Science* 636 (July 2011): 65.
10. Dale Eickelman, *The Middle East: An Anthropological Approach* (Hoboken, NJ: Prentice Hall, 1989): 128.
11. Randal Collins, 'Patrimonial Alliances and Failures of State Penetration', *Annals of the American Academy of Political and Social Science* 636 (July 2011): 21; Charrad, 'Central and Local Patrimonialism', 53; Michael Bratton and Nicholas van de Valle, *Democratic Experiments in Africa: Regime Transitions in Comparative Perspective* (Cambridge, UK: Cambridge University Press, 1997): 83.

12. Cullen S. Hendrix, 'Measuring State Capacity: Theoretical and Empirical Implications for the Study of Civil Conflict', *Journal of Peace Research* 47 no. 3 (May 2010): 274–6.
13. Robert H. Bates, *Essays on the Political Economy of Rural Africa* (Cambridge, UK: Cambridge University Press, 1983): 90.
14. Catherine Boone, 'Rural Interests and the Making of Modern African States', *African Economic History* 23 (1995): 1–36.
15. Daniel Posner, *Institutions and Ethnic Politics in Africa* (Cambridge, UK: Cambridge University Press, 2005): 6. It bears mention that Posner's definition of tribe is not kinship based. See Posner, 1.
16. Jeffrey Herbst, *States and Power in Africa: Comparative Lessons in Authority and Control* (Princeton, NJ: Princeton University Press, 2000): 41–2.
17. Jocelyn Sage Mitchell and Justin J. Gengler, 'What Money Can't Buy: Wealth, Inequality, and Economic Satisfaction in the Rentier State', *Political Research Quarterly* 72 no. 1 (2019): 75–89; Jessie Moritz, 'Reformers and the Rentier State: Re-Evaluating the Co-Optation Mechanism in Rentier State Theory', *Journal of Arabian Studies* 8 (2018): 46–64.
18. See Hale, *Patronal Politics*.

2

DEFINING KINSHIP

Kinship is a genuine belief in common familial descent from a real ancestor between group members. As an identity, kinship is an unusually strong form of social orientation. Kinship groups based on kinship identity have the power to connect many different people under a common banner, and kinship authority can serve as a powerful idiom for allocating power within these groups. As a concept, kinship helps scholars to unlock important social science puzzles concerning the relationship between identity politics and resource distribution in states. Understanding its role in each of these issue areas requires first explaining what kinship is and how it operates as a political phenomenon.

Tracing the evolution of kinship as an academic concept is a useful starting point for this explanation, impacting the applicability of the model to the Brazilian Surui, Ugandan Vonoma, the Cambodian Khmer Loeu, and other kinship groups. Different groups may understand kinship in different ways. However, definitional clarity helps scholars determine how well the term applies to different groups and eliminates some of the conceptual clutter in the field created by a myriad of similar terms. Differences between words like 'tribe', 'caste' and 'clan' are often ambiguous.[1] In contrast to these terms, kinship refers not only to a type of group but also a modality of organisation. By better defining and understanding kinship in this way, scholars can also better theorise the political role these groups play both in societies and in their interaction with states. Definitional clarity also prevents analytical ambiguity that contributes to the conceptual stretching of kinship.[2]

The Study of Kinship

While political science has often used functionalist definitions of kinship, anthropologists have given considerable thought to defining the term. Kinship is based on a notion of common descent, but this concept is not as clear as it first appears. Married couples do not share common descent inherently, but they are in a sense kin. Adopted children may be considered kin by their families. Close family friends may also be treated as kin with the friendly moniker 'aunt' or 'uncle'. Brothers and sisters may be addressed without reference to birth order in some societies but not in others.[3] Genetic definitions may provide a scientific means of understanding kin, but socially, two individuals usually accept each other as kin without conducting blood tests on each other and comparing their genomes.[4] Thus, kinship can be determined through socially constructed meanings that may or may not be based on a demonstrated common genetic descent.

Anthropologists have long considered whether kinship is a purely biological concept or the product of social construction. Early work in social science, including that of Max Weber, considered it an important part of the relationship between individuals and the groups in which they lived. Scholars like Lewis Morgan (1870) identify primordial ties as the basis of an individual's relationship to a group. Later anthropologists (Firth, Fortes, Leach, and Levi-Strauss) accepted these conceptions in their work. Finding evidence of kinship ties in unrelated groups across different continents, they considered these ties as a fact to be discovered rather than a system of relationships that were socially constructed.[5] Social scientists outside of anthropology accepted these ideas as well.[6]

By the 1940s, however, anthropologists began to note that the political salience of these kinship ties was affected by context and circumstance. The insight that kinship groups may represent conflict 'in terms of lineages' and 'express social obligations in a kinship idiom' reflected the understanding that context shapes the political meaning of kinship.[7] Evans-Pritchard's 'segmentary model' created greater conceptual ground for kinship as a dynamic political identity rather than a fact divorced from a greater political context. The saying 'I against my brother, my brother and I against my cousin, and all of us against the stranger', neatly conceptualises this model in which membership in different kinship segments becomes more or less salient depending on circumstances.[8]

Eventually, anthropologists observed that socially constructed entities could activate 'the elements of intense mutual attachment, independent of primordial ties'.[9] In other words, people could behave as if these ties existed regardless of whether they actually did. In contrast to primordialist accounts, constructivists pointed out that social and economic factors often shaped the articulation of such identities.[10] They understood kinship groups as a 'unit of substance' defined by 'corporate organization use for pastoral practices'.[11] The group was a mode of collective action that efficiently allocated sparse resources among members of the group. For example, Bedouin 'depended on their animals for much of their own livelihood and sustenance . . . a household's livestock . . . still contribute to subsistence'.[12] For example, Arab Bedouin tribes were constructed as a 'unit of substance' defined by 'corporate organization use for pastoral practices'.[13] Some accounts went even further, questioning the concept of kinship itself. Schneider argued the term was 'vacuous' and had 'little justification as an analytic construct'.[14]

While anthropologists continued to put analytical stock in the concept of kinship, work on the subject throughout the 1980s reflected the idea that kinship was the product of social construction. This observation manifested itself in work framing kinship not as a biological reality but as a 'system of symbols and meanings'.[15] Swagman's definition encapsulates these perspectives, arguing that kinship is 'the genuine belief in familial connections between members of a political unit . . . defined by a reference to a distant apical ancestor . . . the convention for naming tribes and tribal segments frequently implies a common descent'.[16]

Decades behind anthropology, the idea of social construction became of interest to political science in the late 1990s and early 2000s. Constructivism argued that identity was not given by biology but constructed by social and political processes. Anthropological work on kinship thus became of interest as well. Previous work in the field had alluded to anthropological conceptions of kinship, but only in passing. Kinship was an element of other models of politics and hardly ever the subject of inquiry on its own terms. Anderson's (1986) work on tribes, for example, invokes kinship as an important basis of regional trade in Tunisia and Libya, but does not formally define the term. Khoury and Kostiner's seminal edited volume on tribes in the Middle East (1990) similarly invokes kinship on a number of occasions without defining formally what kinship is.[17]

As constructivism gained traction, however, political science began to take on questions of kinship itself. Some accounts in the discipline understand kinship groups as those that 'have their roots in a culture of kin-based norms and trust . . . [and] serve as an alternative to formal market institutions and official bureaucracies'.[18] Others point out that kinship groups 'share an organizational identity and network. Norms of loyalty, inclusion of members, and exclusion of outsiders continually reinforce the kin-based identity.'[19]

Alternative conceptions understand kinship largely in terms of patronage. They argue that 'the formal equality of kinship reflects the equal access of all recognized members . . . to its production and the inaccessibility of that production to outsiders'.[20] Accounts of tribal kinship in Northern Rhodesia, for example, use the definition 'Are you (or were your parents) subjects of Chief X?' versus 'descendants of Chief X'.[21]

Defining Kinship

Conceptions of kinship in political science agree that it is socially constructed but diverge on how kinship impacts politics. There is convergence, however, on the idea that kinship groups create durable forms of social organisation. This book's definition of kinship, a crystallisation of Swagman's, is based on the underlying reason for this durability: *a genuine belief in common familial descent from a real ancestor between group members.* As opposed to tracing common descent from a mythical ancestor, kinship in the Arabian Peninsula states is based on a genuine belief in descent from a real person. While kinship might operate similarly in cases where people trace descent to a mythical figure, this book limits its scope to kinship as understood in this set of critical cases.

In addition, *these paths of descent create hierarchies of power.* Kinship may or may not be a salient marker of authority in a particular political context. When it is, relative proximity to an apical ancestor grants a person more status within a kinship group. The power generated by this hierarchy is called kinship authority. Those closest to the apical ancestor may enjoy higher status and greater access to resources and power, but authority within kinship groups is diffused throughout its various segmentations.[22] Kinship groups are an example of a hierarchical organised group. Certain aspects of kinship hierarchies – specifically, the nature of kinship identity within these hierarchies – make them uniquely resistant to change compared to other hierarchies. It is this unique durability that makes kinship authority in bureaucratic states different from other kinds of authority. It also helps explain why variation in the salience of kinship authority occurs after state building across similar states.

The special nature of kinship authority originates in the particularly 'sticky' nature of kinship identity as an in-group. Sticky identities are hard to change by virtue of the markers that indicate membership in a certain in-group (e.g. ethnic identity).[23] Kinship is unique among identities because it is super-sticky (extremely hard to change). This is because it delineates not only an in-group but a unique orientation within that in-group. A member of the al-Otaibi tribe is socially oriented not only by belonging to that kinship group, but also by being the son and grandson of a real and unique individual. No other al-Otaibi exists in that exact same orientation.

The super-stickiness of kinship makes it a durable identity. Since it is very hard to change, one's kinship identity is a strong method of social orientation and kinship groups can effectively inhabit a political space and procure access and resources for their members. This is especially true in cases where resources are vital and limited because kinship hierarchies provide a stable means of resource distribution. Additionally, members of kinship groups are often obliged to come to the aid of their compatriots in need of defence, payment of blood money or dowries, or economic relief.[24] Durability and better chances of access to vital limited resources mean an overall higher likelihood of group survival.

Kinship groups in the Arabian Peninsula states are formed from the networks between those who profess a connection to a common real ancestor. As such, the scope of this book is limited to this specific iteration of kinship. Idioms of kinship based on a mythical ancestor, spirit or totem may well resemble an idiom based on a real person. However, to minimise variation on the independent variable, and to avoid overgeneralising a bounded set of cases, this book will focus on groups with real ancestors as the point of common descent in kinship groups.

These individuals who profess descent from a common ancestor share a genuine belief that their descent is shared. As such, the networks formed by these links of common descent are very durable. Durability, for its part, is a politically useful characteristic. It makes arrangements of power more stable within kinship groups and reduces the likelihood of conflict among kinship group members since the identity of an individual is tied directly to that of other individuals.

Kinship groups are not only groups, but also hierarchies. These hierarchies are durable for similar reasons that individual kinship identity is durable. The path connecting an individual to a real common ancestor is unique. This path is part of a network of other individuals who affirm the uniqueness of that path. Kinship hierarchies also serve as the basis for a determination of 'proximity' between a given kinship group member and the apical ancestor. This determination is based on the number of individuals between them in the hierarchy, although close personal relationships can play a role as well.

Kinship hierarchies are useful not only for forging a common identity but also for survival and the provision of resources. Proximity to an apical ancestor makes it possible to conceptualise the kinship group as a hierarchy. While all kinship groups have the potential to be hierarchical, hierarchies only matter in certain groups. It is no coincidence that such kinship groups tend to exist in environments with vital limited resources. Kinship hierarchies serve the political purpose of determining access to resources. Obtaining resources as a group offers a better chance for success than individuals going it alone. Durable, personal and internalised kinship ties incentivise members to look out for the good of all members since these members share 'common blood'. Furthermore, kinship hierarchies ensure that the division of resources within the group will occur in a stable manner. Different kinship groups may be more or less effective at providing their members with resources. However, they offer a better alternative than trying to obtain resources alone, especially when it is a matter of life and death.

Kinship hierarchies provide stable resource provision not only within the kinship group but between kinship groups as well. Kinship hierarchies rarely exist on their own. Rather, they are one of multiple kinship hierarchies that exist in a given area. Interaction between these kinship hierarchies is based on the common need to access a limited set of vital resources. These interactions are governed not only by purely material considerations but by norms. These norms reduce conflict that could disrupt access to the vital limited resources. They determine the responsibilities of kinship hierarchies that enter into alliances. They also determine procedures of conflict resolution (for example, blood money) that reduce the chances of violent escalation that would disrupt resource access.

These norms, based in kinship identity, have the power to compel kinship groups to do things they would not like to do (forgive a murder or tribal raid, for example). Kinship groups, in turn, have the power to compel their members to do things they would not like to do (marry a specific person, support a personal enemy who is a kin group member in a fight). The ability of kinship to compel is the basis of kinship authority. Kinship authority is political in that it determines access to power and resources. It is the basis of organisation in the pre-state period where kinship groups exist and is based on the durability of kinship identity and the utility of kinship hierarchies for obtaining vital limited resources. Kinship authority is affected by the environment in which it exists.

Kinship in Political Science

How should political scientists think about kinship? Drawing upon work in other fields is useful, but this work must fit into a political science framework. It should provide analytical leverage and theoretical rigour while also enhancing the quality of empirical analysis. Thus far, most political science work on kinship has focused on the extent to which it guarantees patronage. This conception is useful but it leaves our understanding of kinship incomplete. We must add to this conception that of kinship as an identity.

Kinship as Guarantor of Patronage

Some constructivist models of kinship are materialist in nature. 'Materialist' means that the primary incentive for the salience of kinship ties is the pursuit of access to material goods or power that can help in attaining those goods. These models identify patronage politics as one example of such a model. They argue that patronage is the predominant driver of the enduring salience of kinship identity. Patronage is a measurable material benefit and, rationally, members of kinship groups could be expected to use their kinship identity to access this patronage.

Modelling kinship as a means of obtaining material goods is useful for political science. Goods and the individuals that receive them are observable. They are tangible evidence, in other words, of the ways in which kinship shapes the allocation of resources. Patronage models of kinship also create a useful basis of comparison with other kinds of political identity and other types of patronage. This generalisability enhances the utility of studies of kinship as a political tool.

While materialist models of kinship provide observable outcomes and a rational causal logic, they risk essentialising kinship groups at the expense of both accuracy and analytical richness. Reducing such groups to one aspect of their functioning may be useful for parsimonious models of certain phenomena. However, it leaves our understanding of such groups incomplete.[25] Tribe (*qabila*) is a major kinship-based political unit in the Arab Gulf states and entire social groups (the *bedu*) are distinguished by their 'tribal heritage'. However, definitions of tribe in political science often proxy kinship groups as analogous to ethnic groups, patronage networks, or economic subsistence units. In reality, tribes act simultaneously as all of these. Tribes can be patronage networks, but they are not only that. When scholars essentialise such kinship groups, they preclude consideration of how these different functions interact with each other.

Essentialising kinship groups as patronage networks does more than obfuscate the multi-faceted nature of kinship politics. Materialist arguments miss the ways in which identity, and not the acquisition of goods or access, drives political outcomes in kinship-based societies. They cannot account for the fact that members of kinship groups act – consistently – in ways that do not advance their immediate material interest. To make sense of these actions, we must understand kinship not only as the basis of patronage, but as an identity as well.

Kinship as Identity

Kinship authority generates behaviour in response to certain primary rules enforced by the relevant agents of social control.[26] This behaviour, however, is not always based purely on material interests. Members of kinship groups act on material interests, but sometimes they act beyond what materialist models would predict. Kinship identity also plays an important political role. Existing accounts have understated this importance as it relates to kinship-based societies.

Kinship's function as a source of authority, like that of most traditional authority, lies in the fact that such practices are understood to have been in place since 'time immemorial'. Framed in this way, continuing these practices is not only about marginal self-interest but also about maintaining a set of practices that others have maintained in the past. This common adherence to certain practices, particularly when performed by an individual's personal ancestors, reinforces the notion of kinship as an identity. Kinship as an identity can facilitate the provision of material goods, but it goes beyond these considerations. Kinship is not only a function of what material goods people can obtain, but also a fundamental component of how they understand themselves. It is this identity aspect of kinship that makes it durable through state building, even when other means of patronage emerge.

We can understand kinship identity as a descent-based attribute similar to those that define ethnic groups.[27] An ethnic group is one in which members share certain sets of mutually recognised physical descent-based attributes.[28] While these physical attributes are necessary for membership, the exact combination is based on social conceptions, and different combinations of attributes become activated at different times. One important characteristic of a descent-based attribute is its 'stickiness'. Stickiness means the 'degree of difficulty associated with changing [an attribute] in the short term'.[29] An example of a sticky attribute would be skin colour, which would be exceedingly difficult to change.

Kinship is a sticky attribute because one cannot simply change one's descent lineage. However, there is another reason kinship is a sticky attribute that drives at its importance as a causal variable. Kinship group identity is unique from other descent-based attributes by virtue of its specificity. It orients its members in relation to all other members of a kinship group in a way few other attributes can. Ethnicity, for its part, uses a socially generated menu of descent-based attributes to delineate an in-group and an out-group. Kinship as an attribute contributes to this delineation but goes one step further. It gives the individual a *specific placement within the in-group* – a unique path connecting that individual with the apical ancestor. Others in the group have their own unique paths. These dual levels of identity make kinship a more durable form of identity than similar forms. For this reason, we can understand kinship as not just sticky, but in fact as *super-sticky.*

Political Effects of Kinship Identity

The super-stickiness of kinship has broad political effects. Most importantly, it regulates power between individuals, kinship groups and states in unique ways. We can understand this power as *kinship authority*. Super-stickiness is at the core of kinship and is the basis for the generation of kinship authority. It also makes this authority durable as a set of rules and norms that regulate behaviour.

Super-stickiness creates durable authority within kinship groups in four ways. First, the specific unique orientation that it gives an individual within a kinship group is ingrained from birth as a fundamental part of her identity. Its basis in 'real' lines of descent makes it difficult to deny, even when an individual might prefer to do so. Super-stickiness, in other words, gives kinship authority the ability to compel individuals with regards to conceiving of their own identity.

Second, super-stickiness links an individual, via a unique path, to other individuals in that same kinship group. Super-stickiness orients a person uniquely in relation to an ancestor, but also in relation to other real descendants of that ancestor. Descent provides not only a link, but also a network. This means that a person's actions within a tribe may affect not only themselves, but other members of the group as well. Kinship authority is durable because group members have the added incentive of protecting the well-being of others in the group.

Third, it allows kinship networks to sanction individuals who violate rules and norms in ways seen as 'damaging' the kinship group. Networks can share information about an individual's behaviour and collectively 'punish' those who refuse to respect kinship authority. This threat of punishment acts as an incentive for individual members of kinship groups to constantly consider the interests of their fellow group members, as well as those of the group as a whole.

Finally, super-stickiness regulates power not only within kinship groups but also between them. It prescribes rules and norms of interaction between individuals from different groups, and between the groups as a whole. Violating these inter-group regulations would introduce instability into a system where violence is otherwise regulated. Instability could create more violence and a breakdown in the political order. Individuals, kinship groups and states could violate these inter-group regulations, but it would come at a higher cost than operating within them.

In this sense, super-stickiness can regulate behaviour not only within kinship groups but also between them. Kinship groups follow informal political rules and norms because of the power of kinship authority rooted in super-stickiness. These rules and norms often centre around a cogent ideological construct and articulate themselves through a certain idiom of kinship that may shift over time.

Among Middle Eastern kinship groups, for example, the concept of *'asabiyya*, commonly translated as 'solidarity' or 'cohesion', has historically served as a guiding ideological principle for tribal relations. In his seminal work *al-Muqaddima*, Ibn Khaldoun notes that 'one cannot imagine any hostile act being undertaken against anyone who has his *'asabiyya* to support him'.[30] The ideological foundation of *'asabiyya* is articulated through a set of concepts which together reflect a particular idiom of kinship relations.[31] This idiom serves as a common template for understanding and articulating the rules and norms upon which kinship relations in many Gulf states are based.

A system of tribal alliances called *shaff* was based on mutual support between groups in order to protect their physical and political well-being.[32] Tribes did not merely form alliances, but rather understood *shaff* as a larger (albeit informal) institution of alliance building. In some societies, *shaff* also regulated behaviour between group members, compelling mutual cooperation.[33] More than a functional alliance, the term connotes a sense of loyalty between tribes. Kinship authority based on the super-stickiness of kinship authority compels this loyalty. Members of the same tribe, and of the same tribal alliance, were compelled to treat each other in certain ways. The kinship authority that originated within the tribe thus regulated behaviour between tribes and their members.

While *shaff* was a system of alliances, a code of hospitality (*dhiafa*) mandated behaviour between groups and individuals, even those at odds with each other. Among tribes in Jordan, for example, the process of tribal conflict resolution is based on the principle of collective responsibility on the part of a stipulated and limited set of patrilineal kinsmen.[34] While not formal in the sense of having a set of written laws or signed treaties, these informal constructs nonetheless are powerful and their terms enforced. In Syria, the sanctity of 'hospitality' was so carefully guarded that a host was obliged to offer protection even to his enemies.[35] Such codes show the non-materialist elements of kinship authority. Even though one is usually incentivised to avoid helping one's enemies, kinship politics carries a greater value for members of these kinship groups than the value of purely material benefits. Interviews with members of kinship groups consistently reflect the importance of this element of kinship identity.

Kinship systems in the Arab Gulf states exemplify a particular idiom of kinship, and one which changed over time. At the same time, several elements of this idiom are not unique to the Gulf states but are shared across societies where kinship authority is salient. Examining kinship, the Gulf region allows us to use a quintessential set of kinship-based societies as cases that illustrate how the theoretical concepts above describe real-world politics.

Kinship Politics in the Arab Gulf States

As an institution, kinship ties in the Arab Gulf mediate access to finite resources by maximising the access of each individual within the group. Kinship groups also have an element of exclusion, denying non-members access to these resources. They are also an important form of political and social identity. For example, one of the most important social cleavages in Arab Gulf states is between traditionally nomadic *bedu* and traditionally urban *hadhar*. An individual is placed into one of these groupings based on into which group her family is designated.

The names of influential tribes in the Arab Gulf region are well-known and respected by other members of the society. Since this power is generated collectively by its members, kinship groups need mechanisms to enforce exclusivity and preserve their reputation. The bad behaviour of one member of the group reflects poorly on all members. One Kuwaiti student explained:

Student: Everything affects the family here. No way will it just affect one person. It depends on what it is, but something has to affect the whole family.

SW: . . . What exactly does that say about the family?

Student: That says that those kind of people come from that family. So you wouldn't want to be associated with anyone from that family.[36]

How Family Names are Constructed in Oman and Kuwait

In the Middle East, tribal kinship is organised at four levels: *qabila* (tribe or mother tribe), *fakhitha* (sub-tribe), *ashira/batan* (large family) and *beit* (house or extended family). The outer boundaries of who is considered 'part' of a kinship group are often socially constructed, depending on resource availability or political uncertainty. Different families may come together to form a confederation under a single family name, or a family may break off from a larger kinship group. While it is the case in many other societies as well, family names in the Arabian Peninsula states can be an indication of a family's origins, livelihood, social position and relative status. Historical information about these families is based on oral sources, or written accounts of oral sources. Different oral sources will sometimes give vastly different accounts of a family's origins based on their personal familial affiliation. As it would in any society, the social and political implications of these accounts make questions of political and social status in the Gulf sensitive. Sensitivity in any society merits scholarly respect, and especially in societies that have been misrepresented historically in Western academia.[37] With that in mind, the information presented here is a simplified model of a very complex system of alliances, confederations and social relations. The presentation of this model reflects an attempt to balance historical accuracy, respect for families in the Gulf, and an appreciation of the sophisticated nature of kinship politics in the Gulf region.

Similar to other descent-based attributes, the ways in which kinship is used as an identity marker are often the product of social or political processes. Furthermore, the inclusion criteria of kinship can shift over time. Sub-groups can break off from the kinship group by 'localising' their kinship. That is to say, they adopt the name of a particular family patriarchy within a broader kinship structure. For example, the name of the Shi'a *Marafie* family in Kuwait is a contraction of the name Mohammed Rafie, a member of the Behbehani family. The Behbehani are a set of families named for their common origins in Behbehan, Iran. The Marafie adopted an apical ancestor as their point of commonality rather than this geographic commonality (although their Behbehani connection remains known in Kuwait).[38] In this case, the identity shifted from geography-based to kin-based.

This localising process also occurs within groups that already use kinship as a means of identity. An interview with a member of the al-Barrack family of the (Sunni) al-Fadhala tribe gives insight into this process:

SW: What was your father's name?

Interviewee 1: My father's name? [*redacted*] al-Barrack al-Fadhala. But we end officially not with al-Fadhala. Just al-Barrack. . . We're originally al-Fadhala from Bahrain.

SW: Before, was the name of the family al-Barrack, or did it change?

Interviewee 2: It's like their grandfather, but their great-grandfather is Fadhala. But we take it very easy. 'We are well known, just say al-Barrack', and they put it in their national and civil ID, everything [was] al-Barrack. But they are originally al-Barrack al-Fadhala.[39]

Family Names in Oman

Family names in Oman are almost always based on tribe and are given in the format 'X son of X grandson of X of family X'. In some cases, interviewees described a 'mother tribe' and 'sub-tribes' which branched off. Some kinship groups have adopted names which denote a certain location of origin. For example, a Lawati family from Muscat has adopted the last name 'Muscati' (from Muscat). Certain al-Baluchi families based in Nizwa have adopted the last name 'al-Nizwani' (from Nizwa). The family names Lawati and Baluchi reference origins in India and Pakistan respectively. Changing the family name to reference the city of residence makes the family seem more 'indigenous' to Oman.[40] It also obscures their Shi'a religious affiliation in an Ibadhi state. These changes are fairly recent (1970 or later), and some interviewees pointed to the discovery of oil in Oman as the turning point.[41]

Family Names in Kuwait

Kuwaiti family names can be divided into four categories: *location of origin*, *historic occupation*, *tribal affiliation* and *personal trait*. Each of these categories in turn convey information about the political status of a family relative to other families. They can also convey information about the family's affiliations or location of origin.

Last names based on *location of origin* denote that the family has historic origins in a particular place. The last name al-Basri for example, means 'from Basra', a city in southern Iraq. These places are usually cities but can also be regions (al-Nejdi from the Nejd region, for example). Location-based last names do not necessarily correlate with affinity. The Behbehani, for example, were originally a coalition of families from Behbehan, but were not all related to each other.[42] In addition, both the Behbehani family and the Dashti family have origins in Iran, but marriages between the two families are fairly uncommon.[43]

Last names based on *historic occupation* tend to denote a particular craft. Al-Najjar, for example, means 'carpenter'. Al-Duwaish means 'a buyer of pearls'. Such occupations were prominent in pre-oil Kuwaiti society. The families bearing these names are often confederations of smaller familial groups which joined together prior to Kuwaiti independence.

Last names based on *tribal affiliation* fall into two subcategories. The first are last names directly invoking the tribe itself: al-Mutairi, al-Shammari and al-Thafiri are major examples. The second subcategory are names of families within the tribe, which the British researcher and colonial administrator J. G. Lorimer first published in English in 1908. Members of families which emphasise tribal identity tend to have an awareness of the major sub-families of a tribe, but those which do not often have less need for awareness of these divisions.[44]

Finally, last names based on *personal traits* convey a particular characteristic of the family. For example, al-Ayar, a subgroup of the al-Saeed family, translates as 'jokester'. Other last names may reference a physical trait or historic event (the name al-Emir, 'the prince', may indicate a historic leadership position, for example). This trait may have a historic basis as well. For example, the Shi'a Qabazard family in Kuwait has a last name that translates from Persian as 'yellow robe', referring to the dress of the family's ancestors. The Qabazard family in Kuwait originated from two brothers from Iran who began work in Kuwait as pearl divers, ship captains (*nakhodas*) and ship owners. Mohammed Qabazard, one of the family patriarchs, was appointed head of the port of Kuwait by the British and was a member of Kuwait's first parliament in 1961. The family became prominent in sea and land trade (including rice and dates) after 1950, including an import-export business with Iran.[45]

Each one of these four categories can give clues about the others. For example, al-Anizi is a last name conveying affiliation with the Aniza tribe. Yet it is also understood in Kuwait that the Aniza are one of the tribes which come from Nejd, the origin of the most prominent tribes in Kuwait. Thus, the last name, while tribal, also conveys information about location of origin and status. Given the social salience of *bedu* and *hadhar* divisions, members of kinship-based societies throughout the Gulf are usually aware of whether a given family has tribal or merchant origins. This information places the family in a particular group in society.

Last names in Kuwait, Qatar and Oman can and have changed to emphasise certain pieces of information over others. This practice reflects the power that different social contexts can have over the activation of different identity attributes. Many families with a last name based on occupation gained little status from their former name. For example, the al-Kanderi family, whose name means 'water carrier', originate from central and south-western Iran. Yet rather than using the names of the various families that were part of their migration to Kuwait, the families' descendants use the name al-Kanderi, which is today a well-known name in Kuwait. Changing the family name created a larger familial network and increased the relative prestige of the individual families which comprised it. Tribal families did the same. The al-Mutair tribe, for example, is a confederation of many different kinship groups.

Gender and Kinship

Gender plays an important role in mediating power relations within kinship groups. Many accounts of kinship politics take for granted that the dynamics they describe apply predominantly to men, and even those that do, often accept a binary conception of gender. In the Arab Gulf states, men tend to gain more benefits from kinship ties than women despite similar proximity to an apical ancestor. On the other hand, kinship groups understand women to have the unique power, through birth and marriage, to create new group members and decide with whom those members are created. In many ways, kinship authority is a structural attempt to regulate this power. Rules and norms surrounding women are also based on the group's desire to have input on a woman's decision that might impact the group as a whole. For example, the engagement and marriage processes involve the families of the bride and groom as well as the couple themselves. Traditionally, women also initiated the process of finding a spouse for their child. A man's mother, grandmother or aunt went to the house of the woman's family and inquired whether there were eligible daughters for her son to marry. If there was such a daughter, the wedding could be held soon thereafter.[46] Often, the wedding was the first time the groom and bride met. One elderly subject from the more Kuwaiti town of Jahra recounted that in 1963, at the age of twenty, he came home from work to be told by his family he was getting married. He did so a few hours later, to his then eighteen-year-old wife.[47]

Marriage in the Gulf states is often functional and based on an obligation to the family or tribe. While some married couples may spend time together, others spend free time in the evenings with same-gender friends and colleagues. Adultery, while illegal, is not unheard of in the region. Divorces have become more common as the stigma surrounding it subsides, and the cost of marriage dowries for many in the Gulf has become prohibitively expensive. Each of these factors speaks to the influence of social and political factors on marriage in the region. This influence operates in all societies, but is magnified where kinship authority is salient because the stakes are higher. A choice of spouse directly affects the reputation of other family members and obligates them to members of that spouse's family. Thus, marriage is not purely between men and women but between entire families in such societies.

Marriage with up to four women is permissible in Islam. However, this is increasingly rare in the Gulf, largely for financial reasons. Today, marriage also involves more agency on the part of the bride and groom. A man will often ask his mother to contact the woman's family to set up a meeting. He may have met the woman at university, work, or at a large family gathering. In the twenty-first century, some couples also make first contact online – via social media or sometimes in internet chat rooms.[48] The couple may meet informally, but the man will initiate the 'formal' meeting between the families after the couple decides they might be interested in marriage. The two will then meet in the presence of close relatives, and perhaps once or twice more if the first meeting is a success. During this time the couple may exchange phone numbers. If the family and the couple decide to proceed, the engagement and marriage date will be set at a gathering called a *khutba*. The official legal marriage ceremony is known as a *milke*. The men's ceremony involves signing the legal documents of marriage and congratulations from the extended family. The women's ceremony involves a small party with a similar congratulatory function. The actual wedding party, or *hafla*, is also usually separate, though rarely some families in Kuwait will have them jointly. Dowries are paid from the groom or his family to the bride, consistent with Islamic law. Unlike in the West, a married woman in the Gulf keeps her family name. Her children, however, will have her husband's family name.

The ties of marriage also have important implications for alliances between families that may stretch back generations. Even in a contemporary context, members of the same or similar families are encouraged to marry each other. Marriage within a family preserves its exclusivity and thus its strength. The marriage is an alliance between two families that are already part of the kinship structure, so no diffusion of resources occurs. It also strengthens internal relations in the family and prevents internal splits or divisions.

At the highest levels, marriages for explicitly political reasons strengthen relations between different kinship groups. For example, Sheikh Jaber al-Mubarak al-Hamad al-Sabah, Kuwait's Prime Minister, married Mutairi women while Mohammed Shahrar, a Mutairi, was head of the Council of Ministers.[49] Such a marriage created an alliance that disincentivised antagonism between the speaker and the royal family.

Social Sanctions

Kinship groups use super-stickiness as a mechanism to enforce certain standards of behaviour. Deviation from these standards in the kinship-influenced societies of the Gulf is designated *'aib*. While the word *haram* indicates behaviour forbidden by Islam, *'aib* is a largely non-religious sanction based on local and regional tradition. It is also open to change based on social context and time.[50] Engaging in behaviour that is *'aib* can damage the reputation of both an individual and his family, though the extent depends on the severity of the *'aib* and in some cases the prominence of the person who committed it. *'Aib* is a social sanction which enforces desirable behaviour – that which preserves the reputation of the kinship group. To preserve one's individual and group reputation is very important since this reputation impacts all members of the group.

In particular, a woman's sexual chasteness and reputation for discretion (sexual and otherwise) are of paramount importance. Honour and reputation often come back to sexual discretion in many societies, and those in the Gulf are no different in this regard. However, while Kuwaiti and Omani female interviewees believed that the pressure was disproportionate on women, they did not describe it in the language of 'oppression' per se. Rather, it was described as more of a double standard or unfair practice. As a female Kuwaiti university student, put it: 'A girl cannot openly date but a guy can. It's counterproductive, I don't know how, because his girlfriend is a girl.'[51] A female Omani student framed it similarly: 'For girls, they judge everything. For men its important but it's not a big a deal . . . Guys can talk to girls but girls should never talk to the guy.'[52]

There are sayings describing society's relative leniency for men versus women. In Kuwait, the phrase *'aib manqoul* means an *'aib* that a man will commit by virtue of being a man. This idea is similar to the Western saying 'boys will be boys'. Another phrase, which one Omani subject explained, is *'aib al-rijaal f'il jaib*, or 'the man's *'aib* is in his pocket'.[53] That is, it can be disregarded by society, at least to some extent. For example, if an Omani man smokes in Muscat, it is technically *'aib* but he faces little sanction for it. A woman smoking, on the other hand, would face a greater social sanction and might be the subject of rumours or gossip.[54] However, Omanis also point out that while women face more pressure than men, both genders have social expectations not to engage in behaviour considered *'aib*.[55]

Religion and Kinship

Islamic law and tradition mediate certain aspects of kinship-based politics in the Gulf. For example, the amount of money to be paid as compensation for a murder (known as *diya*, or blood ransom) is based on verses in the Quran [al-Nisaa' (2:92–3)]. In addition, a dowry (*mahr*) is given by the groom or his family to the bride, a practice consistent with Islamic tradition and also in the Quran [al-Nissa' (4:4)].

However, religion is not the sole basis of customs surrounding kinship in the Gulf. While Islam permits a man to have up to four wives, such a practice is rare in the younger generation of Kuwaitis, Qataris and Omanis. Tribal and family tradition is also the basis of local regulations and customs alongside religion. For example, while Omani women dress to cover all skin except their hands and face (which are also covered in many parts of Oman's interior), they cite adherence to tradition rather than an Islamic mandate as the reason for doing so. Many women in Oman's interior will wear conservative but brightly coloured clothing, while women covering for religious reasons often dress in black. Some woman will in fact cover their face while in their home town in the interior, but uncover it in Muscat. Thus, tradition also plays an important role in kinship politics that should not be confused with religion. Traditional clothing in the region is also not an indication of traditional approaches to other aspects of life. Many women who dress conservatively also embody an individualist lifestyle based on more recent political and social movement in the Gulf region. Similarly, women who dress less conservatively may still be close adherents to other traditional tenets of family or religious life.

This chapter has provided a theoretical framework and empirical background on kinship, and how kinship politics manifest themselves in the Arab Gulf. It defines kinship as *a genuine belief in common familial descent from a real ancestor between group members*. Introducing the concept of super-stickiness, it showed how the unique strength of kinship identity impacts relations not only within kinship groups but also between them. The chapter then outlined key elements of kinship politics at play in the Arab Gulf states. Kinship is a salient political variable at play in many societies. However, it manifests itself differently even across societies that are otherwise similar. Having taken a systematic account of what kinship is, we can now begin to explain systematically what kinship does.

Notes

1. Kanchan Chandra, 'What is Ethnic Identity and Does it Matter?', *Annual Review of Political Science* 9 (June 2006): 402, 413. Furthermore, such terms are often used interchangeably in translations from Arabic to English because of different conceptualisations of the groups. In Arabic, there are multiple sub-groups including *usra, beit, batan, ashira* and *qabila*.
2. Giovanni Sartori, 'Concept Misinformation in Comparative Politics', *American Political Science Review* 64 no. 4 (1970): 1034. See also Scott Weiner and Dillon Tatum, 'Rethinking Identity in Political Science', *Political Studies Review* 19 no. 3 (2021): 464–81.
3. For example, *gēgē* (older brother) or *mèimei* (younger sister) in Mandarin-speaking societies.
4. See also Lawrence A. Hirschfeld, 'Kinship and Cognition: Genealogy and the Meaning of Kinship Terms', *Current Anthropology* 27 no. 3 (June 1986): 219.
5. David Schneider, *A Critique of the Study of Kinship* (Ann Arbor, MI: University of Michigan Press, 1984): 168.
6. See Max Weber, 'The Origins of Ethnic Groups', in John Hutchinson and Anthony Smith (eds), *Ethnicity* (New York, NY: Oxford University Press, 1996): 35–40; Clifford Geertz, 'Primordial Ties', in Hutchinson and Smith (eds), *Ethnicity*, 40–4; Steven Grosby, 'The Inexpungable Tie of Primordiality', in Hutchinson and Smith (eds), *Ethnicity*, 51–6.
7. E. E. Evans-Pritchard, *The Nuer: A Description of the Modes of Livelihood and Political Institutions of a Nilotic People* (Oxford, UK: Oxford University Press, 1940): 143.
8. Rivka Azoulay thoughtfully analyses the segmentary model in the Kuwaiti context. See Rivka Azoulay, *Kuwait and Al-Sabah: Tribal Politics and Power in an Oil State* (London, UK: I. B. Tauris, 2020): 106–8.

9. Edward Shils, 'Primordial, Personal, Sacred and Civil Ties', *British Journal of Sociology* 8 no. 2 (June 1957): 133–4.

10. Eugen Weber, *Peasants into Frenchmen: The Modernization of Rural France, 1970–1914* (Stanford, CA: Stanford University Press, 1976): 294; Yuri Slezkine, 'The USSR as a Communal Apartment, or How a Socialist State Promoted Ethnic Particularism', *Slavic Review* 53 no. 2 (Summer 1994): 417–19.

11. Emmanuel Marx, 'The Tribe as a Unit of Subsistence: Nomadic Pastoralism in the Middle East', *American Anthropologist* 79 no. 2 (June 1977): 344.

12. Donald P. Cole, 'Where Have the Bedouin Gone?', *Anthropological Quarterly* 76 no. 2 (Spring 2003): 238, 245.

13. Marx, 'The Tribe as a Unit', 343–63.

14. Schneider, *A Critique*, 185.

15. David Schneider, *American Kinship: A Cultural Account* (Chicago, IL: University of Chicago Press, 1968): 8.

16. Charles F. Swagman, 'Tribe and Politics: An Example from Highland Yemen', *Journal of Anthropological Research* 44 no. 3 (Autumn 1988): 255.

17. Lisa Anderson, *The State and Social Transformation in Tunisia and Libya (1830–1980)* (Princeton, NJ: Princeton University Press, 1986); Philip S. Khoury and Joseph Kostiner (eds), *Tribes and State Formation in the Middle East* (Los Angeles, CA: University of California Press, 1990).

18. Kathleen Collins, 'Clans, Pacts, and Politics in Central Asia', *Journal of Democracy* 13 no. 3 (July 2002): 142.

19. Kathleen Collins, 'The Logic of Clan Politics', *World Politics* 56 no. 2 (January 2004): 232.

20. Anderson, *The State and Social Transformation*, 28.

21. Daniel Posner, *Institutions and Ethnic Politics in Africa* (Cambridge, UK: Cambridge University Press, 2005): 1.

22. Ernest Gellner, *Muslim Society* (Cambridge, UK: Cambridge University Press, 1981): 117.

23. Chandra, 'What is Ethnic Identity and Does it Matter?', 414.

24. Philip Carl Salzman, 'Tribes and Modern States: An Alternative Approach', in Uzi Rabi (ed.), *Tribes and States in a Changing Middle East* (Oxford, UK: Oxford University Press, 2016): 208.

25. Layne concurs with regards to Bedouin kinship groups in particular. See Linda Layne, *The Dialogics of Tribal and National Identities in Jordan* (Princeton, NJ: Princeton University Press, 1994): 13.

26. Daniel M. Brinks, 'Informal Institutions and the Rule of Law: The Judicial Response to State Killings in Buenos Aires and Sao Paulo in the 1990s', *Comparative Politics* 36 no. 1 (October 2003): 4–5.

27. While some kinship groups can be ethnic groups, not all ethnic groups are kinship groups. This is because ethnicity can be based on a plethora of other descent-based attributes that have little to do with kinship. Members of a particular group need not believe in common descent from an apical ancestor to be co-ethnics, but they do in order to be kin.

28. Kanchan Chandra, 'Attributes and Categories: A New Conceptual Vocabulary for Thinking About Ethnic Identity', in Kanchan Chandra (ed.), *Constructivist Theories of Ethnic Politics* (New York, NY: Oxford University Press: 2012): 98.

29. Chandra, 'What is Ethnic Identity and Does it Matter?', 414.

30. Ibn Khaldoun, *al-Muqaddimah: An Introduction to History – Abridged Edition*, trans. Franz Rosenthal (Princeton, NJ: Princeton University Press, 2015): 166.

31. See P. H. Gulliver, *Neighbours and Networks: The Idiom of Kinship in Social Action Among the Ndendeuli of Tanzania* (Berkeley, CA: University of California Press, 1971).

32. John C. Wilkinson, *The Imamate Tradition in Oman* (Cambridge, UK: Cambridge University Press, 1987): 93.

33. Peter Lienhardt, *Shaikhdoms of Eastern Arabia* (New York, NY: Springer Publishing, 2001): 84, 93.

34. Richard T. Antoun, 'Civil Society, Tribal Process, and Change in Jordan: An Anthropological View', *International Journal of Middle East Studies* 32 no. 4 (November 2000): 446.

35. Sulayman N. Khalaf, 'Settlement of Violence in Bedouin Society', *Ethnology* 29 no. 3 (July 1990): 232.

36. Interview, Salmiya, Kuwait, 6 March 2014.

37. Early scholarship on Arab societies often had an orientalist framing, which makes some members of these societies reluctant to participate in research conducted by a Western scholar.

38. Interview, Shuweikh, Kuwait, 6 March 2014.

39. Interview, Nuzha, Kuwait, 15 February 2014.

40. This legitimacy is particularly important given that the Lawati and Baloushi families have origins outside Oman. In addition, while these families are Shi'a, a majority of other Omanis are Ibadhi.

41. Interview, al-Khuweir, Oman, 21 March 2014.

42. Interview, Shuweikh, Kuwait, 6 March 2014.

43. Interview, Jahra, Kuwait, 12 January 2014.

44. Interview, Nuzha, Kuwait, 15 February 2014. Several Arabic-language books and websites (e.g. www.kuwaitpast.com) list the sub-families of each major tribe. See, for example, Mat'ab bin Othman al-Sa'eed, *Urbanized Nejdi Family Lineages in Kuwait* (Kuwait: Maktaba Afaq, 2011) (Arabic); Khalid al-Mubailesh, 'Kuwaiti Families in the Old Neighborhoods and Quarters', *KuwaitPast.com*, 2007 (Arabic).

45. See Rivka Azoulay, 'The Politics of Shi'a Merchants in Kuwait', in Steffan Hertog, Giacomo Luciani and Marc Valeri (eds), *Business Politics in the Middle East* (London, UK: C. Hurst & Co., 2013): 76; Interview, Shuweikh, 6 March 2014.

46. While interviewees speculated that it might occur in peripheral areas, forced marriages in Kuwait and Oman are likely rare. In Kuwait, if a woman refuses to marry a man, the process is concluded. In the words of several interviewees, 'That's it. It's over.' In Oman, al-Azri notes 'various indications . . . forced marriage and marriage below the age of 18 continues to be practiced'. See Khalid

M. al-Azri, *Social and Gender Inequality in Oman: The Power of Religious and Political Tradition* (New York, NY: Routledge, 2013): 77.

47. Interview, Jahra, Kuwait, 12 January 2014.
48. Interview, al-Khuweir, Oman, 19 March 2014.
49. Interview, Salmiya, Kuwait, 24 February 2014.
50. An Omani woman in Muscat would not be expected to cover her face in public. However, for the same woman to bare her face in her family's village could be considered *'aib*. Interview, al-Khuweir, Oman, 19 March 2014.
51. Interview, Salmiya, Kuwait, 6 March 2014.
52. Interview, German University of Technology, Oman, 26 March 2014.
53. Interview, al-Khuweir, Oman, 19 March 2014. Other Omanis were not familiar with the phrase or mentioned it was not 'Omani' per se.
54. Interview, Ramal Boshar, Oman, 28 March 2014.
55. Interview, Ramal Boshar, Oman, 24 March 2014.

3

RESOURCE ACCESS AND THE POLITICAL SALIENCE OF KINSHIP

It is puzzling that states with similar state building experiences see differences in the salience of kinship authority. While factors occurring during state building – colonialism, the extent of infrastructure, and ruling family politics – can shape aspects of kinship salience, pre-existing conditions play a crucial role as well. Existing accounts tend to overlook these preconditions in their analysis of state building, particularly in cases that involve a strong outside influence. However, politics in kinship-based societies did not begin with Western intervention. The nature of kinship politics before this intervention set important constraining factors on the state-building process. These constraints in turn played a key role in shaping politics, including the salience of kinship authority, after state building.

Whether kinship authority has governing or instrumentalised political salience after state building is a function of access to vital limited resources. This access can be either competitive or cooperative. When access is competitive, different kinship groups compete for these resources. While groups can form ad-hoc arrangements, the inherently competitive nature of access precludes stable long-term cooperation. During state building, therefore, rulers reach out to individual kinship groups to disrupt kinship authority and bring them within the purview of the bureaucratic state. This kind of outreach, however, incentivises kinship groups and their members to reassert kinship authority since doing so preserves access to patronage. While the government expands its bureaucratic apparatus and extends it into non-urban areas, kinship authority instrumentalises bureaucratic authority to provide patronage and political access. Furthermore, the government's nationalist narrative in

36

these cases will also reify kinship authority by centring it in narratives of the state's heritage. Thus, after state building in such cases, kinship authority will have governing salience, meaning that it relegates bureaucracy to a tool for obtaining resources and political power.

In contrast, when access is cooperative, kinship groups form proto-bureaucracies to manage access to resources. These proto-bureaucracies are run by members of kinship groups who have the assent of local kinship group members, but their authority comes from their knowledge of the bureau-cratic system of resource management. Proto-bureaucracies therefore act as an intermediary between kinship authority and bureaucratic authority. They are structured similarly to government bureaucracies, but their staff have assent to govern from the local population based on their authority as mem-bers of kinship groups. During state building, the government diminishes kinship authority and embeds these proto-bureaucracies within its governing apparatus. This process, while not always undertaken with the enthusiastic consent of those it affects, allows the bureaucracy to instrumentalise kinship authority as a means to create assent to bureaucratic rule. Additionally, the state's national narrative will downplay kinship authority in favour of a ter-ritorial story that emphasises a common heritage across different groups in the state. As a result, kinship authority at the end of state building will have instrumentalised salience, meaning that it will be used by the state's bureau-cracy as a means of distributing patronage (specifically, resources and political power) and attaining assent to rule.

The elements and operationalisation of kinship salience are given in greater detail in Chapter 7. Generally speaking, however, the political salience of kin-ship authority refers to the specific ways in which kinship allocates access to power and resources. When kinship has governing salience, kinship author-ity instrumentalises bureaucratic authority by using bureaucratic institutions to provide resources and political access for pre-existing kinship networks. When kinship has instrumentalised salience, the opposite is true – bureaucratic authority subsumes kinship authority as a means of attaining bureaucratic gov-ernance over a population. Measuring salience involves two components. The first relates to questions of governance. Are kinship groups and their leaders part of the state bureaucracy or do they have authority independent of formal state recognition? How important is kinship authority for obtaining resources and political access? Who are the primary arbiters of inter- and intra-group dis-putes? The second component relates to kinship authority's ability to constrain the behaviour of kinship group members. Is 'purity' emphasised among kinship groups? Do social constraints like 'aib constrain behaviour? Are dating and marriage constrained by kinship authority? A systematic evaluation of these empirical questions allows us to evaluate kinship salience in both an observable and replicable manner.

State formation is a complex process and kinship salience manifests itself in a plethora of ways. Thus, the model presented in this chapter engages a well-defined scope of state-building cases. Despite the temptation to adopt monocausal models for parsimony's sake, it is important for scholars to acknowledge that single factors rarely produce complex outcomes on their own. Patterns of access to vital limited resources are the key driver of kinship salience after state building. However, the previous chapter identifies other factors – patronage politics and state capacity – which play a necessary if insufficient explanatory role. The book's focus on patterns of resource access as a primary driving factor impacting kinship salience should not be read as an implication that no other variable matters. In the empirical chapters, historical details of each case demonstrate the multitude of factors that played a role in shaping the salience of kinship. Nonetheless, the path-dependent role of preconditions to state building, under-theorised in many accounts, is the critical element of the political processes that produce governing or instrumentalised kinship salience.

This chapter proceeds in two parts. Part one explains why resource access is competitive or cooperative in the first place and describes the differences between competitive and cooperative resource access patterns. Part two offers a model of state building consisting of three stages: infrastructure expansion, bureaucracy extension, and nationalism building. It shows how pre-existing patterns of resource access constrain a government's choices with regard to each state to produce governing or instrumentalised kinship salience.

Part One: Before State Building

Whether a kinship group has cooperative or competitive access to vital limited resources is the product of two factors. The first is whether the kinship group attempting to obtain the resource is nomadic or settled. The second is whether the resource is dispersed or concentrated. These factors are usually closely dependent. Nomadic groups tend to be nomadic because resources are dispersed, and settled groups tend to be settled because resources are concentrated.

Kinship Groups

Kinship groups can mediate access to power and resources by delineating an in-group and an out-group. Kinship identity creates a super-sticky association between an individual and other members of the kinship group. This collective sense of identity can then become the basis of political association.

It can also be the basis by which others are excluded from the association. In addition, kinship ties are based on a hierarchy of proximity to an apical ancestor. This hierarchy allows for the distribution of power and resources, with those at the top getting more and those at the bottom getting less.

The super-sticky nature of kinship makes it an attractive framework for political association. Al-Naqeeb (1991) explains that governments use tribes as corporate solidarities to distribute political and economic patronage, and that tribes in turn adapt in order to make themselves useful for such processes. Kostiner (2016) adds that tribes benefit states by fighting for them, maintaining order and loyalty, and creating patrimonial trust.[1]

Kinship features close interpersonal ties that are often affirmed from birth and are difficult to break. Furthermore, they pay dividends to each member of the kinship group. Yet not all kinship groups are political. The fact that kinship groups are hierarchical does not mean these hierarchies are always activated for political purposes. When this political activation of kinship hierarchies does occur, it tends to be among groups where access to vital limited resources is low because of either a lack of the resource or a lack of the means to obtain it. In such cases, associations of people are limited by the availability of access to resources. Because kinship is based on close ties that incentivise collective action and interpersonal trust, it is often the best means to determine access.

Vital Limited Resources

Vital limited resources are a major factor in the political salience of kinship. 'Limited' means that access to the resource is competitive in the economic sense (one person's use of the resource detracts from another person's ability to use the resource). 'Vital' means that the resource is essential for sustaining life. Water is a quintessential example of a vital limited resource in many societies. Arable land, where it is limited, is another example. Different vital limited resources may have unique characteristics. This book focuses on water as such a resource. Water is easy to transport and can also be divided easily by volume or by timed access. However, while the type of vital limited resource we study may affect specific configurations of competitive and cooperative access, it would have little effect on how states interact with the kinship groups accessing it.

Vital limited resources exist in one of two configurations – dispersed and concentrated. Dispersed resources exist in small quantities and in many different sites spread across a particular environment. Concentrated resources, on the other hand, exist in large quantities in a particular place. Whether a resource is dispersed or concentrated affects the living patterns of kinship groups. At best, dispersed resources may sustain a population for a few months to a year. Concentrated resources, however, may sustain a population for decades. Different configurations of resources thus incentivise different kinds of living.

Kinship groups, for their part, can be either settled together or nomadic. Settled groups, as the name implies, stay in one place – often with other kinship groups. These groups live in the same locality, have permanent living structures, and likely have fixed public spaces like markets and meeting houses. Nomadic groups, in contrast, move from place to place as conditions (seasons, resource availability) dictate. The temporary settlements of these groups may have a certain organisation (rows of tents, for example), but do not exist at a fixed geographic location. A third category of kinship group are seasonal migrants. Groups that are seasonally migratory move only twice per year, usually between settlements. Most of the year, they are in a fixed location. Thus, their behaviour is similar to settled groups.

Different combinations of resource configurations and living patterns can exist in theory. However, the most likely combinations (and thus the most useful to model) are dispersed/nomadic and concentrated/settled. When resources are dispersed, kinship groups are most likely to be nomadic. Accessing the resource requires moving from site to site where the resource exists. Nomadism is simply a practical approach. A nomadic approach to obtaining dispersed resources offers flexibility. Kinship groups that can pack up and move fairly easily can stay in one site as long as necessary, and then move to a different site as resources dictate. In theory, there could be a set of

Resource Configuration	Kinship Group Living Patterns	
	Nomadic	**Settled**
Dispersed	Mobility improves access.	*Settlement inefficient for access.*
Concentrated	*Nomadism inefficient for access. Difficult to regulate.*	Regular interaction makes conflict-free access more likely. Easy to regulate.

Figure 3.1   Pairings of resource configurations and kinship group living patterns

groups that were nomadic but made use of a concentrated resource. However, nomadism is usually employed as a sustenance strategy by groups in areas where resources are sparse. If the resource were concentrated it would remove the major advantage of a nomadic lifestyle. Access to a certain concentrated resource would also be hard to regulate given the absence of a permanent presence at or near that resource. Additionally, a concentrated/nomadic configuration is not an empirically common occurrence for vital limited resources, and certainly not with water in particular.

Concentrated/settled is a most likely pairing for two reasons. First, since different kinship groups are settled together, they are forced to have regular interaction. Regular interaction between entities does not guarantee conflict-free access but it creates a shadow of the future that incentivises it and, given mutual interests, makes access without conflict more likely.[2] While conflicts may break out from time to time, ongoing conflicts would be unsustainable since they would jeopardise the access of all kinship groups to the vital limited resource. Second, collaborating to obtain resources and dividing them up according to pre-arranged agreements is significantly less challenging when groups are in one place versus moving around.[3] In theory, a settled community could draw upon dispersed resources by sending out groups to gather the resource and bring it to the village. This would be fairly inefficient, however, given the effort required to obtain sufficient quantities of the resource.

Resource Access Patterns (Independent Variable)

Resource access patterns are the means by which sets of kinship groups attain vital limited resources. They refer to processes, norms and behaviours regulating access to these resources specifically. It is possible to model these patterns as competitive or cooperative.

Competitive access means that different kinship groups are in ongoing contestation over access to a vital limited resource. It refers to situations where allocation of the resource has a constant potential to shift based on the outcome of this contestation. Contestation itself can be violent or non-violent. Violent contestation may entail a raid or attack on a site where the resource is present. In such a case, one kinship group takes the resource by force. Non-violent contestation may come about as part of an agreement or alliance. A stronger kinship group may grant resource access to a weaker group in exchange for allegiance against another kinship group. They may also accept tribute in monetary or non-monetary form (e.g. cattle).

Both violent and non-violent contestation in competitive access are regulated by norms. Since kinship groups are structured similarly and have similar kinds of authority, it is not surprising that they should mandate similar ways of interacting with other kinship groups. These norms are an extension of kinship authority and they are more likely to be adhered to than norms governing relations between non-kinship groups. Kinship authority is a form of traditional authority, and its appeal to 'time immemorial' offers an increased probability of norm adherence by kinship groups. This is because the norms governing inter-group behaviour come from the same kinship authority that governs individual groups and empowers their leaders. Failure to adhere to inter-group norms would undermine the same authority that empowers the leader, and is disincentivised. In addition, because kinship groups are hierarchical networks, the effect of one group member's failure to adhere to norms impacts the entire group. Kinship group members thus experience the systemic effects of norm violation on a more personal level. This personal effect also reduces the chances of norm violation.

Blood payments are an example of a norm that kinship authority helps to enforce. The concept is designed to prevent the emergence of protracted feuds between kinship groups. If a member of one kinship group kills a member of a second kinship group, that second group may retaliate by killing a member of the first group. However, the first group may see this as an affront and kill another member of the second group. This back-and-forth can escalate into a decades-long inter-group feud that creates instability for all kinship groups within a given tribal system. Blood payments are designed to prevent this protracted violent conflict. Rather than killing a member of the other group, the second group can demand a blood payment. The amount of this payment may be negotiated between the groups in an ad hoc meeting, or it may be set by the state. Religious texts may also mandate certain amounts of payment. In exchange for the blood payment, the afflicted kinship group forgives the group making the payment and agrees not to seek revenge in the form of killing. The issue is considered settled and protracted violent conflict is avoided.

A kinship group making a blood payment has no material guarantee that the recipient of the payment will not defect on the bargain. However, since the recipient kinship group operates according to traditional kinship authority, and since blood payment is a traditional means of politics, the likelihood of compliance is higher than for other kinds of groups. Kinship authority may also delineate sanctions for a group that fails to adhere to the norms surrounding blood payments. A group which defected might be ostracised from the system or the target of a confederation of groups who would come to the aid of the afflicted one. Also, it would usually be against that group's self-interest to destabilise the system of kinship relations in which it exists since the potential for conflict would be raised.

While norms endure over time, contestations that occur under competitive access occur repeatedly for two reasons. First, with limited resources, a kinship group is under constant pressure to gain more access. In the nomadic societies that tend to have competitive access, one cannot simply produce more of a vital limited resource like land or water. While competitive access is somewhat market-based, the highly inelastic nature of supply makes the system fragile. Second, because kinship groups with competitive access tend to be nomadic, inter-group interaction is ad hoc. Nomadic groups do not have the same kind of constant contact as their settled counterparts. This lack of contact makes it unlikely that nomadic groups will be able to create the kind of iterated bargaining that produces cooperation. Thus, nomadic kinship groups tend to have competitive access to vital limited resources.

Cooperative access means that different kinship groups work together to manage access to a vital limited resource. Among settled kinship groups, iterated contact raises the possibility of cooperation for access. Cooperation is not guaranteed, but it is incentivised given that different kinship groups can already manage living in the same location without substantial conflict. Cooperation also is more efficient since it requires only one system to provide resource access for all kinship groups rather than separate ones for each.

An inter-group system of resource management requires creating a new institution. The institution requires expertise to build, manage and oversee access for multiple hierarchies of resource distribution. These functions are bureaucratic because they require knowledge of the administrative system itself. However, the small size of such an institution makes it shy of being a full bureaucracy. As such, we may refer to such institutions as proto-bureaucracies.

Proto-bureaucracies function similarly to bureaucracies and manage access to vital limited resources between kinship hierarchies. Unlike the interactions governing access in a competitive access environment, they are not ad hoc, but rather administrate on a regular basis. Since proto-bureaucracies manage a specific system in a specific location, they are usually not very big. For small villages, a proto-bureaucracy may require only two or three people to successfully manage resource access. In larger towns or cities, more staff may be required. Critically, members of a proto-bureaucracy are members of kinship groups, but they have bureaucratic authority based primarily on their knowledge of the administrative system. In this regard, the staff of proto-bureaucracies have assent from the population to govern based on their acceptance of kinship authority, but the coercive capacity provided of bureaucratic authority. In some cases, they may even hold coercive power over the leaders of kinship groups. During state formation, proto-bureaucracies bridge the gap between kinship and bureaucratic authority by serving as an extension of state bureaucratic authority but possessing assent to govern based on kinship authority.

Competitive and cooperative access are the independent variables that explain variation in the political salience of kinship authority after state building. Competitive access is most common when groups are nomadic and draw upon a dispersed vital limited resource. The limited contact between groups and their constant movement makes norms the most likely means of regulating interaction. While norms may reduce the severity of conflict, competitive access means that disputes are handled on an ad hoc basis. These disputes are ongoing and part of a constant renegotiation among kinship groups for resource access. In contrast, cooperative access is most common among settled groups that draw upon a concentrated resource. Repeated interaction between groups increases the likelihood of forming a proto-bureaucracy to administer the resource. Proto-bureaucracies administer access between different kinship groups, but they are bureaucratic in that their function is based on individuals with knowledge of the administrative process. As opposed to norms that regulate behaviour under traditional kinship authority, proto-bureaucracies regulate behaviour using bureaucratic authority. This makes them an important element in state building.

Part Two: Kinship Salience during and after State Building

Having established that patterns of vital limited resource access can be competitive or cooperative, we can now turn to explaining the political effects of these differences. State building necessitates interaction between kinship groups and the bureaucratic state. The nature of kinship authority before state building shapes this interaction in fundamental ways.

State Building

State building is the context in which kinship authority develops governing or instrumentalised salience in a given state. It is also the period during which kinship and state bureaucratic authority first interact with each other. In a study of market institutions in the Middle East, Chaudhry (1997) defines state building in terms of bureaucracy: 'The elimination or co-optation of existing forms of authority and exchange that might challenge the existence of the state and expansion and centralization of the fiscal, legal and regulatory instruments of the state.'[4] This definition captures the idea that state building includes bureaucratic expansion and centralisation, a concept directly relevant to a process-tracing study of kinship in bureaucratic states. Critical to the bureaucratic expansion and centralisation process is the creation of physical infrastructure.[5] Thus, 'state building' in the context of this book refers to *a process by which a state creates or repurposes infrastructure within its borders to expand and centralise its governance.*

State building is in many ways an ongoing process. We can, however, define the end of the major state-building process in analytically useful ways. State building is a process by which the state gains enough administrative control to be the main provider of public services such as water and electricity provision, trash collection, records keeping, and land distribution. At the end of this process, such states will have developed (1) settled, or at least non-nomadic, populations; (2) a national-level bureaucracy for service provision; and (3) local branches of this bureaucracy that administer non-urban populations.

In many cases, the state-building period coincides with a new major inflow of capital. This inflow can be revenue from natural resource extraction, or a subsidy that a colonial benefactor provides. The state uses these revenues to contract major infrastructure projects that allow it to reach a critical minimum of resource provision. The source and duration of this revenue inflow is observable, which allows us to determine when state building begins and ends. State building infrastructure projects begin with a contract, treaty, law or edict signed on a certain date. They end when infrastructure projects commissioned under that document are complete, or at least, when construction work on them ceases. When enough projects have been completed to satisfy the three conditions above (settled population, national bureaucracy, local administrative branches), the state can be said to have reached a critical minimum that marks the end of the state-building period.

Components of State Building

For each element of state building, different patterns of resource access create different configurations of governance. These patterns are based on state interactions with kinship groups. Breaking down the state-building process in terms of each element helps to explain how these different patterns produce states with variation in the political salience of kinship authority.

State building can take many paths and there are conflicting ideas about whether modern bureaucratic governance enhances or degrades kinship authority. On the one hand, modernisation does not inherently threaten kinship. Inkeles' study of six cases of modernisation revealed that 'becoming modern was not at all consistently associated with the rejection of, or defaulting on, traditional obligation'.[6] Kostiner and Khoury point out that 'tribes were given a renewed role through their participation' in identity conflicts that arose from state formation.[7] In general, kinship continued to play an important role in the politics of many Middle Eastern states following state formation. On the other hand, 'the negative side of modernization was [that] . . . the ecological integrity and political autonomy of tribes were eroded . . . the change in tribal settlement patterns had political and socio-cultural implications'.[8] In other words, modernisation perpetuated but sometimes degraded the salience of kinship identity. For its part, kinship can change during state building as well. Recent work on Kuwait, for example, highlights the increasing importance over time of kinship group leaders as elite intermediaries with the state.[9] Assessing these processes is also helpful for understanding state building and modernisation in states with a history of kinship-based governance.

Existing accounts of state building indicate that kinship salience after state building is the norm.[10] However, there is no inherent reason that kinship should be salient after state building at all. In fact, bureaucratic states can destroy or eliminate kinship authority altogether. There are three reasons a state would do this. First, if kinship authority could seriously challenge not only the state's authority but its existence as a governing entity, the state may opt to demolish kinship authority within its borders. Kinship may pose not only an alternative to bureaucratic state governance but a direct and immediate challenge to it. In such cases, and if the state has the resources to demolish kinship authority, we might expect the state to do so out of the desire for survival. Second, where the cost of mitigating the challenge is less than the cost of ongoing management of kinship authority, states may opt for demolishing kinship authority rather than dealing with constant management. The challenge of kinship authority in this case is not existential, but it would impose significant costs on the state for as long as such authority continued to exist. Finally, if the state's claim to authority is predicated on a governing logic to which kinship authority is antithetical, the state may opt to demolish kinship authority. For example, it could be risky for a Marxist government's claim to authority to allow kinship authority to be salient given that kinship ties are a means for concentrating capital. The state would risk undermining a major pillar of its claim to rule.

Despite these rationales, the European disappearance of kinship authority is the global exception rather than the rule. The elimination of kinship authority was also often motivated by systemic political factors rather than states that were often weak.[11] Thus, this book focuses on states where kinship retains salience while acknowledging that this is not universally the case.

In other societies, different stages are necessary for successful state building, and in different sequences. For many historically kinship-based societies, however, state building is a sequential attempt to introduce three elements to a non-urban population. The scope of the model presented in this chapter is limited to these cases.

This book theorises a path-dependent process of state building that occurs in three stages. In stage one, the ruler builds or expands physical and bureaucratic infrastructure. In stage two, it uses this infrastructure to extend the

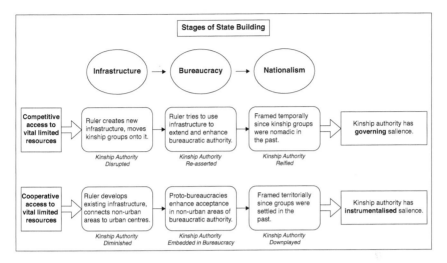

Figure 3.2   Effects of resource access on kinship salience after state building

bureaucratic authority from the urban centre to non-urban areas. In stage three, the state creates a nationalist idiom which underpins a narrative of the state's heritage and political origins. It bears noting that in the most relevant cases for the present theory, each element followed the next in the span of a few decades rather than a few centuries. It bears mention that this pathway of state building, while common, is not the only one. In some African cases, for example, bureaucratic authority and nationalism arose often with insufficient infrastructure. In China, shifting versions of nationalist idioms pre-date national infrastructure and the bureaucratic state by millennia. Thus, while the pathway examined here is both important and generalisable, we should not understand it as exclusive.

Stage one: infrastructure

The term infrastructure as used here includes roads, electric and phone lines, water, and buildings. States provide infrastructure for two reasons. First, infrastructure is a prerequisite for ruling bargains in which the state provides resources to subjects in exchange for loyalty. Second, infrastructure is a prerequisite for central bureaucratic governance. It provides a physical means for states to exert authority over populations in non-urban areas, and to connect these non-urban areas to a central bureaucratic authority.

Irrigation is one of the most important types of infrastructure. For this reason, it features prominently in early accounts of modernisation and the 'hydraulic civilization'. The management of water through irrigation required discipline and organisation, as well as a knowledge of science.[12] The technical expertise and knowledge required for irrigation also underlie bureaucratic authority. Irrigation is one example of the kind of infrastructure that may be useful for distributing a vital limited resource and creating bureaucratic governance.

State capacity is an important factor in the way in and extent to which rulers create infrastructure. They must have the capital and the technical knowledge to build roads, utility lines and water pipes that will be the basis of state governance. However, a ruler's ability to extend infrastructure is constrained by the nature of the population that infrastructure is serving. Specifically, the population's pre-existing resource access affects what infrastructure during stage one will be more effective for extending state bureaucracy during stage two of state building. This is especially true in non-urban areas where rulers may not yet project sovereignty.

Given the objective of expansion and centralisation, a state undertakes infrastructure building in one of three ways: it can extend it into areas where the population already lives, it can supplement or enhance existing infrastructure, and it can create new areas where infrastructure is provided and move populations into these areas. The decision to take each approach is shaped by patterns of resource access before state building and state interaction with non-urban populations during that time period. Furthermore, since infrastructure is physical, each of these patterns of infrastructure building is observable.

The salience of kinship after state building is determined by resource access among the specific groups to whom the state reaches out. States may exhibit subnational variation with certain kinship groups that have competitive access to resources while others have cooperative access. For the purposes of this model, the groups that have direct contact with the state at the beginning of the state-building period are most relevant.

Where access to vital limited resources is competitive before state building, kinship groups are usually nomadic and lack an overarching institution mediating this access. In such cases, rulers and ruling families create and expand infrastructure to provide services to these nomadic non-urban populations, gain territorial control over non-urban areas, and connect infrastructure in these areas to infrastructure in the centre. Simultaneously, the objective of infrastructure creation is to extend the bureaucratic reach of the state. Since infrastructure is stationary, this poses a challenge when non-urban populations are nomadic. To overcome this challenge, rulers' families engage in a particular type of infrastructure building called sedentarisation. They create new infrastructure and incentivise kinship groups to move onto this infrastructure. Once this process is completed, these groups and their members will then be beholden to the state for resource access and the state's provision of infrastructure can become part of a ruling bargain of loyalty-for-resources. Sedentarisation involves not only a disruption of nomadic lifestyles but also a disruption of kinship authority and kinship-based governance. Settled populations are significantly easier for states to govern through bureaucratic authority. Thus, settling competing kinship groups on new infrastructure is a critical part of state building in such cases.

These processes disrupt kinship authority but do not erase it. Critically, rulers and ruling families reach out to and engage the non-urban population *as kinship groups* as opposed to individuals or other political identities. Since these groups are also hierarchical, rulers economise their efforts by engaging with group leaders rather than the entire tribe. Kinship group hierarchies also serve as ready-made patronage networks. Rulers and ruling families offer kinship groups a ruling bargain of infrastructure and provision of services in exchange for loyalty. This process of engagement, however, indicates government recognition of kinship groups and their internal hierarchies mediated by kinship authority. While kinship authority does not cause rulers and ruling families to engage in this way, it is nonetheless perpetuated by the process of government outreach and sedentarisation.

In contrast, when access to vital limited resources is cooperative, kinship groups use proto-bureaucracies to mediate access. Rulers and families can take advantage of the existing infrastructure proto-bureaucracies manage by expanding it and linking it with infrastructure at the centre, where the seat of government resides. For example, they may pave local dirt roads and link them to a national highway. Rulers and ruling families may create some new buildings that are safer or nicer and move populations into them, but these buildings are usually in the vicinity of existing settlements since it minimises the magnitude of change for the local population. Creating completely new infrastructure and moving populations onto it in this case would be unnecessary and could actively damage the state's attempt to extend bureaucratic authority through this infrastructure.

While the population in this case still consists of kinship groups, the critical difference is the existence of proto-bureaucracies. Since proto-bureaucracies already manage infrastructures of resource provision, the ruler can incorporate them as part of infrastructure building rather than conducting outreach to kinship groups. Kinship authority does not disappear during this stage but is diminished as local infrastructure managed by proto-bureaucracies begins to be grafted onto state infrastructure.

In summary, based on whether kinship groups have competitive or cooperative resource access before state building, a ruler will either (in the former case) build new infrastructure and move kinship groups onto it, or (in the latter case) enhance existing local infrastructure and link it to infrastructure in the centre. Infrastructure is a critical step in state building because it allows the future state to control its population's access to resources through bureaucratic means.

Stage two: bureaucratic authority

Stage two of state building involves the extension of bureaucratic authority beyond the centre into non-urban areas. This authority is often intricately connected to property and land ownership in the context of state building.[13] Infrastructure provides a vector for this process to occur. Just as resource access constrains steps the ruler can take at stage one, it further constrains the actions it can take with regard to the extension of bureaucracy.

The extension of bureaucracy and a bureaucratic apparatus is the most important part of state building since without bureaucratic institutions there is no state. For our purposes, it is also the stage at which kinship authority and bureaucratic authority come into direct contact since both mediate resource access for the non-urban population. Stage two is thus a critical juncture at which kinship authority either reasserts itself following the disruption of sedentarisation, or becomes embedded in the state's bureaucratic apparatus.

Bureaucratic institutions not only provide services, but also shape beliefs and attitudes.[14] Some of the most important such institutions are schools, which provide mass education to a population. Schools allow modernisation through teaching career skills and create a common 'durable national loyalty' to a state from among many different populations within it.[15] They can also create significantly more pro-modernisation values and attitudes in the children who attend them.[16]

In addition to creating buy-in for the state-building project, schools also create bureaucrats to administer the state's affairs. Russian nation building in Turkmenistan, for example, involved the construction and operation of schools to educate Turkmen boys. These boys then grew up to be members of a Russian bureaucratic class.[17] In France, the military served as a vector for literacy and the inculcation of French nationalism among the population. The imposition of national bureaucratic authority through mass education gave soldiers a more universally 'French' identity.[18] Poor road conditions made getting to schools practically impossible for the rurally based students who often were a majority in their parishes.[19] In addition, landlords often kept students home to tend the fields. The success of French nationalism has its roots not only in nationalist ideology taught in schools, but in physical improvements to roads and advances in agricultural technology that allowed children to study without jeopardising crop yields.[20]

When resource access is competitive, rulers build new infrastructure and move kinship groups onto it. They will then try to use this infrastructure to govern using bureaucratic authority. Sedentary populations are more easily governed through bureaucratic authority than nomadic ones. Individuals living in a discrete domicile can more easily receive basic services, and can also be more easily held accountable since the government knows, literally, where they live. Sedentarisation disrupts kinship authority by introducing a competing provider of resources and changing spatial relations between kinship groups and their members. It creates an opportunity for the state to introduce bureaucratic authority. The ruler extends bureaucratic authority using the infrastructure onto which sedentarised populations are settled. They provide electricity and water, but monitor, regulate, and perhaps even tax its use. They build roads but implement rules for their usage and also implement license systems governing who can operate vehicles on them. Central state authority also extends to these sedentarised areas through services like education. Schooling takes place in buildings constructed by the government, which are staffed by teachers paid by the government and use curricula approved by the government.

At the same time, this process is constrained by the ruler's outreach to individual kinship groups that preceded sedentarisation in three ways. First, since the population was engaged as kinship groups, kinship identity reasserts itself as an important identity marker for interactions vis-à-vis the state. Second, while the state provides access to vital limited resources, other resources will still be mediated through kinship authority. Even though the government becomes the main provider of services, kinship hierarchies continue to be necessary for managing service provision to individuals.[21] Finally, kinship authority sustained in both these ways will begin to instrumentalise bureaucratic authority. This means that it will attempt to use the institutions and resources of the bureaucratic apparatus in ways that sustain kinship authority. For example, subsidies may be released to the population through kinship group leaders who then distribute these subsidies through hierarchies regulated by kinship authority. Members of kinship groups with official status in the bureaucracy may favour members of their kinship group over others consistent with kinship authority. Ultimately, while the ruler extends bureaucratic authority, it becomes a tool for kinship groups to obtain resources and political access.

When resource access before state building is cooperative, the ruler improves existing infrastructure and links it to infrastructure in the centre. Proto-bureaucracies already mediate access to vital limited resources among a settled population. Their staff have bureaucratic authority in that their coercive power originates in expertise on the governing process itself. However, they are also members of local kinship groups and are embedded in these groups' hierarchies. These parameters constrain the ruler's options during the extension of bureaucratic authority.

Dissolving proto-bureaucracies would risk angering local populations and, more importantly, activating kinship hierarchies to resist the state's imposition of bureaucratic authority. Thus, the ruler instead will embed proto-bureaucracies into the state's bureaucratic apparatus. Staff in these proto-bureaucracies retain their positions in the proto-bureaucracy, but it becomes a part of state-wide bureaucratic institutions. This arrangement avoids backlash from the local population since little changes at the local level in terms of which staff oversee which functions of resource access. Embedding proto-bureaucracies also represents the instrumentalisation of kinship authority by the bureaucratic state. The state uses the population's acceptance of kinship group members who staff the proto-bureaucracy to reduce local friction as it expands its bureaucratic authority.

Stage three: nationalism

The successful extension of bureaucratic authority requires non-urban populations to assent to the state's rule. States use nationalism to enhance this assent. Nationalism is not strictly necessary for state building but it can enhance the extent of this assent. As with the elements of infrastructure and bureaucracy, nationalism too varies based on patterns of resource access before state building.

The idea of nationalism is tied to bureaucratic governance. As Gellner describes, its imposition involves 'the general diffusion of a school-mediated, academy supervised idiom, codified for the requirements of a reasonably precise bureaucratic and technological communication'.[22] Nationalism in kinship-based societies encourages loyalty to the state and its leadership above kinship ties. However, nationalism is often difficult to achieve when the state's population consists of multiple kinship groups whose kinship hierarchies remain politically salient. By creating a nationalist idiom by which the state's leadership is the vanguard of the national project, loyalty to nationalist ideals means loyalty to the leadership as well. Infrastructure is crucial for spreading this nationalist idiom. In particular, mass literacy allows for easier communication by the state and more reliable storage of history and national myths than in other areas.[23] Kinship identity sometimes factors into these histories and national myths, and did so frequently in the Arab Gulf states.[24] Saudi Arabia, for example, emphasised genealogy and family lineage as the basis of national citizenship. The bureaucratic apparatus of the state set out to record on paper what until that point had been oral histories of kinship lineages.[25]

States can generate assent to rule by providing resources and political access and threatening punishments. They can also appeal to a sense of duty and pride rooted in nationalism. By tying the ruler into the national narrative directly, states can link loyalty to the ruler with patriotism and fulfilling one's nationalist duty. Nationalism is also important to state building because it represents the creation of a story about the state-building process itself. In societies where kinship authority exists, the nationalist story must acknowledge the past importance of these groups while also providing a story about why their role has changed now, and why this change is good. The idiom upon which these stories are based is constrained by the process of state building up to this point.

When resource access is competitive before state building, the ruler sedentarises the population and tries to extend bureaucratic authority through newly created infrastructure. Describing this process as the 'taming' of kinship groups would understandably generate backlash. Instead, the state reifies the role kinship groups played in state building using a temporal idiom of nationalism. In other words, it glorifies the historic moment at which kinship groups collectively settled and formed the modern state. Membership in the national project is described in terms of when one's kin settled in the new state. Thus, even at the end of state building, the importance of kinship groups is part and parcel of the nationalism upon which the state legitimates itself.

In contrast, when resource access is cooperative before state building, the ruler expands existing infrastructure and links it to infrastructure in the centre. The state bureaucratic apparatus embeds proto-bureaucracies staffed by members of kinship groups. Since state building consists of expanding the state's authority into non-urban areas, the nationalist idiom in such cases is territorial. Membership in the nation is determined by the state's borders and bureaucratic control. Temporal idioms in this case would serve only to reiterate the fact that alternatives to bureaucratic authority existed. Additionally, since these groups were already settled before state building, it makes little sense to define membership in terms of when each group arrived. At the end of state building, therefore, these nationalist narratives promoted by the state downplay the historic role of kinship authority.

To summarise, state building commonly involves three elements: infrastructure, bureaucratic authority and nationalism. State building can take place along two different paths as each of these elements comes into play during state building. Each path is shaped by patterns of access by kinship groups to vital limited resources before state building.

When access to resources is competitive, states extend infrastructure to their nomadic non-urban kinship groups. This extension of infrastructure gives the state control over the means of access to resources. Control of resource access creates the basis for the state's bureaucratic authority over these kinship groups. The state's nationalist projects in such cases will be based on the timing of when kinship groups came onto the state's infrastructure.

When access to resources is cooperative, states enhance local infrastructure and extend infrastructure from the national grid to local towns and villages. They make use of existing proto-bureaucracies by embedding them into the state's bureaucratic apparatus. This embedding process enhances the population's buy-in to bureaucratic authority. Nationalist idioms in such cases will be based on territory, with the national infrastructure serving as the linkage between one town or village, and the other towns or villages where nationals live.

Case Selection

The cases of Kuwait, Qatar and Oman presented in the following chapters constitute a most similar case comparison of the relationship between access to vital limited resources and kinship salience. Such a comparison explores variation of the independent and dependent variables while holding most other factors constant.[26]

This book selects cases from among the Arab Gulf states to explain how differences in resource access affect the political salience of kinship authority. The Gulf region has been the site of major social science scholarship on kinship politics and state formation. Furthermore, water resources in the Arab Gulf are a quintessential example of the vital limited resources that are key to this book's argument. Water is a common example of a vital limited resource and is a good starting point for inquiries into how these resources are accessed. Furthermore, the similarity of cases in the Arab Gulf allows us to control effectively for other variables. While recognising that the Gulf states are not a monolith, states in the region share similar kinds of kinship hierarchies, state building and administration that make the region an excellent set of cases for studies of kinship authority and state formation.

Kuwait, Qatar and Oman are Arab Gulf states with histories of kinship-based rule. As Arab Gulf states, they have many important factors in common that serve as scope conditions for the theoretical model. These factors include a similar experience of Western influence over the state-building process, sparse access to water, kinship-based governance before state building, and a state government created through direct intervention by an outside actor. Many states across the Middle East, Africa and South America exhibit such conditions. Cases lacking any one of these four factors may exhibit different causal processes and thus are outside the parameters of the model.

However, expanding the model presented here through future research would provide explanatory leverage for these cases since it is based on quintessential elements of state building that can be changed.

A key difference between Kuwait and Qatar on the one hand and Oman on the other is their resource access patterns, explained earlier in this chapter. Kuwait and Qatar are examples of competitive access before state building while Oman is an example of cooperative access. This rest of this chapter provides an introduction to each case, including the history of leadership in the country and an explanation of urban resource access. It then illustrates and compares competitive resource access in Kuwait and Qatar to cooperative access in Oman.

In Kuwait and Qatar, kinship identity has governing political salience. In Oman, it has instrumentalised political salience. This variation between cases avoids the problem of selection on the dependent variable.[27] Kuwait and Qatar have a number of factors in common that make them useful for a comparative study of kinship authority and state building. Most importantly, water is a vital limited resource in both, and kinship groups were important to resource access in both places before state building. They both had non-urban kinship groups that interacted with the state during the state-building process. This element is critical for testing alternate explanations of state capacity, since the argument is that both these kinships groups and the state itself affect outcomes at the end of state building.

On the major variables listed above, Kuwait, Qatar and Oman are comparable. Some differences do exist, however. Firstly, Oman is considerably bigger than Kuwait or Qatar. Oman's leadership needed to project power into a wider area than did Kuwait's leadership. In addition, while many of Oman's tribes exist within the state's borders, Kuwait and Qatar's small size means that some of their tribes are split between Saudi Arabia and (in the Kuwaiti case) Iraq. However, the model is based on the kind of resource access network rather than its size. What truly matters is whether access to resources within the purview of kinship structures was competitive or cooperative.

Most importantly, Kuwait, Qatar and Oman vary in terms of the salience of kinship authority. In Kuwait and Qatar, kinship authority has governing salience whereas in Oman it has instrumentalised salience. Additionally, Kuwait and Qatar both have extensive kinship networks that have been the subject of attention for multiple historians and social scientists, allowing the current analysis to draw upon a wide body of existing scholarly work. Kuwait, Qatar and Oman are not the only Arab Gulf states with a history of tribal politics before, during and after state building. However, they provide the best comparison that holds other exogenous factors constant. Anomalies in the state-building process rule out Arab Gulf states like Saudi Arabia, the United Arab Emirates and Yemen. Bahrain's small physical and population size and island geography also make it a difficult comparison given that competition for resources often crossed national borders in the Gulf region.

Kuwait and Qatar most closely resemble the typical case among both the Arab Gulf states, and the universe of cases more broadly. Oman, in contrast, serves as an exception that proves the rule. Showing meaningfully different outcomes in the salience of kinship in Kuwait and Qatar versus Oman demonstrates the importance of pre-state conditions. While competitive access to vital limited resources in Kuwait and Qatar created governing kinship salience after state building, cooperative access in Oman created instrumentalised kinship salience after state building. The following three chapters illustrate how the theoretical patterns of resource allocation described in this chapter played out in an empirical context.

Notes

1. Joseph Kostiner, 'The Nation in Tribal Societies: Reflections on K. H. al-Naqib's Studies on the Gulf', in Uzi Rabi (ed.), *Tribes and States in a Changing Middle East* (Oxford, UK: Oxford University Press, 2016): 222.
2. Robert Axelrod and Robert O. Keohane, 'Achieving Cooperation under Anarchy: Strategies and Institutions', *World Politics* 38 no. 1 (October 1985): 226–54.
3. See Karl A. Wittfogel, *Oriental Despotism: A Comparative Study of Total Power* (New Haven, CT: Yale University Press, 1976).
4. Kiren Aziz Chaudhry, *The Price of Wealth: Economies and Institutions in the Middle East* (Ithaca, NY: Cornell University Press, 1997): 6.
5. Krasner and Risse also note the importance of infrastructure to state building while recognising the public goods provision this infrastructure facilitates. See Stephen D. Krasner and Thomas Risse, 'External Actors, State-Building, and Service Provision in Areas of Limited Statehood: Introduction', *Governance* 27 no. 4 (October 2014): 546.
6. Alex Inkeles, *Exploring Individual Modernity* (New York, NY: Columbia University Press, 1983): 24.
7. Philip S. Khoury and Joseph Kostiner, *Tribes and State Formation in the Middle East* (Los Angeles, CA: University of California Press, 1990): 16.
8. Joseph Kostiner, 'Transforming Dualities: Tribe and State Formation in Saudi Arabia', in Philip S. Khoury and Joseph Kostiner (eds), *Tribes and State Formation in the Middle East* (Los Angeles, CA: University of California Press, 1990): 244.
9. Azoulay, *Kuwait and al-Sabah*, 69.
10. See Lisa Anderson, *The State and Social Transformation in Tunisia and Libya (1830–1980)* (Princeton, NJ: Princeton University Press, 1986); Edward Schatz, *Modern Clan Politics: The Power of 'Blood' in Kazakhstan and Beyond* (Seattle, WA: University of Washington Press, 2004); Adrienne Lynne Edgar, *Tribal*

Nation: The Making of Soviet Turkmenistan (Princeton, NJ: Princeton University Press, 2004); Kate Baldwin, *When Politicians Cede Control of Resources: Land, chiefs and coalition-building in Africa.* Afrobarometer Working Papers, Working Paper No. 130 (2011).

11. Francis Fukuyama, *The Origins of Political Order: From Prehuman Times to the French Revolution* (New York, NY: Farrar, Straus and Giroux, 2011): 229–31; Avner Greif and David D. Latin, 'A Theory of Endogenous Institutional Change', *American Political Science Review* 98 no. 4 (November 2004): 643.

12. Wittfogel, *Oriental Despotism*, 29.

13. Christian Lund and Catherine Boone, 'Introduction: Land Politics in Africa – Constituting Authority Over Territory, Property and Persons', *Africa* 83 no. 1 (February 2013): 2.

14. See Alex Inkeles, 'Industrial Man: The Relation of Status to Experience, Perception, and Value', *American Journal of Sociology* 66 no. 1 (July 1960): 1–31.

15. Harris Mylonas and Keith Darden, 'Threats to Territorial Integrity, National Mass Schooling and Linguistic Commonality', *Comparative Political Studies* 49 no. 11 (September 2016): 1447.

16. Michael Armer and Robert Youtz, 'Formal Education and Individual Modernity in an African Society', *American Journal of Sociology* 76 no. 4 (January 1971): 621; Donald B. Holsinger, 'The Elementary School as Modernizer: A Brazilian Study', *International Journal of Comparative Sociology* 14 no. 3–4 (1973): 200.

17. Edgar, *Tribal Nation*, 31.

18. Eugen Weber, *Peasants into Frenchmen: The Modernization of Rural France, 1870–1914* (Stanford, CA: Stanford University Press, 1976): 298.

19. Weber, *Peasants into Frenchmen*, 320.

20. Weber, *Peasants into Frenchmen*, 323.

21. Al-Haj refers to the provision of benefits to individual as 'instrumentalized kinship'. See Majid al-Haj, 'Kinship and Modernization in Developing Societies: The Emergence of Instrumentalized Kinship', *Journal of Comparative Family Studies* 26 no. 3 (Autumn 1995): 324.

22. Ernst Gellner, *Nations and Nationalism* (Ithaca, NY: Cornell University Press, 1983): 57.

23. Keith Darden and Anna Grzymala-Busse, 'The Great Divide: Literacy, Nationalism, and the Communist Collapse', *World Politics* 59 no. 1 (October 2006): 98.

24. See Miriam Cooke, *Tribal Modern: Branding New Nations in the Arab Gulf* (Los Angeles, CA: UCLA Press, 2014).

25. Nadav Samin, *Of Sand or Soil: Genealogy and Tribal Belonging in Saudi Arabia* (Princeton, NJ: Princeton University Press, 2015): 193.

26. Jason Seawright and John Gerring, 'Case Selection Techniques in Case Study Research: A Menu of Qualitative and Quantitative Options', *Political Research Quarterly* 61 no. 2 (June 2008): 304.

27. See Barbara Geddes, 'How the Cases You Choose Affect the Answers You Get: Selection Bias in Comparative Politics', *Political Analysis* 2 no. 1 (1990): 131–50.

4

STATE BUILDING IN KUWAIT

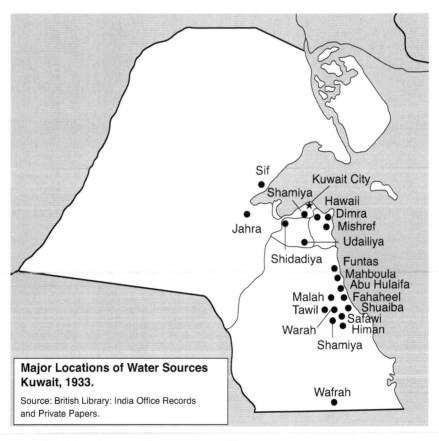

Major Locations of Water Sources Kuwait, 1933.

Source: British Library: India Office Records and Private Papers.

Figure 4.1   Major locations of water sources in Kuwait, 1933

Tribal and kinship identity in Kuwait is central to public and political life. Kinship authority has largely instrumentalised the state bureaucracy. The right tribal last name can be a key to a license, doctor's appointment, building permit, or well-paying job. Government ministry jobs that offer a comfortable salary and short hours are often distributed according to kinship affiliation. For the highest status families, major life events like weddings and funerals can warrant a visit from the Emir. Families and family lineage are often a matter of public knowledge and families pride themselves on the accuracy and completeness of increasingly popular family trees. Social life in Kuwait involves weekly *diwaniya* meetings where male members of a family gather to drink tea or coffee and talk business and politics. This governing salience of kinship identity in Kuwait, however, was not a foregone conclusion. Rather, patterns of resource access before state building constrained the Kuwaiti ruling family's options in a path-dependent way such that kinship now has governing salience in the country.

Kuwait's competitive access to vital limited resources before state building set the country on this path toward governing kinship salience. Before state building, kinship groups in Kuwait had control over resources in constantly shifting territories known as *diyar*. To establish territorial control, Kuwait's leadership reached out to these groups in an attempt to bring them under the purview of the state. The outcomes of this process reified the importance of kinship authority in an otherwise bureaucratic Kuwaiti state.

During state building, the Kuwaiti government sedentarised kinship groups onto newly created infrastructure in order to disrupt kinship authority. However, these groups settled together and resisted government attempts to split them up, reasserting kinship authority. The government used the infrastructure it had built to try to extend its bureaucratic authority. This authority, however, was mediated by patronage networks established and governed by kinship authority. As a result, these networks began to instrumentalise the state bureaucracy to obtain resources and political access. Finally, Kuwait developed a nationalist project reflecting a temporal idiom. In other words, the 'most Kuwaiti' families are ones who were present in Kuwait earlier. This nationalist project stabilised the ruling family's hold on power and enhanced buy-in to the state-building project. At the same time, it reified kinship authority by glorifying kinship groups with an early presence in the state as important political constituencies. As an outcome of this process, kinship authority after state building has governing political salience in Kuwait.

Introduction

Kuwait is a parliamentary monarchy at the northern end of the Gulf nestled between Iraq to the north and Saudi Arabia to the west and south. It is roughly the size of the US state of New Jersey. The word Kuwait comes from *kut*, or fort, a nod to the history of conflict in the northern Nejd desert in which Kuwait is situated. Kuwait gained independence in 1961 after sixty-two years as a British protected state. Kuwait's head of state is the Emir, who is always from the royal al-Sabah family. The al-Sabah comprise roughly 1,200 Kuwaitis out of a total and growing Kuwaiti population of 3 million in 2021.[1] The Emir is chosen by consensus within the royal family, but Kuwaitis elect a fifty-seat parliament, the *Majlis al-Umma*, with ten members elected from each of Kuwait's five electoral districts. The *Majlis* proposes its own legislation and has the power to interpolate members of the cabinet. However, the Emir can dissolve the parliament and call for new elections.

Kuwait's governance is bureaucratic, consisting of ministries and agencies that ensure the adequate provision of services. This governance is regulated by the country's 1962 constitution, a document widely respected in the country. In Kuwait, the Emir appoints a Prime Minister who oversees a Council of Ministers, at least one of whom must be an elected member of the *Majlis al-Umma*. These individuals oversee Kuwait's ministries. The Emir receives advice and guidance from an Emiri Diwan, a council of ministers appointed from among the major families in Kuwait. Nonetheless, the Emir's role as leader of the al-Sabah family is a vital component of his mandate to rule.

The Ruling Family of Kuwait

The al-Sabah family rules Kuwait. The family is part of the 'Utub tribal confederation and is named for Sabah bin Jaber, the first ruler of Kuwait City who lived between 1718 and 1762. The current ruling family consists of descendants who trace their lineage back to Mubarak al-Sabah, who entered into a

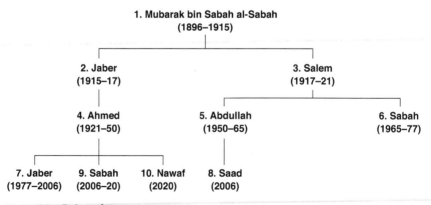

Figure 4.2   Rulers of Kuwait since 1896

treaty with Britain in 1899 making Kuwait a British-protected state. While the family consists of roughly 1,200 members – all of whom have special status in Kuwait – political leadership is concentrated today in the hands of a small group of family patriarchs who are descendants of Mubarak's son Jaber.

The al-Sabah settled in Kuwait City along with their other 'Utub counterparts sometime before 1750. Prior to their arrival, Kuwait was under the rule of the Bani Khalid tribe. However, their power declined over time due to antagonism with the Ottomans, major tribal leaders, and eventually the death of the Bani Khalid sheikh, Sulaiman bin Muhammad al-Hamad, in 1752. He was replaced by Sheikh Sabah bin Jaber al-Sabah.[2] Under his rule, the Awazim helped build a protective wall (the *Soor)* around Kuwait City and repelled attacks in the desert areas surrounding it.[3]

In the nineteenth century, the al-Sabah were among a number of powerful families vying for influence in the Nejd region that encompassed Kuwait and northern Saudi Arabia. The al-Rashid family, a branch of the large Shammar tribal confederation, controlled a large swath of land in modern-day Saudi Arabia. This polity, called the Emirate of Ha'il, lasted from 1836 until 1921 when the Emirate's Rashaida leaders surrendered to Saudi forces following a military defeat.[4]

The al-Saud family was also a major player in the region's politics and it had extensive interaction with the al-Sabah. The dynasty was consolidated in 1720 when Saud ibn Mohammad ibn Miqrin deposed his nephew Musa.[5] In 1744, Saud's son Mohammed allied with Muhammed ibn abd al-Wahhab, founder of the Wahhabi religious movement. His son and Abd al-Wahhab's daughter were married as a show of faith in this alliance.[6] The combination of Saudi military power and Wahhabi ideology proved formidable at first. However, the alliance suffered a series of setbacks – first from the Sultan of Egypt Mohammed Ali in 1818 and then by the al-Rashid who captured Riyadh in 1891 in the Battle of al-Mulayda. In 1902, the city was recaptured by Ibn Saud.[7] At that time, the leader of family was Ibn Saud (Abd al-Aziz al-Saud), who was born sometime between 1876 and 1880. He formed a force called the Ikhwan in 1912 who were based in communities called *hujar*. By 1916, there were twenty such *hujar* with a population of 60,000 men.[8]

The al-Saud and al-Sabah both originate from the Aniza tribe. They are connected through Lulua al-Thaqib, the influential mother of Mubarak al-Sabah, who came from the same family (though a different branch) as Saud.[9] When they were driven out of Riyadh in 1891, the al-Saud took refuge in Kuwait under the auspices of the al-Sabah. They also took on joint campaigns, including one against the Mutair tribe and its leader Faisal Duweesh in 1903.[10] Most importantly, the British had alliances with both the al-Sabah and the al-Saud. However, the families often competed for tribal influence and territory, leading to a delicate political game in which tribal influence was the prize. After Mubarak had helped Ibn Saud defeat the Ajman in 1916, for example, Sheikh Jaber authorised Sheikh Salem to grant some of these Ajman refuge in Kuwait.[11]

Preconditions to State Building in Kuwait

State building often involves a set of interactions between a ruler in the urban centre and kinship groups in non-urban areas of the state. As the urban centre develops infrastructure and the ruler expands his governing apparatus from a small group of advisors into a bureaucratic government, his power can then be projected out to the non-urban areas. Assessing conditions in the urban centre before state building therefore helps to frame the incentive structure of the ruler with regards to state building. Rulers reaching out to non-urban kinship groups is the core of state building, but understanding the full extent of the ruler's capabilities and constraints contextualises this process. It helps us understand the ruler – and later the government's – incentives and motivations for taking certain actions and making certain decisions during state building.

Preconditions in the Centre

Kuwait City arose as a shipping port. The secluded waters of Kuwait Bay offered maritime merchants and shipowners protection from the rougher waters – and pirates – of the Gulf. Port cities along the Gulf were waypoints for global trade routes linking Europe, the Middle East, Africa and India. Ships began their journey at Basra, near the southern tip of Iraq. Travelling south, some sailed along the southwestern coast of Iran, while others travelled along the Arabian Peninsula. After passing through the Strait of Hormuz and along the coast of northern Oman, the ships would either travel south to Africa for resources like wood, or east to India for spices.

Arab Gulf towns were also regional bases for pearling vessels and their crews. The pearl trade was a major element of Kuwait's economy. Pearl divers worked on ships for months at a time to collect pearls that would be sold at regional (and eventually international) markets. Ship captains, or *nakhodas*, would sail out into the Gulf with pearl divers aboard. These divers, without breathing assistance, worked twelve- to sixteen-hour days, diving as deep as sixty feet (eighteen metres) under the water to the rocky seabed.[12] They would collect oysters by hand and place them into a mesh basket that hung from their necks before being pulled to the surface by a rope. The pearls from these oysters would be brought back to shore, weighed and sold in the pearl market in Kuwait City. Pearl diving was not a lucrative occupation nor a pleasant lifestyle. It required men to be away from their families for months at a time while the ship was at sea. Furthermore, pearl diving was a debt-based system. Pearl divers were paid an advance by the *nakhoda* and then worked to pay back their debt in the number of pearls retrieved. *Nakhodas* in turn were in debt to pearl merchants, who were in turn often indebted to pearl buyers. This debt-based system worked against the accumulation of wealth for those at the lower levels of the system. It also stunted the economic growth of Kuwait City since these indebted individuals were also consumers.

Kuwait City before state building consisted of densely packed neighbourhoods where houses were made of mud-brick. The streets were unpaved. The city itself was protected by a wall, which protected it from tribal invaders from the west. People living outside the city, however, participated in commerce within the city limits, and the city was a centre of both land- and sea-based trade.[13] Importantly, Kuwait City was not merely an isolated coastal town. It was, rather, a cosmopolitan crossroads that fostered interaction between Kuwaiti merchants, captains and sailors from the Middle East, Africa, India, and beyond. These interactions contributed to Kuwaiti infrastructure as well. For example, wooden ceilings were not uncommon in Kuwaiti houses. This is surprising given that Kuwait has little vegetation and no forests. Because of the shipping trade, however, it was possible to ship wood to Kuwait from forests in East Africa and India.[14]

Kuwait City was also home to several merchant families. These families, some of whom were members of kinship groups stretching across the Arabian Peninsula, were involved in the shipping and pearling trade. In addition to these merchant families, Kuwait City and its surrounding areas were inhabited by seasonal migrant tribes including the Awazim. Some estimates place the group at 25 per cent of Kuwait's total population before state development.[15] The Awazim were seasonal migrants. During the summer months, many worked as farmers, fishermen, pearl divers or ship captains (*nakhodhas*). Members of the tribe often, though not always, worked alongside each other on these ships. In the winter, they moved west into the desert and raised camels, sheep and goats.[16] By 1908, 250 Awazim families lived in Kuwait City in a quarter bearing their name. They also inhabited the town of Jahra, to the west of Kuwait, and were the original inhabitants of Dimna, an oasis and fishing village to the west which today is the Salmiya area of Kuwait City. Such oases were dispersed throughout Kuwait and the northern Nejd desert.

Water Access

Until the twentieth century, Kuwait City had few native water resources. Most of the city's water came from two lines of wells outside the city. One was to the southeast in what is today the Dasma neighbourhood, and the other was to the southwest near what is today the Shamiya neighbourhood.[17] Kuwait also had palm groves, situated at oases and settlements along the coast. These groves required water that was fresh, but not necessarily potable. They were irrigated via ditches that drew from underground water sources.[18] The plantations varied in size from a few hundred to a few thousand date trees. Both nomadic and seasonally migratory groups – or their leaders – owned these groves, and the al-Sabah family also owned a number of date groves in the region.[19]

While each house in Kuwait City had a well, the water was often brackish and unsuitable for drinking.[20] By 1908, population growth in the town made existing water resources insufficient, especially in periods of low rainfall.[21] To address this shortfall, Kuwait began obtaining water from the Shatt-el-Arab at the southern Iraqi port of Fao about sixty miles away. Water came via a boat (*duba*) and it was stored in a small reservoir near Shuweikh beach.[22] In some cases, women would bring empty tins directly to the beach to fill with water from the boat when it arrived.[23] The water was cooled and stored in leather bags, and distributed once or twice per day by donkey, wagon or water truck (called a *tenek*, from the English word 'tank') by private entrepreneurs, many of whom were Persian. Each time the water carrier made a delivery, he put a chalk mark outside the entrance to the house. When the house's tally reached ten marks, the water carrier would ask the family for payment. A bag of water cost one half rupee.[24] Prominent residents of the city also sponsored the construction of tanks and provided free water to others in the city. These tanks were also funded in certain cases by endowments (*awqaf*).[25]

As Kuwait's population expanded, the supply of water and other resources quickly became insufficient. Between 1909 and 1912 several bazaars opened and a set of new pearling ships began operating from Kuwait City. The demand for housing was so great that the wages of those involved in house construction doubled. Water also became more expensive, and old brackish wells that had fallen out of use were re-opened out of sheer demand.[26]

As Kuwait City's population continued to grow, responsibility for providing access to water resources fell more and more heavily on the leadership. Local collective action was no longer sufficient for this access and Mubarak came under considerable pressure to respond to the shortage. On 9 November 1912, he sent an unusually deferential letter to Percy Cox, the Political Resident in the Persian Gulf, requesting help to address the lack of drinking water in Kuwait City.[27] In his analysis accompanying the letter, Kuwait's Political Agent William Shakespear noted: 'The Shaikh is convinced that he must make some adequate arrangement for a proper water-supply at once, he does not care at what cost as the necessity is so great.'[28]

It was these pressures that led – one year later – to Kuwait's first attempt at water desalination. In 1913, Sheikh Mubarak contracted Kuwait's first desalinisation plant with the assistance of the British government, and built under the auspices of Strick Scott and Co., LLC. The plant was designed to produce 100,000 gallons of fresh water every twenty-four hours.[29] However, by 1919 the plant was still not producing sufficient water, and that which it did produce was salty and discoloured. The new emir, Sheikh Salem, demanded a refund for the ineffective plant, and in March 1931 he and Strick Scott agreed to a refund of 250,000 Rs.[30] Kuwait did not build a new desalinisation plant until 1951. By this time, water access had become enmeshed with the Kuwaiti state-building project.

Water shipment to Kuwait from Iraq expanded throughout the early twentieth century. By 1933, forty boats were in use to bring about 35,000 gallons of water per day, which came from the Shatt al-Arab at the rate of six boats per day.[31] These water resources expanded in 1939 with the establishment of a company to manage the shipment of 8,500 gallons of water per day to Kuwait City. This shipping of water from the Shatt to Kuwait continued into the 1950s.[32] According to the British Political Resident, 'Artesian wells could probably be sunk . . . which may render the population completely independent of the Shatt-el-Arab water, but this would cost money and throw out of employment the men employed in the water-carrying trade.'[33] Ultimately, Kuwait pursued the creation of larger, more effective desalination plants. The first of these plants opened in 1951 in Ahmedi and new plants later opened as water demand continued to rise.

Authority in the Centre

The outcome of kinship salience is a function of how rulers extend authority into non-urban areas during state building. However, configurations of authority in the centre before state building are a relevant precondition that set conditions for the state-building process and provide information about state capacity. Conceivably, for a ruler to extend his authority into non-urban areas he must have some measure of authority in the first place. Often, this authority existed over families in an urban centre.

Historically, the merchant families of Kuwait City were its source of economic strength.[34] Kuwait's economy was supported by shipping, trading and pearl-diving. Businesses were based on trade over land and sea and were characterised by mobile assets. The ruling family generated income from merchant family business by imposing tariffs on marine activities. In exchange, it provided merchant families with security. However, the ruling family's dependence on merchant families and their employees created vulnerability because merchant families could work together to wrest political concessions.

Perhaps the most prominent example of such a vulnerability occurred in 1907. In that year, Mubarak al-Sabah raised taxes on the ship captains (*nakhodas*) to fifteen rupees per diver and ten rupees per 'puller up irrespective of catch'.[35] Mubarak also introduced an import tax, a house tax, a pilgrimage tax, and price controls. The purpose of these taxes was to fund military excursions in the desert tribal areas to the west, where Mubarak was in competition with Ibn Saud and his *Ikhwan* fighting force.[36] In protest of these expensive taxes, three major shipping merchants left Kuwait with their employees and pearling ships and resettled in Bahrain: Hilaal al-Mutairi, Shamlaan bin Ali and Ibrahim al-Madaf.

In response to this devastating blow to Kuwait's economy, Mubarak sent his son, Sheikh Salem, to Bahrain to entice the merchants back. After a meeting hosted by Bahrain's Sheikh Eisa bin ʿAli al-Khalifa, Salem convinced al-Madaf and bin Ali to return. However, Hilaal al-Mutairi remained adamant. Mubarak was forced to go to Bahrain himself under the guise of a visit to Sheikh Eisa al-Khalifa. Only then did Hilaal al-Mutairi and his men return to Kuwait.[37]

This incident demonstrated that Kuwaiti merchants' businesses did not rely on being present in a given territory. Their mobile resources allowed these merchants to leave the authority of one ruler and easily enter the territory of another. While Kuwait's sheltered location on a bay made it ideal as a trading post, other cities along the Gulf were successful trading cities as well. Thus, merchants' abilities to leave and come back to Kuwait gave them considerable leverage over the ruling family.

Building on previous successes, the merchant families formed a municipality – without the assent of the government – in 1930. It was a bureaucratic body that addressed education and social affairs and had technical staff that included directors, a clerk, tax collectors, market cleaners, guards and auditors. This body was independent of the ruling family and was elected by 250 prominent members of the merchant families.[38] Kinship did not necessarily determine who was elected to the council, but access to the electorate was determined by membership in a kinship group and authority within that group. Furthermore, kinship protected the council from the scorn of the ruling family: the Emir's cousin, Abdullah Salem, was president of the council. This was no coincidence. Mubarak's son Salem was the Emir of Kuwait from 1917 until his death in 1921. Following his passing, the royal family had passed over Abdullah Salem in favour of his first cousin Ahmed Jaber to be the new Emir. The choice created dissent from within the Salem branch of the family. Abdullah Salem's presidency of the council gave it political insulation despite challenging the power of the Emir. However, it was also a tool by which Abdullah Salem could pressure his cousin after being snubbed by the ruling family.[39]

It was in this municipality, Crystal argues, that merchant family opposition to the ruling family coalesced.[40] Between March and August of 1938, merchant families began to agitate in Kuwait City, leading Sheikh Ahmed al-Jaber to allow the formation of a *majlis* (council). While it was short lived, this twenty-member council had considerable powers in state affairs as compared to others in the Gulf.[41]

Preconditions in Non-urban Areas

Kuwait's non-urban population competed for vital limited resources. The results of this competition were often a matter of sheer strength. Bigger and more powerful tribes gained more access to resources than their smaller and weaker counterparts. Many of these powerful tribes were instrumental to Kuwaiti state building and retain considerable influence in the modern era.

Water Access

Nomadic and migratory kinship groups lived off water resources located predominantly in non-urban areas.[42] The descendants of such groups are known today in Kuwait and across the Arabian Peninsula as *bedu*. These kinship groups controlled areas of land known as *diyar* (singular: *dirah*). A group's *dirah* could extend over hundreds of square miles, and its boundaries were often both dynamic and disputed.[43] The multiple families within a kinship group lived together in clusters of large black tents and made use of the oases and wells within the borders of the *dirah* for their water needs.[44] Tribal strength and ad hoc arrangements with other groups in the area determined access to these oases.

The *dirah* was the critical link between kinship and resources in Kuwait and the Nejd desert. A kinship group's control of a *dirah* meant access to its oases and water. In the northern Nejd, each tribal group was aware of the others' territorial claims.[45] One tribe could make use of water sources in another tribe's *dirah*, but only via prior arrangement with that tribe. Kinship authority also regulated the boundaries and norms surrounding *diyar*. This is not to say, however, that this regulation always prevented conflict. Competition over the desert's limited resources incentivised frequent raids between tribes. These raids occurred even when one tribe granted another permission to enter its *dirah*.[46] For example, in 1860, the sheikh of the Aniza, Ibn Hithal, permitted the Thafir tribe to migrate from their *dirah* to the Aniza *dirah*. However, a conflict erupted soon thereafter when Ibn Hithal seized Thafir camels after entering the *dirah*.[47]

The *dirah* was also a link between territory and people, a critical element for ruling families seeking greater sovereignty. Kinship group alliances with the al-Sabah gave the family greater control over the legitimate use of force – a key aspect of state formation and nation building.[48] Alliances also translated into political influence for the ruling family since it gave them influence over territory. Kinship groups also benefitted from these alliances because in the event of a raid by another group, it could appeal to the ruling family to induce the raiders to return stolen livestock.

Authority in Non-urban Areas

Kinship groups in Kuwait in non-urban areas largely managed their own affairs. Weaker tribes paid tributes (*zakat*) to stronger ones, and ad hoc meetings could be called to mediate conflicts. Kinship authority governed the interactions between these groups through a set of customary laws and practices (*'urf*), alliance systems (*shaff*), a focus on solidarity (*'asabiyya*), and a code of hospitality (*dhiafa*).[49]

The more tribal alliances a ruling family had, the more bargaining power it had vis-à-vis British, Ottoman, Russian, German, and other foreign interests. In exchange for alliance with a royal family, a tribe would gain the protection of that family. Tribal alliances also gave the less powerful tribe recourse in the event of a raid, since it could appeal to the ruling family to induce the raiders to return stolen livestock. These alliances were informal agreements between major families and tribes.

Among the most influential tribes in the Nejd were the Mutair and Shammar. The Mutair are a tribal confederation led by the Daweesh family, which itself is part of the Al Dushan branch of the Mutair tribe.[50] Leadership within the family was based on kinship, passing from father to son, and starting with Faisal Daweesh, the patriarch of the Mutair ruling family. Daweesh was the grandson of the Ajman sheikh Sultan ibn Hithlain, and was known for his light complexion and good looks.[51] The Mutair are historically nomadic, although they had a settled presence in villages throughout Nejd. They were known in particular for raising camels.[52] While the Mutair are considered (and historically considered themselves) *bedu*, Hilaal al-Mutairi and his descendants were a powerful Mutair merchant presence in Kuwait City during the early twentieth century.

The Shammar are a tribe originating from Nejd. They are led by the al-Rashid family who ruled the area of Jabal Shammar, starting in 1835 under the leadership of Abdullah bin Rashid.[53] Like the Mutair, the Shammar formed from a coalition of families including the Taghlib, 'Abs and Hawazin.[54] The Shammar emir resided in Ha'il in the Nejd region and had a personal guard of between 800 to 1000 men.[55]

Impetus for Government Outreach to Kinship Groups

Major families like the al-Sabah in the Gulf region competed with each other for territorial control. These conflicts had increasingly high political stakes as Western powers moved into the region following the demise of the Ottoman Empire after the First World War. This territory, however, was inhabited and controlled by kinship groups. The leaders of these groups realised that they could improve their status by garnering favour with outside powers and creating competition between different outside powers for their allegiance.

Beginning in 1858, the British Raj solidified territorial control over India, Pakistan and Bangladesh. The Middle East, however, was the site of territorial competition given its geo-strategic characteristics. As the centre of global trade routes, the region was highly valuable for international influence. Britain had strong influence in Persia and its political residency in the Gulf region was in Bushir, a port city on the southwestern coast of modern-day Iran. However, it faced considerable competition from the Ottomans whose empire extended into Kuwait through 1915. Britain also faced competition from Germany, which sought to extend the Baghdad Railway into Kuwait, and Russia, which attempted to align itself with Arab leaders against the Ottoman Empire.[56]

In order to gain influence in the Gulf region, Britain began to appoint ruling families in the various territories it sought to control. To attain this coveted position, however, required that the family be sufficiently powerful and have sufficient control over territory and kinship groups in the Gulf. Thus, competition for territory and power between powerful families was not just about gaining control of vital limited resources. It was also a matter of currying favour with colonial governments. These relationships were later the basis for creating protected states that eventually gained independence.

Competition for colonial favour incentivised ruling families to reach out to kinship groups. Because kinship groups controlled territory, an alliance between a leading family and a kinship group extended the territorial influence of the major family. This meant that the major family could appeal to the colonial power with the promise of larger territorial control. In addition, kinship group members themselves were of value to major families, for two reasons. First, these men and women were subjects who acquiesced to the leading family's authority. This control over subjects was a form of state power. Second, the men of the kinship group were fighters. Since resources were limited, men from various Nejd families would go on raids, stealing livestock or camels. Sometimes the raiders were sent by the ruling families themselves, and were captured or killed during the raids.[57] They would also need to defend their own stock from theft by a competing tribe. Bringing these men under a unified banner created a fighting force that could defend colonial territory. Fighting men were particularly critical for the al-Sabah, who faced periodic attacks on Kuwait City and the outlying town of Jahra from the Ajman and other groups.[58]

The state-building process in Kuwait began as it did elsewhere in the Gulf – with the signing of a pact. In 1899, the British government concluded a treaty with Mubarak al-Sabah, the patriarch of Kuwait's ruling dynasty. Mubarak agreed to let the British control Kuwait's foreign affairs. In turn, the British allowed Mubarak to deal with domestic politics given his 'alliances with various tribes in the interior of Arabia [in which] he considers himself quite secure'. In exchange for his allegiance, the British also gave Mubarak 15,000 rupees and assistance in reducing the illegal arms trade in the region.[59] Most importantly, Mubarak and his family also became the rulers of Kuwait. The agreement gave Britain a foothold in a territory still under Ottoman influence, but did not give them full control over Mubarak himself, much to the chagrin of Britain's Foreign Ministry. Expressing regret over the deal, Secretary of State for Foreign Affairs Henry Petty-Fitzmaurice complained, 'We have saddled ourselves with an impossible client in the person of the Sheikh. He is apparently an untrustworthy savage.'[60] While it may have lacked the full support of politicians in London, this alliance set into play a state-building process through which kinship authority would ultimately endure in Kuwait.

Kinship alliances between the major families and tribes were eventually standardised in bureaucratic proceedings. As the British created protectorates in the Gulf region, the issue of territorial control took on new-found importance for ruling families. In 1922, the British convened the Uqair Conference to delineate the borders of Saudi Arabia, Kuwait and Iraq. Led by Sir Percy Cox, the British High Commissioner to Iraq, the conference was designed to solve tribal territorial issues that had been the subject of dispute between ruling families. Tribes aligned with Ibn Saud had been carrying out raids on Kuwait and tribal groups aligned with the Emir, Ahmed bin Jaber al-Sabah. The delineation of a border would serve as an agreement that would prevent further raids. Despite the high stakes for Kuwait at the conference, the Emir did not participate in the negotiations. Rather, Kuwait's interests were represented by Major John Moore, the British political agent in Kuwait. For this reason, and due to pressure from Ibn Saud (who reportedly broke down in tears during one conversation with Cox), Kuwait ceded two-thirds of the territory it controlled. During the conference, the parties used the tribal *diyar* as a basis for land claims.[61] Such strategies allowed kinship authority to endure at a time when statehood was being introduced into the region. While the Uqair Protocol created formal territorial arrangements enforced through bureaucratic means, it also perpetuated power allocations based on kinship authority. Rather than representing a transition from kinship to bureaucracy, the protocol represented the reification of kinship-based power arrangements.

State Capacity

As Kuwait developed into a modern state under British protection, the creation of government ministries became a key element in bureaucracy extension. The creation of these ministries is often understood, accurately, in terms of rentier patronage. Prior to the discovery of oil, the Kuwaiti government's revenue came from tariffs on trade. Trade was profitable but not lucrative to all who participated in it. While merchants in pre-state building Kuwait enjoyed some degree of affluence, others in Kuwait City did not. The pre-state debt economy prevented wealth accumulation and entrenched limits on economic advancement.

Kuwait lies on top of one tenth of the world's oil reserves. While originally the state's revenue came from a combination of British payouts and customs taxes on merchants doing business in Kuwait City, oil revenues quickly became the primary source of income for the Kuwaiti state. They also funded the country's state-building project. The Kuwait Oil Company was established by the Anglo-Persian Oil Company in 1934. In 1938, the first commercial quantities of oil were discovered at the Burgan Field, directly to the south of Kuwait City. The first shipment of crude oil from Burgan occurred in 1946.[62]

When oil wealth suddenly became available, the state had literally more revenue than it knew how to handle. British authorities observed that Kuwait's leaders did not 'really understand the extent of development taking place . . . [al-Sabah] Shaikhs are extravagant in their demands and regard the exchequer as a bottomless purse.'[63] Ministries often served as clearing houses for the distribution of this revenue. It is no coincidence that until April 1975, Kuwait's Ministry of Finance and Ministry of Oil were one government body.[64] Employment in Kuwait's ministries became 'an aim in itself and had become a means of indulging nepotism'.[65]

Some analyses of the discovery of oil in the Gulf describe it as the point at which states gained clear dominance over other political entities.[66] Yet as Crystal points out, 'rulers were able to manipulate newly reinforced family ties to penetrate and control the new oil-induced bureaucracy's top positions . . . Political kinship . . . was in fact a response to the oil-induced bureaucratic state.'[67]

Oil, and the state capacity it creates, is often given as an explanation for certain patterns of state development. Rentier theory, for example, tells us that states with income from oil or other natural resources are less likely to be democratic than states whose income comes from taxation and the private sector.

Oil rents are a financial resource. However, having a resource is not equivalent to knowing what to do with it – a key point that many state capacity arguments miss. The way a state ultimately spends its resources affects state-building outcomes and is partially dependent on the pre-existing infrastructure and governance conditions in the state, particularly in non-urban areas.

Kuwait's leadership was at first overwhelmed with the amount of money it had available to spend. While this shock led to 'lavish provision by a beneficent state', this provision was itself shaped by pre-oil conditions.[68] State capacity arguments can tell scholars when states have the ability to create these provisions, but they cannot alone explain the means by which provision itself occurs. State building in Kuwait illustrates this point. It was not purely the result of oil resources, but also of pre-state conditions among non-urban kinship groups that determined Kuwait's path of state building.

Stage One: Infrastructure

The first step in Kuwait's state-building process was the extension and creation of infrastructure. Because resource access was competitive before state building, Kuwait built infrastructure and moved non-urban kinship groups onto this infrastructure. In order to accomplish this goal, however, the government preserved kinship hierarchies and made accommodations for kinship authority. It did this even when the express purpose of infrastructure building was to strengthen the state's bureaucratic authority.

When the state began gaining revenue from its export of oil, the resulting influx of capital revolutionised living in Kuwait. The city, which had once been comprised of stone and mud-brick houses, suddenly transformed into a bustling metropolis with highways and office buildings. Kuwait City's population skyrocketed, jumping from 160,000 in 1952 to 250,000 in 1953.[69]

Oil's effects on kinship went far beyond the ruling family. As an immediate effect, oil allowed nuclear family members more contact with each other. Prior to oil, many men worked on shipping vessels, either as pearl divers, sailors or captains (*nakhodas*) for months at a time. The discovery of oil created opportunities to make a living in Kuwait itself as the government offered jobs to *nakhodas*. Fathers and uncles would go to work and come back once per week rather than twice per year. Money also meant funding for education. Women as well as men took advantage of these new opportunities and many achieved college degrees from Kuwait University, which opened in October 1966, or from institutions in Britain and the United States.[70]

By 1951, Kuwait was exporting nearly 28 million tons of oil per year.[71] The sudden influx of oil revenue prompted the Kuwaiti government to expand Kuwait City, with the creation of new neighbourhoods. In 1952 the government established a Development Board to oversee the planning of the expanded city. The Development Board enlisted the help of the British firm Minoprio, Spencely and MacFarlane to accomplish this task. In 1952, Kuwait's Emir, Abdullah Salem al-Sabah, signed off on the firm's master plan for the expansion of Kuwait City. The plan called for turning the existing city into a downtown area. It also called for the creation of urban, commercial and residential zones in neighbourhoods that extended outward in concentric rings.[72] Among the first of these new neighbourhoods were Kaifan, Shamiya, al-Faiha and al-Roba.[73] These residential areas would be equipped with water, electricity, roads and other infrastructure required in the residential area of a modern metropolis.

These new residential suburbs were of little use, however, unless Kuwaitis moved there, either from their urban houses or non-urban dwellings. The government thus began to issue permits on a first-come first-served basis to individual Kuwaitis wishing to move into these new suburbs that also offered an improved standard of living. As the sons and daughters of Kuwait City's residents moved into the newly created suburbs, they built houses near each other using government loans. This proximity solidified kinship ties and the political influence of that family in that particular area of Kuwait.[74]

New Kuwaiti infrastructure was not only for Kuwait's historically urban families. The government settled nomadic non-urban kinship groups as well. This settlement was key to the state building process in Kuwait because it brought formerly non-urban populations within the purview of bureaucratic governance. The process, however, involved major adjustments to a modern urban lifestyle for a population that had previously lived in tent clusters. In the early 1960s, Kuwait's government sought the assistance of another British firm, Colin Buchanan and Partners, to create a way to successfully sedentarise its tribal population. In 1971, the firm designed a plan to settle the *bedu* into permanent housing.[75] It called for the creation of 'shanty towns' to be built in non-urban areas as an intermediary step between nomadism and sedentarisation. Once the *bedu* had adjusted to settled life, they could be moved into more permanent housing. Then, the shanty towns would be dismantled and the government would prevent new ones from being built. The development plan set a ten-year timeframe for the demolition of all shanty towns outside of downtown Kuwait City.[76]

The 1971 plan, like prior Kuwaiti government initiatives, engaged the tribes as kinship groups. It called for settling the *bedu* population at the edge of Kuwait City as the first stage in a 'transition from desert to urban living'. It still allowed for the presence of 'wandering Bedouin', at least at first, and envisioned such communities as depots for obtaining water, supplies and medical attention. Water as a vital limited resource also featured prominently in the government's plans. Colin Buchanan and Partners suggested that the state create 'places where the wandering Bedouins could get water and supplies'. It also suggested that *bedu* could use newly sunk wells for agriculture. The firm believed this kind of rural settlement plan would be more successful than forcing the *bedu* into urban areas where their lifestyle would change drastically.[77] In other words, they would be less likely to reject state building were it to occur in a more incremental fashion. Successful state building would also give Kuwait's government control over the provision of water, electricity and other key resources.

The plan, which underwent updates three times between 1971 and 1990, reflected an awareness by Kuwait's leaders and urban designers that patterns of living rooted in kinship authority would not be easily changed.[78] Given the crucial importance of bringing kinship groups within the purview of the state, however, Kuwait tried to gradually introduce bureaucratic governance. The 1971 development plan reflects the assessment that, over time, kinship authority in Kuwait would diminish as *bedu* became habituated to a more sedentary suburban lifestyle. As the government tried to extend bureaucratic authority, however, it found consistently that kinship authority reasserted itself rather than diminishing.

Stage Two: Bureaucratic Authority

Infrastructure building in Kuwait was a basis for the extension of the state's bureaucratic authority because it allowed the government to gain control over kinship groups' access to resources. Water infrastructure and public works infrastructure like roads, houses and electricity were particularly critical to this process. In addition, infrastructure allowed the government to promote loyalty to the state through education, and the provision of social services guaranteed by citizenship laws. Infrastructure acted as a vector for the state to extend bureaucratic authority into non-urban areas.

Kuwait's leaders were constrained in this process, however, by their initial outreach to these populations *as* kinship groups. While sedentarisation disrupted kinship authority it did not destroy it altogether. Government patronage to these groups was often mediated by the leaders of kinship hierarchies. In addition, kinship group members sought to maintain kinship hierarchies by continuing to favour fellow kin group members, even as they entered bureaucratic institutions as officials. By 1969, members of non-urban kinship groups in Kuwait worked as civil servants, clerks and policemen. They were also heavily represented within Kuwait's armed forces.[79] Nonetheless, kinship continued to influence the behaviour of these kinship group members as kinship authority instrumentalised the bureaucratic authority of the state. Kuwait built neighbourhoods with roads and houses for sedentarised kinship groups to live in, equipped them with water and electric infrastructure, and built public schools and universities. It furthermore created citizenship laws to serve as an underlying legal framework for accessing this infrastructure. Nonetheless, when it tried to use this infrastructure to expand bureaucratic authority, kinship authority reasserted itself.

Authority over Housing

Water and public works infrastructure connected government-controlled resources to individual subjects of the state who were sedentarised. The patterns of this sedentarisation, however, reflect a reassertion of kinship authority. During state building, Kuwait's government issued permanent housing permits for *bedu* as well as for their urban *hadhar* counterparts. Colin Buchanan and Partners suggested this process take place with respect for kinship ties: 'there is a strong case,' they argued 'for directing future Bedouin settlement into relatively small units containing a number of entire *batns* [sic].'[80] The basis for this recommendation was the prevention of conflict and social unrest. The firm sought to strike a balance, noting that 'These communities would be likely to retain an effective degree of social cohesion . . . but they would not be so rigid as to inhibit the process of assimilating the Bedouin into the urban environment.'[81] Again, the salience of kinship authority was sufficiently high that development plans had to account for it even when designing a means to bring the *bedu* under the purview of bureaucratic governance.

These permits were issued by the government bureaucracy without regards to kinship affiliation. However, house owners from different tribes often engaged in mutual swaps with each other so as to live near their respective families. In Jahra, for example, Shammari and Thafiri families sometimes swapped houses to be near their respective tribes.[82] Despite attempts to impose bureaucratic authority, Kuwait's government was unable to prevent kinship authority from shaping patterns of settlement in its own residential areas.

Since kinship group members settled together, Kuwait's social geography continued to reflect an organisation based on kinship authority. Tribe members had frequent in-person contact since they lived in the same neighbourhoods, and often managed their local affairs as a tribe despite living in neighbourhoods created by a bureaucratic government.

In 1961, Kuwait offered citizenship to members of the Ajman tribe, with social services and housing, in exchange for military service.[83] At the time, many tribal groups in Kuwait were living in shanty towns. Some Ajman families had lived in Kuwait City since at least 1908.[84] However, most lived in shanty towns in Jahra, as well as in al-Wafra in the south and al-Shamiya in the north. They settled in these towns in the hope of gaining employment in Kuwait's oil industry or in its security services. The houses in these towns were made of wood or fibre board, and water came in via truck – a 2,000 gallon tank cost twelve dollars.[85] These towns were illegal under Kuwaiti law, but the ruling family recognised that as a kinship group, the Ajman could be powerful allies against merchant family pressure. Thus, they brought the Ajman under the auspices of the state by offering citizenship.

To facilitate this process, the government moved the Ajman from shanty towns into more permanent housing infrastructure. The government placed this infrastructure closer to the urban centre to avoid perpetuation of a nomadic lifestyle. It also encouraged tribal families to settle separately from one another. This encouragement, however, fell on deaf ears as tribe members tended to settle in the same areas. The Ajman were one of a number of tribal groups who gained citizenship in Kuwait during this time period. Of the roughly 220,000 people who gained citizenship between 1965 and 1981, the majority were *bedu*.[86]

The 1971 development plan reflects the salience of kinship authority in the government's settlement plans. It recommends that 'control over development normally exercised by the [government's] planning authority would be waived in the designated shanty areas'. This loosening of bureaucratic authority would allow 'these settlements [to] be free to evolve in their own way, reflecting the social and family structure of the inhabitants'.[87] In other words, the success of infrastructure building for kinship groups required accommodating pre-existing kinship authority. Despite sufficient capacity for state penetration, Kuwait's government accepted the plan's recommendation and refrained from disputing totally the salience of kinship authority.

This is not to say that *bedu* were antagonistic to the bureaucratic state. Interviews with *bedu* who lived during this time in Kuwait indicate that, generally, the changes introduced by sedentarisation were welcome.[88] A sixty-year resident of Jahra recalls growing up in a large tent and moving to a house for the first time in 1967, paying 4,000 KD for it to the government in installments. The man reflected upon the move favourably, noting that 'everybody wanted to move into a house because there was electricity and air conditioning'.[89] Another fifty-seven-year-old interviewee spoke favourably of moving into a house for the first time in 1981, living before in a settlement of twenty–thirty tents.[90] Kinship authority remained important through this process. Yet it is not accurate to say that *bedu* resisted bureaucratic authority altogether. Rather, the ultimate effect of state building in Kuwait was that kinship authority instrumentalised bureaucracy, using it for resource provision and political access in ways that also preserved pre-existing kinship hierarchies.

Authority over Water and Electricity

Kuwait expanded its water capacity to accommodate not only sedentarised tribes but also a growing population. In 1951, the Kuwait Oil Company commissioned the construction of a desalination plant in Mina al-Ahmadi with a capacity of 80,000 gallons of fresh water per day. The Mina plant was followed by larger plants in Shuwaikh in 1953, Shuaiba North (1965) and South (1971), Doha East (1978) and West (1983), and South Zoor (1988). While Kuwait's 1971 plans make little specific mention of water, the installation of water pipes and this expansion of desalination infrastructure were part and parcel of Kuwait's broader state-building process.[91] While *bedu* still used wells, particularly for watering their camels, they slowly fell out of use as the government gained control over the provision of water. Desalinated water was easier to access and available consistently, as opposed to well water which rose and fell with seasonal precipitation. Additionally, water from the government was distributed through infrastructure that support townships and settlements built for bureaucratic governance. As such, water infrastructure acted as a vector for bureaucracy in Kuwait.

The first electric power in Kuwait came from a kerosene-powered generator and lit Saif Palace.[92] The first power plant for Kuwaitis, however, began production in April 1934 in Sharq with a capacity of three kilowatts. Following the Second World War, a larger plant was opened in 1949 in al-Mirqab, and another that used the steam created at the Shuwaikh desalination plant to power its generator in 1952. Similar plants opened at desalination plants elsewhere in Shuwaikh and in Doha throughout the 1970s and 80s.[93] Electric power was a major advance for Kuwaitis. It allowed for the installation of electric lights rather than kerosene lamps. Most importantly, however, it allowed for air conditioning in private houses. Climate controlled housing proved a major incentive for sedentarisation in a region whose summer temperatures are regularly above 40°C.

Following state building, kinship authority no longer determined water access. Electricity and the climate control it provided offered a further incentive for *bedu* to accept bureaucratic authority. Yet since kinship groups settled together, government control over these resources did not diminish entirely the importance of kinship authority in other aspects of Kuwaiti politics.

Authority over Education

Prior to state building in Kuwait, schools existed primarily in the urban centre. In many cases, they were run out of a private home by a teacher of Quranic recitation called a *mutawa'a*, who received fees for each individual student.[94] These Quranic schools, with gender-segregated classes of about thirty, formed the majority of schools until the opening of the Mubarakia

School in 1911 and the Ahmedia School in 1921. Funded by urban merchant families, these schools offered not only Islamic Studies education but also instruction in reading, writing, mathematics and commerce. Their teachers were paid monthly with a stack of Indian rupee coins, and their skills were in high demand. One of the original teachers at Mubarakia interviewed for this book was sixteen at the time and recalled teaching in order to make more money for her family. At a time when fifty rupees per month could support a family of ten, her monthly salary was 100 rupees.[95]

Schools were a critical part of the government's attempt to turn a sedentarised population into loyal subjects of the bureaucratic state. Kuwait's 1971 development plan for the *bedu* also included plans for schools, proposing one nursery school for every two clusters of 1,500 people, and one secondary and intermediate school for every eight such clusters.[96] These schools would give students contact with the bureaucracy from a young age, inculcate national values, and help the state generate acceptance for bureaucratic authority among the *bedu*.

During state building, Kuwait's new Ministry of Education began building public schools that served both boys and girls of both *bedu* and *hadhar* origin. This free compulsory education created a literate young population as well as a captive audience to build assent to bureaucratic authority. Kuwait's schools not only served to prepare students to be successful members in Kuwaiti society, but also gave Kuwait's government influence over the ideas and beliefs of a new generation. Using the educational bureaucracy, Kuwait could build assent to bureaucratic governance and loyalty to the ruling family through classroom instruction and eventually, a national curriculum. The government also supported higher education through the founding of Kuwait University, which quickly expanded from hosting a few hundred students its first year of operation to tens of thousands over the course of a few decades.

Schools served as important tools of bureaucratic authority in Kuwait. At the same time, students returned home at the end of the day to their families and the kinship groups in which they were embedded. Furthermore, at school itself, students sometimes self-segregated by kinship group, congregating together outside of classes.[97] At universities, similar self-segregation persisted. Since Kuwait is a relatively small country, furthermore, many college students did not live in dormitories but rather returned home to their families at the end of the day. Ultimately, public education in Kuwait shaped perceptions of bureaucratic authority but life outside of the school reasserted the importance of kinship.

Authority over Citizenship

Building a citizen population was another fundamental element of Kuwaiti state building. States without citizens have no subjects over whom to exert authority in the first place. A series of citizenship laws determined who in Kuwait fell under the government's formal authority. At the same time, these laws also bound the government by forcing it to engage with pre-existing configurations of kinship authority that had already been established among some of these citizens.

The Kuwaiti government's immediate impetus for granting citizenship to tribal *bedu* groups was self-interest. Merchant families, a tide of non-Kuwaitis who came to fill skill gaps in the country's economy, and external pressures on Kuwait's sovereignty all challenged the stability of the government's rule.[98] Yet it is important to understand citizenship laws in Kuwait within the broader context of state building. Pressures on the government impacted which tribes received citizenship, and they explain the timing at which groups were given citizenship. The idea of using citizenship to extend the government's bureaucratic authority, however, was not uniquely Kuwaiti. Citizenship was a means of extending bureaucratic authority but it was also a means of creating a patronage network separate from those established by kinship groups. Prior to state building, patronage came in the form of money, guns and military protection. In a state-building environment, however, citizenship guaranteed access to the resources provided by a government's bureaucratic authority, mediated through infrastructure. For the government, extending citizenship entailed patronage commitments, but also expanded its bureaucratic authority over non-urban populations who lived within the state.

Until 1948, 'citizenship' in Kuwait was informal and determined by loyalty to the Emir. In December 1948, Emir Ahmed bin Jaber approved two citizenship laws that granted citizenship to members of the ruling family, those settled in Kuwait City since 1899 and their descendants, and Arab and/or Muslim men born in Kuwait and their descendants.[99] The law was also subject to other influences. 'Kuwaiti nationality can be bought for a few rupees', notes a 1954 report on Kuwait's military from the British residency.[100] Kuwait's 1959 citizenship law was the most comprehensive. It expanded the definition of 'citizen' to those who were settled in Kuwait City before 1920 and their descendants. While the law was written with several provisions for naturalisation, the 'original' Kuwaitis were defined as the urban merchant families.[101]

Kuwait's citizenship laws and the amendments that followed them diluted the power of often oppositional merchant families by granting citizenship to tribal groups loyal to the leadership. They also expanded Kuwait's population and the state's bureaucratic authority over tribal groups. Not all tribal groups were included in this process. Kuwait's stateless *bidoon* tribes, for example, were excluded by amendments passed between 1960 and 1987. Yet other tribal groups were brought under the purview of the state, often in exchange for military service.[102]

Since the military is a bureaucracy based on logistical infrastructure, military service was one way in which the state could bring tribal men within the bureaucratic purview of the state. Military salaries also were (and remain today) a source of patronage. To encourage military service, the state paid tribal leaders to encourage tribe members to join.[103] This payoff reinforced the power of these leaders' kinship authority and emphasised the importance of kinship group membership even as the state attempted to impose bureaucratic authority. While tribal leaders' kinship authority was not formally embedded into the bureaucratic state, it was nonetheless an important aspect of the government's state-building process.

Kuwait's citizenship laws played a role in emphasising the timing of settlement. By defining a year of settlement (1920) as the basis for nationality, the law created distinctions between 'original' Kuwaitis and those who arrived later. The merchant families of Kuwait and long-settled tribal groups like the Awazim formed the core of this inner circle of nationhood. While the Awazim bear the claim of 'original' Kuwaitis, they have not been a high-status tribe in the country's history. In other words, a claim to national identity was based on timing of settlement, even when the family in question did not have high status. Low-paid pearl divers and sailors are also examples of Kuwaitis who received citizenship but were not necessarily high status.

Kuwait's government responded to kinship groups with competitive access to resources by creating infrastructure and moving groups onto it. These initiatives were constrained by pre-state conditions and the salience of kinship authority. The 1971 development plan reflects these constraints. The path taken to settle the Bedouin, however, turned out to be very different from what Colin Buchanan and Partners had recommended. Given the copious resources the Kuwaiti state invested in the 1971 development plan, it is surprising from a state penetration perspective that its overall implementation was never realised. The state had the resources to implement the plan, including the ability to penetrate into non-urban areas of the state. Yet it did not do so. This is because pre-existing conditions in Kuwait constrained the state's ability to disrupt kinship authority.

Despite its overwhelming revenues, Kuwait's government faced constraints in spending. While it sought to expand bureaucratic authority, this expansion required the inclusion of non-urban kinship groups. These kinship groups, however, had agency in the process of bureaucratic expansion in that they could accept or reject it. Thus, while ministries were indeed sources of patronage and the use of state capacity, the way this patronage was distributed was neither a predetermined outcome nor the sole purview of the state. Rather, it was constrained by the state's previous relationship with non-urban kinship groups and their kinship authority.

Legislative bodies, ministries and citizenship allowed Kuwait to extend bureaucratic authority outside of its urban centre. Historically nomadic groups came within the purview of the bureaucratic state, and Kuwait's government gained control over the distribution of resources for these groups. Bureaucratic outreach to tribes as kinship groups was constrained by kinship authority. Because previous emirs had given payouts to individual tribes in exchange for loyalty before state building, kinship hierarchies remained salient. Individual group members continued to use them to obtain resources, and tribal leaders continued to enjoy privileged (if informal) status with Kuwait's leadership. When it came time to settle tribes in Kuwait, these hierarchies continued to play a key role.

Stage Three: Nationalism

While Kuwait gave citizenship to non-urban kinship groups to balance other constituencies, national unity remained a priority. Kuwait's leadership used nationalism to unite the various constituencies upon which it relied for power. It also used nationalism to connect the well-being of the state to the rule of the al-Sabah family. Because of pre-state patterns of resource distribution in Kuwait, this nationalism took on a temporal idiom. Such an idiom, which glorified the tribal families that participated in the founding of Kuwait, reified kinship authority as part and parcel of the Kuwaiti national narrative.

Kuwaiti nationalism is based on an appeal to history. The state seal features a dhow on the water, a reference to Kuwait's past participation in maritime trade in the Gulf region. Below this image is a hawk of Quraish. The hawk is a symbol of the Banu Quraish tribe, to which the Prophet Mohammed belonged. In addition to appealing to Kuwait's Muslim character, the hawk also appeals to historic symbols associated with Islam's founder. Nationalism in Kuwait is encouraged by the country's public education system, although many children (particularly non-Kuwaitis) attend private schools. Nationalist ideas are written into the state's curriculum, an example of the use of bureaucracy to spread nationalist ideals.[104] Pictures of the Emir and Crown Prince appear on billboards and posters throughout the country. Criticism of the Emir is illegal in Kuwait as it has the potential to stir national disunity. Interestingly, while the state appeals to maritime trade and the hawk of Quraish as elements of its national symbolism, the ruling family was neither involved in maritime trade nor is it descended from the Quraishis. Rather, the family frames its nationalist right of rulership on the development of the modern Kuwaiti state. As one example, many of the planned neighbourhoods surrounding Kuwait built after the 1970s bear the names of previous emirs.

Pearl diving also became a national symbol of Kuwait. Other Gulf states have adopted this national symbolism as well. Kuwait's state seal bears a dhow, a ship used for transport, trade, fishing and pearl diving, hearkening back to the historic trade of its inhabitants. Kuwait City today hosts a maritime museum with models of various ships and exhibits linking shipping and pearl diving to Kuwait's national narrative. While the museum presents a historical perspective, it is managed by Kuwait's National Council for Culture, Arts and Literature. The linkage of pearl diving and Kuwaiti nationalism connects the traditional trade of Kuwaitis in the past with a sense of Kuwaiti nationalism in the present. This linkage also frames merchant families and those who worked for them as true Kuwaitis, linking their experience with the broader national experience of Kuwait.

While nationalism is often based on the idea of a shared homeland, a territorial nationalist idiom would have proven difficult for Kuwait. Since its borders tended to be in non-urban areas, they most directly impacted tribal groups whose lifestyle was nomadic rather than sedentary. However, these kinship groups were often transnational, meaning that their sense of affinity with others did not stop at the border checkpoint. Throughout the expansion of ministries, building of infrastructure and extension of bureaucratic authority, kinship had remained salient. As Kuwait developed a nationalist idiom, it was forced to respond to this salience. While territorial idioms proved successful in other parts of the Middle East (indeed, borders in the region have changed little overall since the 1950s), such an idiom would not have worked in Kuwait.

A temporal idiom of nationalism also resonated well with the concept of tribal purity. Kinship groups with well-established lineages stretching back hundreds of years were seen in Kuwait and the broader Arab Gulf as 'purer' than their counterparts whose origins were less clear. A temporal idiom of nationalism, by which those whose ancestors were present in Kuwait during its pre-state days, resonated with tribal populations. As one Kuwaiti historian described nationalism in the 1950s, 'the Arab tribes envisioned the state as if it were a tribe, so they devoted their loyalty to it . . . the tribe is a social unit that takes on the national character'.[105] Defining membership in the nation similarly to membership in the tribe, therefore, was a choice shaped by pre-state conditions of kinship authority.

This is not to say that nationalism was wholly successful in Kuwait. The idea of being a Kuwaiti national was often tied up with entitlement. A British Embassy official in 1962 observed '"Kuwaitiness" is exclusive and negative . . . It is the peculiar malaise of the Kuwaitis that they are unable to inspire loyalty and devotion in those who serve them.'[106] In addition, Kuwait was affected by the rise of pan-Arab nationalism, a sentiment which competed with that of Kuwait's monarchic rule. Secret British documents from the early 1970s reveal considerable fear that the Kuwaiti ruling family would be overthrown in a nationalist *coup d'état*.[107] An assassination attempt in May 1985 on Emir Jaber al-Ahmed al-Sabah illustrates the very real danger Kuwait's leadership faced at the time.

A programme of Kuwaiti nationalism served to create assent to rule by the Kuwaiti population and keep rebellious elements in check. The success of this nationalism, however, depended on the incorporation of kinship into Kuwait's national story. The effect of this incorporation was the reification of kinship authority in Kuwait, since it was now part and parcel of the national narrative of the bureaucratic state.

Conclusion

State building in Kuwait was a process driven by the state but constrained by kinship authority. Prior to state building, kinship groups in non-urban areas competed for access to water, a vital limited resource. They formed territories (*diyar*) whose boundaries shifted constantly and were a source of constant dispute. As colonial powers moved into the Arabian Peninsula, they sought out ruling families to manage the domestic politics of the protectorates these powers controlled. Ruling families realised they could enhance their power and territorial claims in order to find favour with these powers by engaging with non-urban kinship groups. They did so, offering money, guns and protection in exchange for loyalty. This transaction gave the ruling family fighting men and expanded territorial claims that they could use to bargain with colonial powers for influence.

Kuwaiti state building was fuelled originally by colonial rents and later by oil revenue. Using this capacity, the government created new suburbs and modern infrastructure that could serve its urban and non-urban populations. This infrastructure building also allowed the government to disrupt kinship by gaining control over resource access and strengthening its bureaucratic authority. For non-urban kinship groups, sedentarisation offered easier access to better resources in exchange for loyalty to and acceptance of a bureaucratic state. As the government extended infrastructure, it also extended bureaucracy to govern these newly settled kinship groups. Ministries operated under bureaucratic authority to govern the population, and used Kuwait's infrastructure as the basis for extending this authority to historically non-urban kinship groups. Roads and electric lines emerged, as well as schools. Citizenship policies provided a legal framework for determining who had access to this infrastructure. Despite these advances, however, kinship authority in Kuwait reasserted itself. It instrumentalised state bureaucracy by distributing the patronage it provided through hierarchies established by kinship authority. Furthermore, leaders of kinship hierarchies continued to play an intermediary role between the government and their kinship group members. Emphasising membership in a kinship group was useful for these members, since it allowed them access to the government's patronage. For the government, it allowed the distribution of patronage that predicated loyalty to the government. Since it had already engaged these non-urban populations as kinship groups, kinship authority endured even as bureaucratic governance emerged in Kuwait.

Nationalism in Kuwait created deeper loyalty to the royal family and the bureaucratic state. The boundaries of the Kuwaiti state were shifted and negotiated over time. Kinship groups competing for resources tended to have a temporary rather than fixed sense of borders. For both these reasons, nationalism took on a temporal idiom. The 'truest' Kuwaitis were those who had settled first, while groups that settled later had less of a nationalist claim. Other nationalist idioms would not have had a chance of success given the importance of kinship groups and kinship authority to the government's rule.

State capacity played an important part in Kuwaiti state building. Without oil revenues and the ability to create infrastructure, Kuwait after state building would have looked very different. However, the existence of capacity itself is insufficient for explaining why, at the end of state building, kinship had governing political salience. The effects of state capacity on kinship authority depend heavily on how that capacity is used. In the Kuwaiti case, this use was constrained by pre-state conditions of kinship groups' resource access. The government was forced to reach out to non-urban kinship groups in particular ways that constrained its ability to instrumentalise kinship authority. Rather, by the end of the state-building period in Kuwait, kinship authority in Kuwait had largely instrumentalised the state's bureaucratic authority.

Notes

1. 'Kuwait', *CIA World Factbook*, https://www.cia.gov/the-world-factbook/countries/kuwait/#people-and society (accessed 29 January 2021).
2. Jill Crystal, *Oil and Politics in the Gulf: Rulers and Merchants in Kuwait and Qatar* (Cambridge, UK: Cambridge University Press, 1990): 16, 20, 21; Selwa al-Ghanim, *The Reign of Mubarak al-Sabah: Shaikh of Kuwait 1896–1915* (New York, NY: I. B. Tauris, 1998): 5–6.
3. Interview, Salmiya, Kuwait, 4 February 2014. After Kuwaiti independence in 1961, the Awazim became prominent in Kuwait's military as well.
4. Madawi al-Rasheed, *A History of Saudi Arabia* (Cambridge, UK: Cambridge University Press, 2010): 25.
5. James Wynbrandt, *A Brief History of Saudi Arabia* (New York, NY: Infobase Publishing, 2010): 107.

6. 'Muhammed bin Saud [1744–1765]', *GlobalSecurity.org*, http://www.globalse-curity.org/military/world/gulf/muhammad-bin-saud.htm.
7. John R. Bradley, *Saudi Arabia Exposed: Inside a Kingdom in Crisis* (New York, NY: Palgrave Macmillan, 2005): 7–8.
8. Wynbrandt, *A Brief History of Saudi Arabia*, 170–2.
9. Alan Rush, *Al-Sabah: History and Genealogy of Kuwait's Ruling Family, 1752–1987* (Atlantic Highlands, NJ: Ithaca Press, 1987): 236.
10. Seif Marzouq al-Shamlaan, *Min Tarikh al-Kuwait* (Kuwait: That al-Silasil Publications, 1986): 148 (Arabic).
11. Rush, *Al-Sabah*, 94. Ali Abdal Moneim Abdal Hamid contends that this animosity originated when Mubarak gave a firearm to Ibn Saud rather than his son Salem. The jealousy over this snub lasted years. See Rush, *Al-Sabah*, 81–2.
12. Ruqaya al-Qalesh, 'Kuwaitis Practiced Pearl Diving for Livelihood, Bearing Risks, Hardships', *Kuwait News Agency*, 24 August 2013, https://www.kuna.net. kw/ArticleDetails.aspx?id=2329735&language=en; Matthew Teller, 'The Pearl Fishers of Arabia', *BBC News*, 15 November 2014, https://www.bbc.com/news/blogs-magazine-monitor-30042226.
13. Farah al-Nakib, 'Revisiting Hadhar and Bedu in Kuwait: Citizenship, Housing, and the Construction of a Dichotomy', *International Journal of Middle East Studies* 46 no. 1 (February 2014): 10.
14. William Lancaster and Fidelity Lancaster, *Honour is in Contentment: Life Before Oil in Ras al-Khaimah (UAE) and Some Neighbouring Regions* (Berlin, Germany: de Gruyter, 2011): 414.
15. Interview, Salmiya, Kuwait, 4 February 2014.
16. 'Awazim (Extract from Gazetteer of the Persian Gulf, Oman and Central Arabia, 1908)', in *Gazetteer of Arabian Tribes, Volume Three*, ed. R. Trench (Cambridge, UK: Archive Editions Ltd, 1996): 59; Interview, Salmiya, Kuwait, 28 January 2014.
17. 'Military Report on the Arabian Shores of the Persian Gulf, Kuwait, Bahrein, Hasa, Qatar, Trucial Oman and Oman [25] (39/226)', British Library: India Office Records and Private Papers, IOR/L/MIL/17/15/141, in *Qatar Digital Library*, http://www.qdl.qa/en/archive/81055/vdc_100023509623.0x000029.
18. Date palms can grow with water as salty as 2,000 parts per million (ppm). Fresh drinking water has a salinity below 1,000 ppm. See 'Kuwait', *FAO Corporate Document Repository*, http://www.fao.org/docrep/W4356E/w4356e0g.htm (accessed 8 January 2015); M. Mumtaz Khan and S. A. Prathapar, 'Water Management in Date Palm Groves', in A. Manickavasagan, M. Mohammed Essa and E. Sukumar (eds), *Dates: Production, Processing, Food, and Medicinal Values* (New York, NY: CRC Press, 2012): 52.
19. John Gordon Lorimer, *Gazetteer of the Persian Gulf, Oman, and Central Arabia, Volume II* (Calcutta, India: Superintendent Government Printing, 1908): 23, 90, 511.
20. Interview via Skype, 14 October 2014.

21. 'File 53/83 I (D 99) Kuwait-Iraq Smuggling [150r] (316/716)', British Library: India Office Records and Private Papers, IOR/R/15/1/531, in *Qatar Digital Library*, http://www.qdl.qa/en/archive/81055/vdc_100023510123.0x000075.

22. 'Administration Report of the Persian Gulf Political Residency for the Year 1912', *Persian Gulf Administration Reports, Volume VII*, ed. Penelope Tuson (Cambridge, UK: Cambridge Archive Editions, 1989): 117; 'An Historic Glimpse', *Ministry of Electricity and Water, State of Kuwait*, 2014, http://www.mew.gov.kw/?com=content&id=73# (accessed 12 August 2014) (Arabic).

23. Farah al-Nakib, *Kuwait Transformed: A History of Oil and Urban Life* (Stanford, CA: Stanford University Press, 2016): 51.

24. Interview via Skype, 14 October 2014.

25. Al-Nakib, *Kuwait Transformed*, 31.

26. 'File 53/47 (D 43) Kuwait Water Supply [5-6] (24/486)', British Library: India Office Records and Private Papers, IOR/R/15/1/511, in *Qatar Digital Library*, http://www.qdl.qa/en/archive/81055/vdc_100023527869.0x000019.

27. 'File 53/47 (D 43) Kuwait Water Supply [7] (25/486)', British Library: India Office Records and Private Papers, IOR/R/15/1/511, in *Qatar Digital Library*, http://www.qdl.qa/en/archive/81055/vdc_100023527869.0x00001a.

28. 'File 53/47 (D 43) Kuwait Water Supply [7] (25/486)', British Library: India Office Records and Private Papers, IOR/R/15/1/511, in *Qatar Digital Library*, http://www.qdl.qa/en/archive/81055/vdc_100023527869.0x00001a.

29. 'File 53/47 (D 43) Kuwait Water Supply [60r] (142/486)', British Library: India Office Records and Private Papers, IOR/R/15/1/511, in *Qatar Digital Library*, http://www.qdl.qa/en/archive/81055/vdc_100023527869.0x00008f.

30. 'File 53/47 (D 43) Kuwait Water Supply [217r] (462/486); [221r] (470/486)', British Library: India Office Records and Private Papers, IOR/R/15/1/511, in *Qatar Digital Library*, http://www.qdl.qa/en/archive/81055/vdc_100023527871.0x00003f.

31. 'Arabia Intelligence Report [21r] (41/52)', British Library: India Office Records and Private Papers, IOR/L/MIL/17/16/5, in *Qatar Digital Library*, http://www.qdl.qa/en/archive/81055/vdc_100023545441.0x000028.

32. *Ministry of Electricity and Water, State of Kuwait*; Interview via Skype, 14 October 2014.

33. 'File 53/83 I (D 99) Kuwait-Iraq Smuggling [151r] (318/716)', British Library: India Office Records and Private Papers, IOR/R/15/1/531, in *Qatar Digital Library*, http://www.qdl.qa/en/archive/81055/vdc_100023510123.0x000077.

34. Crystal emphasises the economic power of the merchant families, treating them as a 'class'. I contend that the reason these families had money in the first place was because of their high family status. While treating these families as a class may explain economic outcomes, it lends limited causal leverage to explaining why kinship structures have a high presence in Kuwait.

35. 'Political Diary of the Persian Gulf Residency for the week ending 26th May (received 3rd June) 1907 – Koweit, 9th to 15th May', *Political Diaries of the Arab World: Persian Gulf 1904–1965, Volume 2*, ed. Robert Jarman (Cambridge, UK: Cambridge Archive Editions, 1998): 193.

36. Crystal, *Oil and Politics in the Gulf*, 24.
37. Al-Shamlaan, *Min Tarikh al-Kuwait*, 155.
38. Crystal, *Oil and Politics in the Gulf*, 46–7.
39. Abdullah Salem eventually became the Emir after Ahmed died in 1950. He ruled from 1950 until 1965. In 1961, Kuwait gained independence and Abdullah Salem became the first Emir of the State of Kuwait.
40. Crystal, *Oil and Politics in the Gulf*, 47.
41. 'Administration Report of the Kuwait Political Agency for the Year 1938 – IV. Local Interests', *Persian Gulf Administration Reports, Volume IX*, 27.
42. Al-Nakib points out, however, that historic residence in or outside of Kuwait City is a poor indicator of whether a family was tribal *bedu* or urban *hadhar*. See al-Nakib, 'Revisiting Hadhar and Badu in Kuwait', 5–30.
43. For example, in 1860, the sheikh of the Aniza, Ibn Hithal, permitted the Thafir tribe to migrate from their *diyar* to the Aniza *diyar*. However, a conflict erupted soon thereafter when Ibn Hithal seized camels owned by Da'ibil bin Badi al-'Areefi of the Thafir. See 'Attiya bin Kareem al-Thafir, *Qabilat al-Thafir: Dirasa Tarikhia L'Ghuiya Muqarina* (Kuwait: Mutab'a Muassasa Dar Al-Siyasa, 1995): 142 (Arabic).
44. The tent, called a *beit sha'ar*, was made of black goat hair and was partitioned with a large rug that split the tent into areas for family and guests, men and women, living quarters from kitchens. One member of the Juwarin tribe recalls his family's *beit sha'ar* was split into areas for parents and children. It included a kitchen, and a small *diwaniya* tent just outside. See Gerald de Gaury, *Review of the 'Anizah Tribe*, ed. Bruce Ingham (Lebanon: Kutub Limited, 2005): 27; Interview, Jahra, Kuwait, 30 January 2014; Mohammed Suleiman al-Haddad, 'The Effect of Detribalization and Sedentarization on the Socio-Economic Structure of the Tribes of the Arabian Peninsula: Ajman Tribe as a Case Study', PhD dissertation, University of Kansas, 1981: 58.
45. Ibn Saud's advisor, Fuad Bey Hamza, once offered the British a list of 150 wells and the tribes affiliated with them. See 'File 53/54 IV (D 119) Kuwait Blockade [118r] (248/440)', British Library: India Office Records and Private Papers, IOR/R/15/1/517, in *Qatar Digital Library*, http://www.qdl.qa/en/archive/81055/vdc 100023548816.0x000031.
46. *Rakaan bin Hathleen: Poet, Cavalier, and Sheikh of the Ajman* (Kuwait: Rabian Publishing and Distribution Company, 2003): 59 (Arabic).
47. Al-Thafir, *Qabilat al-Thafir*, 142.
48. See Max Weber, *Politics as a Vocation*, trans. H. H. Gerth and C. Wright Mills (Philadelphia, PA: Fortress Press, 1972); Charles Tilly, *Coercion, Capital, and European States: AD 990–1992* (Malden, MA: Blackwell Publishing, 1992); Eugen Weber, *Peasants into Frenchmen: The Modernization of Rural France, 1970–1914* (Stanford, CA: Stanford University Press, 1976).
49. Evans-Pritchard's segmentary model suggests it is possible to generalise such kinship groups configured 'as segments of a larger system in an organization of society in certain social situations, and not as parts of a kind of fixed framework'. See Evans-Pritchard, *The Nuer*, 149.

50. 'Appendix I: Divisions of Mutair, 'Ajman, 'Awazim, Rashaida, Shammar and 'Aniza Tribes (Extract from The Arab of the Desert, 1949)', in *Gazetteer of Arabian Tribes, Volume Ten*, 263; 'Muteir (Two Extracts from Handbook of Arabia, 1916)', in *Gazetteer of Arabian Tribes: Volume Ten*, 18.

51. 'Faisal ad Dawish of the Mutair (Memorandum on Jibali Raid, by Special Service Officer, Diwaniya, 3 January 1928 [AIR 23/33])', in *Gazetteer of Arabian Tribes, Volume Ten*, 136.

52. 'Mutair (Extract from Handbook of Arabia, 1916)', in *Gazetteer of Arabian Tribes, Volume Ten*, 17.

53. Ibrahim Jarallah bin Dakhna al-Sharifi, *The Golden Encyclopedia of Individuals of the Tribes and Families of the Arabian Peninsula: Part Five* (Ann Arbor, MI: University of Michigan Press, 1998): 1799 (Arabic).

54. 'The Shammar (Two extracts from Handbook of Arabia, 1916)', in *Gazetteer of Arabian Tribes, Volume Thirteen*, 67.

55. 'Chapter XI (Two extracts from: Lady Anne Blunt, A Pilgrimage to Nejd, 1881)', in *Gazetteer of Arabian Tribes, Volume Thirteen*, 41.

56. '(Confidential) Memorandum Respecting Kuweit, October 30, 1901', *Records of Kuwait, 1899–1961, Volume 1*, ed. Alan Rush (Cambridge, UK: Cambridge University Press, 1989): 190.

57. See, for example, 'Administration Report of the Koweit Political Agency for the Year 1906–1907', *Persian Gulf Administration Reports, Volume VI*, 74; 'Diary of the Persian Gulf Political Residency for the Week Ending the 7th May 1905', *Political Diaries of the Arab World: Persian Gulf 1904–1965, Volume 1*, 83; 'No. 6 of 1929: Summary of the News from the Arab States for the Month of June 1929', *Political Diaries of the Arab World: Persian Gulf 1904–1965, Volume 8*, 411.

58. 'Summary of News of his Britannic Majesty's Political Residency in the Persian Gulf for the Month of April 1916', *Political Diaries of the Arab World: Persian Gulf 1904–1965, Volume 6*, 214; 'Administration Report for the Kuwait Political Agency for the Year 1916', *Persian Gulf Administration Reports, Volume VII*, 77. These conflicts are largely relegated to the past, and today the Ajman in Kuwait enjoy a good relationship with the ruling family.

59. 'Telegram to Foreign (Sd. Meade, 8/1/99)', *Records of Kuwait, 1899–1961, Volume 1*, 111; 'Lieutenant-Colonel Meader to Government of India (Confidential) January 30, 1899', *Records of Kuwait, 1899–1961, Volume 1*, 124–5; 'Translation of Above, Lt-Col P.Z. Cox to Shaikh Mubarak, 17 May 1910, (R/15/5/45)', *Records of Kuwait, 1899–1961, Volume 2*, ed. Alan Rush (Cambridge, UK: Cambridge University Press, 1989): 723.

60. 'Memorandum by the Marquess of Landsdowne, Foreign Office, March 21, 1902', *Records of Kuwait, 1899–1961, Volume 1*, 224.

61. See H. R. P. Dickson, *Kuwait and Her Neighbours* (London, UK: George Allen & Unwin, 1956): 273.

62. 'Brief History of Kuwait Oil Company', *Kuwait Oil Company*, 2012, https://www.kockw.com/sites/EN/Pages/Profile/History/KOC-History.aspx.

63. 'Mr. Pelly to the Foreign Office, 20th March, 1953', *Records of Kuwait, 1899–1961, Volume 3*, ed. Alan Rush (Cambridge, UK: Cambridge University Press, 1989): 379.

64. 'Research Department Memorandum: The Economy of Kuwait, 1950–68, 3 March 1970 (RR 6/9)', *Records of Kuwait, 1966–1971: 1968*, ed. Anita Burdett (Cambridge, UK: Cambridge University Press, 2003): 639.

65. 'Despatch from Mr S. Falle, Kuwait, to Mr A. Acland, Foreign Office, 1 July 1970', *Records of Kuwait, 1966–1971: 1970*, 27.

66. See, for example, Gregory F. Gause III, *Oil Monarchies: Domestic and Security Challenges in the Arab Gulf States* (New York, NY: Council on Foreign Relations Press, 1994): 23.

67. Crystal, *Oil and Politics in the Gulf*, 12.

68. '(1736/63) British Embassy, Kuwait, June 16, 1963', *Records of Kuwait, 1961–1965*, ed. Anita Burdett (Cambridge, UK: Cambridge Archive Editions, 1997): 108.

69. Dickson, *Kuwait and Her Neighbours*, 40.

70. Interview, Nuzha, Kuwait, 15 February 2014. Kuwait University's College for Women existed from 1966 until 20 November 2013, when it became the College of Life Sciences. See 'A Brief History', *Kuwait University*, http://www.kuniv.edu/ku/AboutKU/BriefHistory/index.htm.

71. 'The Persian Gulf Administration Reports from the Year 1951', *Persian Gulf Administration Reports, Volume XI*, 213.

72. Al-Nakib, *Kuwait Transformed*, 99–100.

73. This process sometimes involved the repurposing of existing structures. For example, the Nuzha area was previously the site of Kuwait's airport. Its runway is now the neighbourhood's main street.

74. Interview, Nuzha, Kuwait, 14 February 2014.

75. 'First Five Year Development Plan 1967/8–1971/2', *Development Plans of the GCC States 1962–1995 (Kuwait 1)* (Cambridge, UK: Archive Editions, 1994): 26–7.

76. Colin Buchanan and Partners, 'Studies for National Physical Plan and Master Plan for Urban Areas, 1971 (December 1971)', *Development Plans of the GCC States 1962–1995 (Kuwait 1)*, 44.

77. Colin Buchanan and Partners, 'Studies for National Physical Plan and Master Plan for Urban Areas, 1971', *Development Plans of the GCC States, 1962–1995 (Kuwait 3)*, 44.

78. The British firm Shankland Cox conducted reviews and updated the development plan. See al-Nakib, *Kuwait Transformed*, 115.

79. 'Mr. Arthur to Mr. Stewart – Kuwait: The Internal Situation, 6 January 1969, Section 1', *Records of Kuwait, 1966–1971: 1969*, 74.

80. Colin Buchanan and Partners, 'Studies for National Physical Plan and Master Plan for Urban Areas, 1971 (December 1971)', 23. Recall from Chapter 2 that *batan* refers to a sub-tribal unit of organisation.

81. Colin Buchanan and Partners, 'Studies for National Physical Plan and Master Plan for Urban Areas, 1971 (December 1971)', 23.

82. Interview, Salmiya, Kuwait, 12 January 2014.

83. Crystal, *Oil and Politics in the Gulf*, 88.

84. John Gordon Lorimer, *Gazetteer of the Persian Gulf* (online: General Books LLC, 2012): 16.

85. Al-Haddad, 'The Effect of Detribalization and Sedentarization', 112–13, 121.

86. Shafeeq Ghabra, 'Kuwait and the Dynamics of Socio-Economic Change', *Middle East Journal* 51 no. 3 (Summer 1997): 364.

87. 'First Five Year Development Plan 1967/8–1971/2', *Development Plans of the GCC States 1962–1995 (Kuwait 1)*, 44.

88. Some Bedouin found their houses too small and rented them out to non-Kuwaitis. See al-Haddad, 'The Effect of Detribalization and Sedentarization', 115.

89. Interview, Jahra, Kuwait, 12 January 2014.

90. Interview, Salmiya, Kuwait, 5 February 2014; Interview, Jahra, Kuwait, 5 February 2014. Obtaining a house was an opt-in system. Requests in outlying areas such as Jahra came mostly from *bedu*.

91. Al-Nakib, *Kuwait Transformed*, 92.

92. Allegedly, the first use of this electric generator was to light the wedding party of Mubarak's son Hamad.

93. Sara al-Mokhaizim, 'Kuwait Marks Over 100 Years of Introducing "Electricity"', *Arab Times*, 6 April 2018, http://www.arabtimesonline.com/news/kuwait-marks-over-100-yrs-of-introducing-electricity/.

94. Interview, Nuzha, Kuwait, 15 February 2014.

95. Interview, Nuzha, Kuwait, 15 February 2014.

96. Colin Buchanan and Partners, 'Studies for National Physical Plan and Master Plan for Urban Areas, 1971 (December 1971)', 28.

97. Interview, Salmiya, Kuwait, 13 March 2014.

98. 'D.M.H. Riches, Esq. to Foreign Office, 12 February, 1958', *Records of Kuwait, 1899–1961, Volume 3*, 248–9.

99. Helen Mary Rizzo, *Islam, Democracy, and the Status of Women: The Case of Kuwait* (New York, NY: Routledge, 2005): 14.

100. 'British Residency, Bahrain, March 20, 1954 (1201279/54G)', *Records of Kuwait, 1899–1961, Volume 3*, 295.

101. 'Nationality Law, 1959', *Refworld*, http://www.refworld.org/docid/3ae6b4ef1c.html.

102. Jill Crystal, *Kuwait: The Transformation of an Oil State* (New York, NY: Routledge, 1992): 75.

103. Crystal, *Oil and Politics in the Gulf*, 88.

104. Rania al-Nakib, 'Human Rights, Education for Democratic Citizenship and International Organizations: Findings from a Kuwaiti UNESCO ASPnet School', *Cambridge Journal of Education* 42 no. 1 (March 2012): 103.

105. *Rakaan bin Hathleen*, 59.

106. 'British Embassy, Kuwait, January 5th, 1962', *Records of Kuwait, 1899–1961, Volume 3*, 487.

107. 'Defence Expenditure Study No. 5: The Kuwait Commitment in the Period to 1970/1: Report by the Defence Review Working Party', *Records of Kuwait, 1966–1971: 1967*, 515; 'Summary and despatch from Mr S. Falle, Kuwait, to Foreign Secretary, 12 March 1968', *Records of Kuwait, 1966–1971: 1969*, 13.

5

STATE BUILDING IN QATAR

Qatar offers a second compelling example of competitive access to resources before state building leading to kinship having governing salience after state building. Its tribal and historical similarity to Kuwait also makes it a useful point of comparison and provides an enriching empirical illustration of a case with governing salience as an outcome. In Qatar, access to vital limited resources was competitive before state building. During state building, the government attempted to consolidate power by building up public administration and engineering settlement patterns. However, kinship authority instrumentalised bureaucratic authority as a result of path-dependent constraints on how the government conducted this state-building process. Like in Kuwait, Qatar's government engaged kinship groups *as* kinship groups, preserving the salience of kinship. As a result, kinship in Qatar at the end of state building had governing salience.

Introduction

Qatar is an Arab Gulf state similar in size to Kuwait. It is surrounded by water on all sides except its southwestern border with Saudi Arabia. Bahrain, a historic rival, controls the Hawar Islands about a mile and a half off the western coast. About 2.6 million people live in Qatar – slightly less than in Kuwait. Over 80 per cent are expatriates.[1] Like Kuwait, Qatar was a British protected state and enjoys substantial oil revenues that give it one of the highest GDPs per capita in the world.

Kinship authority played a large historical role in governance in Qatar. Prior to the arrival of the ruling Al Thani family, seasonal migrant tribes inhabited small fishing villages along the coast. These included the al-Musallam in Huwaylah, the Sudan in Fuwayrat, and the Maadhid and Al bin Ali in Doha.[2] Access to Qatar's water resources, similar to Kuwait, was competitive between kinship groups prior to state building. Governmental attempts to bring these tribes within the purview of bureaucratic governance were constrained by pre-existing patterns of resource access. As a result, kinship authority in Qatar has governing salience.

The Ruling Family of Qatar

The Al Thani ruling family of Qatar is a part of the Bani Tamim, a massive tribe which spans the Arabian Peninsula and Levant. Like the Al Sabah in Kuwait, the Al Thani rose to prominence through diplomacy. In the late 1800s, the family formed a relationship with the Ottomans, who controlled Qatar until 1915. However, the Al Thani maintained deeper and longer-term relations with the British beginning with the Anglo-Bahraini 1868 treaty, which ended a year-long conflict between Bahrain and Qatar. Though concluded between Britain and Bahrain, the treaty implicitly recognised Qatar as separate from Bahrain and recognised Mohammed bin Thani as the ruler of Qatar.[3] Since then, his descendants have served as emirs of Qatar, though not always following the death of their predecessor. Several of Qatar's emirs have abdicated in favour of their sons, and two have been deposed. In 2013, Hamad bin Khalifa, who himself had deposed his father Khalifa bin Hamad, abdicated in favour of his son Tamim bin Hamad.

Preconditions to State Building in Qatar

In 1905, Qatar was home to roughly 27,000 members of various tribes.[4] The leaders of these tribes made political decisions and mediated disputes. These included rulings on issues involving dowries, access to wells, and crime. Norms grounded in kinship authority formed the basis for many of these decisions.[5] As in Kuwait, the major sources of income among merchant *hadhar* were pearl diving, fishing, trade and craftsmanship. While these professions were not occupied upon strict tribal lines, some had tribal majorities. Craftsmen, for example, were most frequently from the al-Murrah tribe.[6] Qatar's small towns were located along the coast or close to channels and bays. Migratory *bedu* also lived in the interior.[7] The Hajir, Ka'aban, and Naim tribes comprised the majority of this population.[8]

Tribal populations in Qatar depended on herding camels and goats to sustain themselves.[9] There was almost no agriculture in the country, and villagers in and around Doha (the modern capital of Qatar) kept only a few horses and cattle which *bedu* tended on their behalf.[10] The city itself was divided into nine quarters linked with narrow streets. It was organised tribally, with the Khalifa, Hajri and Sulati each residing in separate districts.[11] There was a small souk consisting of about fifty shops.[12]

Preconditions in the Centre

Doha, like other cities along the Arab Gulf coast, was a depot for international shipping routes which ran through the region. While it grew quickly following state building, the city began as a small settlement whose ruling family did not project power much outside city limits. This limited projection of power constrained the ruling family's options during state building by forcing it to reach out to non-urban kinship groups whose access to vital limited resources at the time was competitive.

Water Access

In the early 1900s, Doha itself had one well about half a mile south of the city, and a group of fifteen wells one mile to the west at Mushairib. Most of the population obtained its water from a well about three miles inland called Bir-al-Jadidah (the new well), but the royal Al Thani family, notables and Turkish officers who were in Qatar at the time obtained water from another set of wells in Na'aijah.[13] At the end of 1953, British State Engineer H. T. Hale was appointed to create a piped water supply and distillation plant for Doha. This updating and expansion of the town's water supply allowed the state-building process in Qatar to proceed by providing sufficient water for a quickly expanding population.[14]

Authority in the Centre

While the Al Thani ruled Doha, they did not project power far beyond the city limits. Thus, and in a manner similar to Kuwait, the merchant families inhabiting the city could simply move out of Doha if a dispute emerged with the ruling family. This gave these families significant bargaining power vis-à-vis the Al Thani.

Preconditions in Non-urban Areas

Non-urban kinship groups had competitive access to water as a vital limited resource. In many cases these groups were transnational. The al-Murrah migrated between Qatar and Saudi Arabia and the Naim migrated by sea between an area in Qatar near Zubarah in the north as well as Bahrain.[15] Like Kuwait, these groups created ad hoc arrangements to resolve conflicts with varying degrees of success.

Water Access

Qatar is one of the most water-scarce countries in the world and, in fact, has no surface water at all.[16] Many early tribal disputes in Qatar revolved around boundaries and the ownership of Qatar's limited number of wells.[17] These wells were distinguished from others in the Gulf by being lined with stone, which was sometimes set in mortar.[18] Like in Kuwait, tribes controlled wells in Qatar. Yet these wells were dispersed and were few and far between.

Authority in Non-urban Areas

Families were closely connected before state building in Qatar. Nomadic and migratory *bedu*, as in Kuwait, had tribal *diyar* to delineate access to water for drinking and raising livestock. The Naim, for example, were seasonal migrants who tended to flocks in a *dirah* outside of Zubarah.[19] For both groups, families were part of larger kinship groups that were administered by a sheikh. The sheikh's power originated in kinship authority. He had the power to resolve problems both inside and outside the kinship group, and represented his tribe to other sheikhs in the Gulf region.[20]

Impetus for Government Outreach to Kinship Groups

Qatar's Al Thani ruling family faced territorial challenges from other ruling families in the region, but in particular from the Al Khalifah in Bahrain. As in Kuwait, these territories lay within tribal *diyar*. Influence over the kinship groups who controlled this land allowed ruling families to claim control over it. In 1937, the Naim tribe turned to Qatar's Emir, Abdallah bin Qasim Al Thani, to mediate an internal dispute. The Emir ordered the tribe's leader in Zubarah to swear loyalty or else pay a tax. In response, the leader appealed to Bahrain's Al Khalifa ruling family. Conflict between the Al Khalifa and Al Thani broke out when the dispute could not be resolved through diplomatic means. The Naim left the area, moving first to Bahrain and later to Hasa in Saudi Arabia. Nonetheless, Crystal points out that 'their right to the territory was never challenged', and they were permitted to re-enter Qatar after the Second World War, settling in al-Ghuwayriyah.[21]

This dispute between Bahrain and Qatar, which was not resolved until 2001, came amidst rapid expansion of the Qatari government's capacity as a result of oil revenues. As in Kuwait, settling nomadic populations and imposing bureaucratic governance was part and parcel of the Qatari state-building plan. Yet these plans were constrained by these kinship groups' pre-existing conditions of resource access.

State Capacity

The basis of Qatar's state-building process was oil revenue. The oil concession in Qatar began in 1935 and was carried out under the auspices of the Anglo-Persian Oil Company. The concession was then transferred in 1936 to Petroleum Development (Qatar) Ltd.[22] Qatar's extensive oil resources combined with a relatively small population gave it strong state capacity. Nonetheless, the government's use of this capacity was constrained by the resource access of non-urban kinship groups. Qatar could not simply impose bureaucratic authority on these populations. Rather, it engaged them as kinship groups during the state-building process.

Stage One: Infrastructure

While oil in Qatar was discovered in the late 1930s, the Second World War delayed attempts to convert oil resources into state revenue. By 1949, oil exports and payments had begun but the Emir, Abdallah bin Qasim, faced the threat of armed opposition unless he increased the allowances of Al Thani ruling family members. He agreed to abdicate in favour of his son, Ali bin Abdullah. Britain agreed to support the new ruler in exchange for a presence in Qatar.[23]

A British adviser created Qatar's first budget in 1953 and government services funded by this budget followed soon after. In addition to electricity and telephone services, Qatar built a jetty, customs warehouse, airport and a police headquarters.[24] Qatar also began building schools, both in Doha and in smaller villages and towns to educate its younger population. As in Kuwait, previously nomadic tribes were settled into these towns and offered permanent housing and social services. This sedentarisation, as it did in Kuwait, disrupted arrangements of kinship authority that had existed for these previously nomadic tribes.

In 1972, the British firm Llewellyn-Davies was tasked with developing Qatar's urban centres. This included demolishing existing houses belonging to Qatari families in downtown Doha to build larger projects, and reclaiming shallow water in north Doha to create government and financial buildings.[25] An American firm, Pereira Architects, made further developments to Doha's waterfront and urban landscape in 1975.[26] These shifts further disrupted kinship authority in Qatar.

Stage Two: Bureaucratic Authority

Bureaucratic public administration in Qatar expanded significantly in 1949.[27] As Qatar began exporting oil, it requested a financial advisor from Britain to manage its oil revenues. The adviser set up departments and slowly began to fill them with bureaucratic officials. These departments were later institutionalised by Qatar's 1970 constitution.[28] Despite the creation of bureaucratic authority in Qatar, however, kinship authority reasserted itself. As they had done in Kuwait, the country's kinship groups instrumentalised these bureaucracies, drawing upon their patronage and distributing it through tribal networks. Since Qatar's government had reached out to these groups as kinship groups, their ability to prevent this instrumentalisation was constrained.

Authority over Housing

Qatar's regions were divided into municipalities that fell under bureaucratic jurisdiction. These began with the capital, Doha, in 1963.[29] The expansion of Doha engulfed pre-existing settlements including Bidda, Jasra and Wadi as-Sail. New towns were also constructed to support the emerging oil industry in Qatar, including Dukhan in the west.[30] In addition, the government made an attempt to settle tribal populations and foster loyalty to the state. The government offered them free housing and job opportunities. Like in Kuwait, many of these jobs were in the military sector.[31] Such initiatives preserved the political salience of kinship authority because the patronage they created was distributed through existing kinship networks.

Similar to Kuwait, *bedu* and *hadhar* are salient identities in Qatar. Qataris also use the term *hawala* to describe a small group of Sunni families who migrated from Persia. Whether urban or tribal, however, the government settled families together during state building. The Naim, for example, were settled in al-Ghuwayriyah, the Al bu Ainain in Wakrah, and the Al Thani and Murrah in Rayyan.[32] As Doha's development continued throughout the 1960s, however, many residents of these towns left to find work in the city.[33] Nonetheless, kinship authority retained salience. In 2002, for example, al-Shawi found that Qatari men preferred to use tribal leaders rather than bureaucratic institutions to resolve disputes, regardless of their age or socio-economic status.[34] Like Kuwait, Qatar had a land distribution policy that was not necessarily conducive to settling family members together. To circumvent this system, family members used *wasta* – a term translating roughly as 'clout' or 'personal connections' – to secure houses together, or have purchased land through the private real estate market and obtained a partial reimbursement from the Qatari government rather than a land grant. Others, like the Jaideh family, purchased a large plot of land and add wings or private suites to the house as family members marry and have children of their own.[35]

While the state provided housing according to its bureaucratic needs, Qataris sometimes resisted or avoided compliance with these official policies. Kinship authority reasserted itself as families resisted or avoided government attempts to resettle them.[36] Additionally, high land prices in Doha itself incentivised illegal land development on the city's outskirts, which posed a problem for the British firm Shankland Cox and its plan to develop the capital.[37]

The development of downtown Doha in 1970 introduced a conflict between bureaucratic and kinship authority in Qatar.[38] On the advice of the British firm Llewellyn Davies, Qatar established a land purchasing plan to develop its urban centre. However, the government faced difficulty acquiring this prime real-estate because it cost more than expected to purchase it from its owners. As a result, funding to develop the acquired properties had been redirected elsewhere. Additionally, some Qataris resented being relocated while their land remained undeveloped decades later. They were reluctant, in other words, to accept new patterns of bureaucratic governance. After remaining unoccupied for years, their homes downtown were rented out to low-income expatriate workers rather than being demolished and the land being developed.[39]

Authority over Water and Electricity

Qatar's first desalination plant opened in 1954 and its first power plant began operation in 1957, with many more added over the following decades.[40] Desalinated water was stored in underground reservoirs and water towers. It was then transported to customers in water tankers. Between 1982 and 1986, Qatar also installed 1.17 million metres of pipes to deliver water directly to its population.[41] In the 1970s, Qatar's State Water and State Electricity departments were merged into the Ministry of Electricity and Water as part of the bureaucratic expansion of the Qatari state.[42] The country continued to add power generation stations and expand electric grids, as well as the network of water pipes, throughout the 1970s and 80s. Starting in 1995, the government commissioned three additional desalination plants that now account for almost all of Qatar's water supply.[43] By creating this infrastructure, Qatar's government gained control over access to water as a vital limited resource. Kinship authority, which had delineated the boundaries of *diyar* in which kinship groups could obtain water, was disrupted as a result.

Authority over Education

Most education instruction before state building in Qatar involved memorising and studying the Quran in one-room schools called *kuttab*. While both boys and girls had access to this instruction, boys from wealthier families also had access to instruction in Arabic and arithmetic. Around 1918, the Madrassa al-Sheikh Mohammed 'Abal-'Aziz al-Mani' opened in Doha. Its namesake, Sheikh al-Mani', had been appointed by Sheikh Abdullah bin Qasim al-Thani to oversee legal affairs in Qatar, and some of al-Mani's lessons involved students simply watching him conduct bureaucratic procedures. Several graduates of the madrassa went on to become high-ranking officials in the Qatari bureaucratic apparatus.[44]

The development of a larger-scale education programme in Qatar began around 1952. In that year, the Emir tasked a committee of four religious scholars with creating a modern education system funded by Qatar's substantial oil revenues. Qatar's Department of Education was formed in 1954. Between 1954 and 1964 alone, enrollment jumped from 1,098 boys to

4,346. Girls' education was expanded starting in 1956, growing from 122 pupils in that year to 3,176 by 1964.[45] Qatar's government also expanded education into villages and temporary settlements outside the centre. However, its ability to do so was constrained by kinship authority. Kinship groups welcomed government schools, but not solely for the educational value they provided. The government paid rent to members of the kinship group for the use of buildings as schools, and teachers paid rent for their houses. In addition, regular tribal migration made it difficult for the government to hold lessons regularly and find teachers who were willing to move along with the kinship group. To deal with this problem more generally, Qatar's government began sedentarising kinship groups in the 1970s. It also paid for cars to transport students who did not live in these settlements to school.[46] Rather than force families to move into areas where schools were established, Qatar's government instead made accommodations for existing living arrangements predicated on kinship authority.

In 1977, Qatar University opened as a result of the merger of two education colleges (one for men and one for women). The university's four-year course of study provided a local option for students seeking higher education who wished to remain in Qatar for the duration of their studies. Remaining at home allowed these students not only to save money on transportation and the costs of dormitory living, but also to maintain kinship ties with their family through regular interaction and contact.

Authority over Citizenship

Qatar's 1961 citizenship law (2/1961) granted citizenship to those living in Qatar since 1930. Children of Qatari fathers were automatically granted citizenship, and foreigners could be naturalised after living in the country for twenty years (fifteen if they were from an Arab country). It also allowed for Qatar to withdraw citizenship from any naturalised person convicted of 'crimes pertaining to honor [*sharaf*]'.[47] This provision (Article 14 Section 2a) exemplifies the instrumentalisation of kinship authority. While citizenship is granted bureaucratically by the state, it can be revoked for violating codes of honour originating in kinship authority. Rules pertaining to the ability of spouses of Qataris to obtain citizenship changed in a series of amendments to the law passed between 1963 and 1989.[48] In 2005, Qatar's Emir issued an updated citizenship law (38/2005). This law preserved the original 1930 cut-off while tightening restrictions on obtaining Qatari citizenship. Throughout each of these amendments, however, the 1930 cutoff remained in place. This suggests preference for the tribal groups that had settled in Qatar by that time. Finally, as in Kuwait, a Qatari woman who marries a non-Qatari cannot pass citizenship to her children.[49] This provision of citizenship law allows Qatar's patronage networks to restrict who acquires access.

Qatar's bureaucratic expansion involved major advances in the provision of resources and the administration of previously nomadic populations. At the same time, kinship authority reasserted itself by constraining how and where the government could extend its bureaucratic authority. The government's initial outreach to non-urban populations as kinship groups constrained its options in this regard.

Stage Three: Nationalism

Similar to Kuwait, Qatari nationalism adopted a historical idiom which reifies the historic role of kinship groups and kinship authority. Ultimately, nationalism in Qatar is constructed as a sense of tribal belonging.[50] Qatar's national anthem, adopted in 1996 and written by a member of the ruling family, links the conceptualisation of Qatar to 'the achievements of our forefathers'. As Crystal notes, Qatar's 'government so publicly embraces Qatar's nomadic pastoral history, essentially the history of the tribes' while also elevating the status of the Al Thani ruling family. Qatar's government publications and heritage sites also emphasise Qatar's history of tribal pastoralism.[51] The Qatari national narrative is also historical, emphasising the country's maritime past in which merchant families engaged in shipping and pearling. The Qatari state seal also bears a dhow, a reference to these families' maritime heritage.

A territorial idiom would not have been successful in Qatar for two major reasons. First, the territorial boundaries of the state were a subject of constant dispute throughout the twentieth century. Disputes with ruling families and major kinship groups alike changed the territory over which the Al Thani projected power. Secondly, many of Qatar's tribes were historically nomadic across national borders. Migration between Qatar, Saudi Arabia and Bahrain was common for many major tribal groups. Thus, territorial definitions of nationhood carry less historical weight than the identity of the groups who arrived in Qatar at particular points in time.

Notes

1. Omer Karasapan, 'Pandemic Highlights the Vulnerability of Migrant Workers in the Middle East', *Brookings*, 17 September 2020, https://www.brookings.edu/blog/future-development/2020/09/17/pandemic-highlights-the-vulnerability-of-migrant-workers-in-the-middle-east/.
2. Jill Crystal, 'Tribes and Patronage Networks in Qatar', in Uzi Rabi (ed.), *Tribes and States in a Changing Middle East* (Oxford, UK: Oxford University Press, 2016): 38.

3. Habibur Rahman, *The Emergence of Qatar* (London, UK: Kegan Paul International, 2005): 79.
4. John Gordon Lorimer, *Gazetteer of the Persian Gulf, Oman, and Central Arabia*, 5 vols (Calcutta, India: Superintendent Government Printing, 1908–15).
5. A. Nizar Hamzeh, 'Qatar: The Duality of the Legal System', *Middle Eastern Studies* 30 no. 1 (January 1994): 80.
6. Crystal, 'Tribes and Patronage', 41.
7. Sharon Nagy, 'Social and Spatial Process: An Ethnographic Study of Housing in Qatar', PhD dissertation, University of Pennsylvania, 1997: 95–6.
8. 'Military report on the Arabian Shores of the Persian Gulf, Kuwait, Bahrein, Hasa, Qatar, Trucial Oman and Oman', British Library: India Office Records and Private Papers, IOR/R/15/1/531, in *Qatar Digital Library*, https://www.qdl.qa/en/archive/81055/vdc_100023509623.0x000076.
9. Ali A. Hadi al-Shawi, 'Political Influences of Tribes in the State of Qatar: Impact of Tribal Loyalty on Political Participation', PhD dissertation, Mississippi State University, 2002: 8.
10. Rahman, *The Emergence of Qatar*, 6–7; John Gordon Lorimer, *Gazetteer of the Persian Gulf, Oman, and Central Arabia, Volume II* (Calcutta, India: Superintendent Government Printing, 1908): 487.
11. Allen James Fromherz, *Qatar: A Modern History* (New York, NY: I. B. Tauris, 2012): 21.
12. Lorimer, *Gazetteer of the Persian Gulf* (1908), 487–8.
13. Lorimer, *Gazetteer of the Persian Gulf* (1908), 491. Lorimer notes that the Turkish military outpost had its own well, which was guarded by eight men in a watch tower.
14. 'Historical Summary of Events in the Persian Gulf Shaikhdoms and the Sultanate of Muscat and Oman, 1928–1953 [68v] (141/222)', British Library: India Office Records and Private Papers, IOR/R/15/1/731(1), in *Qatar Digial Library*, https://www.qdl.qa/en/archive/81055/vdc_100023415995.0x00008e.
15. Crystal, 'Tribes and Patronage', 42.
16. Victoria Scott, 'Managing Water Supply a Key Challenge Facing Qatar, Expert Says', *Doha News*, 26 November 2013, http://dohanews.co/managing-water-supply-a-key-challenge-facing-qatar-expert-says/.
17. Al-Shawi, 'Political Influences of Tribes', 9.
18. 'Gazetteer of the Persian Gulf. Vol. II. Geographical and Statistical. J G Lorimer. 1908', British Library: India Office Records and Private Papers, IOR/L/PS/20/C91/4, in *Qatar Digital Library*, https://www.qdl.qa/en/archive/81055/vdc_100023515719.0x00002e.
19. Crystal, 'Tribes and Patronage', 43.
20. Al-Shawi, 'Political Influences of Tribes', 9.
21. Crystal, 'Tribes and Patronage', 44.
22. 'File 82/27 VIII F 91 QATAR OIL [31r] (70/468)', British Library: India Office Records and Private Papers, IOR/R/15/1/633, in *Qatar Digital Library*, http://

www.qdl.qa/en/archive/81055/vdc_100023800656.0x000048; 'File 82/27 VIII F 91 QATAR OIL [40r] (90/468)', British Library: India Office Records and Private Papers, IOR/R/15/1/633, in *Qatar Digital Library*, http://www.qdl.qa/en/archive/81055/vdc_100023800656.0x00005c; 'File 82/27 VIII F 91 QATAR OIL [210r] (436/468)', British Library: India Office Records and Private Papers, IOR/R/15/1/633, in *Qatar Digital Library*, https://www.qdl.qa/en/archive/81055/vdc_100023800658.0x000025.

23. Anthony Toth, 'Qatar: Historical Background', in Helen Metz (ed.), *Qatar: A Country Study* (Washington, DC: Library of Congress Federal Research Division, 1993).
24. Toth, 'Qatar: Historical Background'.
25. Khalid Al Thani, 'The Development of Qatar Over the Past Few Decades', *The Peninsula*, 16 November 2017, https://www.thepeninsulaqatar.com/article/16/11/2017/The-development-of-Qatar-over-the-past-few-decades.
26. Nayla al-Naimi, 'The Morphology of Urban Qatari Homes', *Building Doha*, 7 February 2017, http://sites.northwestern.edu/buildingdoha/2017/02/07/morphology-of-urban-qatari-homes/.
27. Abdallah Yousef al-Maliki, 'Public Administration in the State of Qatar: Origin, Development, Problems, and Current Directions', PhD dissertation, Golden Gate University, 1989: 28–9.
28. Al-Maliki, 'Public Administration', 64, 71.
29. Al-Maliki, 'Public Administration', 73.
30. Nagy, 'Social and Spatial Process', 97; Crystal, 'Tribes and Patronage', 44.
31. Al-Shawi, 'Political Influences of Tribes', 2.
32. Crystal, 'Tribes and Patronage', 44.
33. Crystal, 'Tribes and Patronage', 44.
34. Al-Shawi, 'Political Influences of Tribes'.
35. Nagy, 'Social and Spatial Process', 172–5.
36. Nagy, 'Social and Spatial Process', 104.
37. Nagy, 'Social and Spatial Process', 121–2.
38. Nagy, 'Social and Spatial Process', 109–10.
39. Nagy, 'Social and Spatial Process', 111.
40. Toth, 'Qatar: Historical Background'.
41. 'History', *Kahramaa*, https://www.km.com.qa/AboutUs/Pages/History.aspx (accessed 31 July 2018).
42. 'Qatar General Electricity & Water Corporation: Adapting Infrastructure for Changing Demands', *IndustryME*, 20 February 2016, https://industry-me.com/features/infrastructure/qatar-general-electricity-water-corporation-adapting-infrastructure-for-changing-demands/.
43. 'Water and Desalination', *Hukoomi – Qatar e-Government*, http://portal.www.gov.qa/wps/portal/topics/Environment+and+Natural+Resources/Water+and+Desalination.
44. Abdulla Juma Kobaisi, 'The Development of Education in Qatar, 1950–1977 with an Analysis of some Educational Problems', PhD Dissertation, University of Durham, 1979: 34–5.

45. Kobaisi, 'Development of Education in Qatar', 39–40.

46. Kobaisi, 'Development of Education in Qatar', 43–4.

47. 'Law No. 2 of 1961 on the Qatari Nationality (repealed)', *Qatar Legal Portal*, http://www.almeezan.qa/LawView.aspx?opt&LawID=2578&language=en (accessed 26 July 2018).

48. Gianluca Paolo Parolin, *Citizenship in the Arab World: Kin, Religion and Nation-state* (Amsterdam, The Netherlands: Amsterdam University Press, 2009): 90.

49. Rehunama Asmi, 'Finding a Place to Sit: How Qatari Women Combine Cultural and Kinship Capital in the Home Majlis', *Anthropology of the Middle East* 11 no. 2 (Winter 2016): 29.

50. A. Hadi Alshawi and Andrew Gardner, 'Tribalism, Identity, and Citizenship in Contemporary Qatar', *Anthropology of the Middle East* 8 no. 2 (Winter 2013): 54; Fromherz, *Qatar* (2012), 29.

51. Crystal, 'Tribes and Patronage', 42.

6

STATE BUILDING IN OMAN

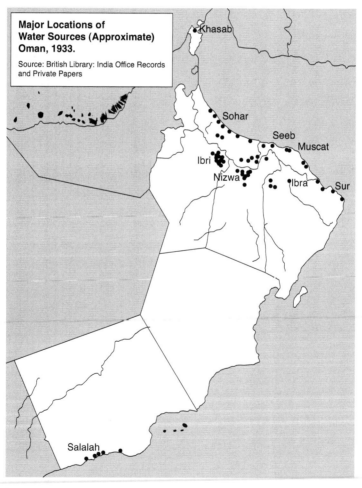

Figure 6.1   Major water sources (approximate locations) in Oman, 1933

O man is officially home to 216 tribes – all of them registered with the government. Certification of tribal membership is a prerequisite for Omanis seeking to obtain a license, passport or other official document. In 2006, the government replaced the al-Tuwaiya and al-Khalifain tribal designations with that of the larger and more powerful al-Harthi tribe. In response, the tribes complained to Oman's administrative courts and several human rights organisations. Oman's government verbally agreed to cease this designation. However, tribe members attest that it has continued. Despite the kinship authority these tribes carry, the government's bureaucratic authority retains the ability to determine which tribes are real in the eyes of the state. Kinship authority in Oman has been instrumentalised by the state's bureaucracy in ways that make it fundamentally different from Kuwait. Functions of kinship authority often serve bureaucratic ends rather than the other way around. As such, kinship authority in the Sultanate has instrumentalised salience.

Oman's cooperative access to vital limited resources created different path-dependent conditions to those in Kuwait, and pre-state conditions are a better explanation of these differences than state capacity. While some kinship groups in Oman were nomadic, many settled in and around towns and villages where they cooperated over access to water. To facilitate this access, these kinship groups formed proto-bureaucracies that had authority over individuals, including leaders of kinship hierarchies. During state building, Oman's government subsumed these proto-bureaucracies within the state's bureaucratic apparatus. Oman began this process by improving infrastructure in non-urban areas of the city, and extending national water and electricity networks to these locations. This process diminished the political salience of kinship authority in Oman by making the government the major provider of resources. Second, the government used this infrastructure to connect local proto-bureaucratic authority with the bureaucratic authority of the state. It used existing buy-in from the population to proto-bureaucratic governance to build assent to bureaucratic authority. By reframing tribal leaders as state officials, Oman's government embedded kinship authority within the bureaucratic apparatus of the state. Finally, Oman used nationalism to enhance loyalty to the state and its leader. Downplaying differences resulting from kinship identity, this nationalism took on a more territorial idiom than it had in Kuwait. The government built up nationalism through the construction of common national symbols across the geographic expanse it governed. The outcome of this state-building process is that kinship authority has instrumentalised political salience in Oman.

Introduction

Oman is a Sultanate on the Arabian Peninsula bordered by the Gulf to the east, the United Arab Emirates to the northwest, Saudi Arabia to the west, and Yemen to the southwest. Its ruler, the Sultan of Oman, is a member of the al-Said royal family who presides over a cabinet of ministers and appoints the eighty-three members of Oman's upper house of parliament, the *Majlis al-Dawla*. Oman's lower house is called the *Majlis al-Shura* and consists of eighty-four elected members.

Oman's national government dates back to the *coup d'état* of 1970 in which Sultan Qaboos bin Sa'id overthrew his father, Sa'id bin Taymur. In so doing, he became the latest in a line of Omani rulers from the Al Busaid family. Dynastic rule is a shared characteristic of leadership in Kuwait, Qatar and Oman. Oman's leadership moves between and across branches of the family. Disputes often arose between these branches. Since 1871, however, power has been concentrated in the hands of the male descendants of Turki bin Sa'id. In January 2020, this trend continued following Sultan Qaboos' death, with the appointment of his cousin, Haitham bin Tareq Al Said.

Kuwait, Qatar and Oman are states that share a history of kinship governance in non-urban areas. However, patterns of resource access in non-urban areas differed between them. In Kuwait, kinship groups outside the city were nomadic and water resources were dispersed. Access to these vital limited resources was competitive. Kinship groups had areas of control – *diyar* – that were a subject of constant renegotiation and dispute. Conflict resolution was ad hoc and governed by norms of intra-group interaction rooted in kinship authority. Kuwait's royal family reached out to individual kinship groups in order to secure a population to govern and fighting men to gain and hold territory against competing regional players.

Oman, in contrast, had towns and villages in which many kinship groups settled. Other groups were seasonally nomadic, settling outside these towns and villages for a few months per year. Both of these groups made use of a *falaj* system – consisting of a series of irrigation channels – to bring water from the mountains directly to the village itself. Because of this concentrated resource and settled population, access to vital limited resources in Oman was cooperative. Different kinship groups in the town or village created a proto-bureaucracy to manage access to water. Led by a *wakil*, this proto-bureaucracy used a cap-and-trade system to manage water resources in an efficient way. If disputes arose between *falaj* systems, a *wakil* acted as a politician to resolve the dispute. If this proved impossible, the *wakil* could appeal to the provincial governor, the *wali*, to mediate. While the *wali*'s primary function was to mediate broader disputes in the province, he also mediated conflicts that arose surrounding these proto-bureaucracies.

The *wakil*, the staff of proto-bureaucracies and the *wali* were all a part of kinship networks. Their tribal and family affiliations were known – to the extent that *walis* were appointed to govern in areas where such affiliations would not be seen as biasing their decisions in favour of one tribe or another. At the same time, their functions as officials were bureaucratic in that they had unique knowledge of a governing system. This overlap between personal identity and official capacity created a framework for local governance in Oman based ultimately on bureaucratic authority. Local populations knew these officials respected kinship authority, even as the government sought to embed this authority within the state's bureaucratic apparatus.

Before state building, Oman's Sultan Sa'id bin Taymur had a relationship with the British government. While more extensive than official narratives in Oman recount, development under Taymur's rule was slow at best. Even after the discovery of commercially useful quantities of oil, development in Oman lagged. State building began as a push by Britain for the Sultan to expand his control over tribes living in areas where oil existed in order to provide safe access to this resource. However, state building accelerated dramatically following the rise of Sultan Qaboos. Following Qaboos' 1970 *coup d'état*, Oman began a massive infrastructure building programme. Whereas Kuwait created suburban infrastructure and moved its non-urban populations onto it, Oman built infrastructure where its settled populations already existed. It extended electricity and water networks from the capital to these non-urban areas, linking the two together. This linkage served as a useful vector for bureaucratic authority. Proto-bureaucracies set up to manage the distribution of water before state building created buy-in among the population to bureaucracy. During state building, the government embedded these proto-bureaucracies into the state's bureaucratic apparatus. To enhance buy-in, Oman also created a nationalist narrative. Unlike Kuwait, where national 'ownership' of the country was a function of when one's family settled there, Oman's idiom of nationalism was territorial. Using unifying symbolism – a common heritage of nobility and military gallantry exemplified by Qaboos himself – Oman created a nationalism that enhanced the population's buy-in to its state-building project.

The Ruling Family of Oman

The Al Said dynasty is a subset of the Al Busaid family and the Albusaidi tribe. Its rise to power, with the help of the British, was an important component of the success of Oman's state building project. Unlike the al-Sabah in Kuwait, the Al Said had established power before the existence of strong British influence. However, British influence was critical for the Al Said's state-building project following the 1970 coup.

The Al Busaid family rose to power following the expulsion of Persian troops present in Oman from 1742–4 and the subsequent demise of the Yaruba

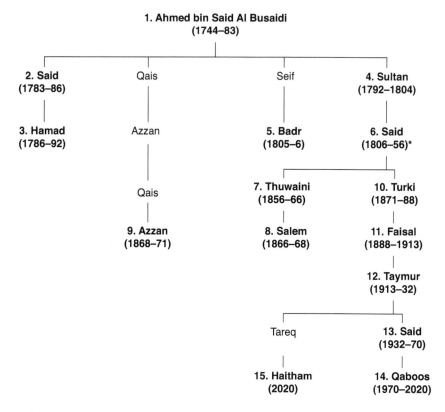

*Co-ruled with his brother Salem bin Sultan from 1804 to 1806 during a dispute with Qais bin Ahmed and Badr bin Seif.

Figure 6.2   Al Busaid rulers of Oman since 1744

ruling dynasty in 1749 with the death of Bal'arab bin Himyar.[1] Ahmed bin Sa'id Al Busaidi, who assumed rule in June 1749, was the first of the dynasty of Al Busaid rulers that has continued since.[2] After Ahmed's death in 1783, his son Sa'id bin Ahmed ruled for a short three-year period. His son Hamad, who came to power in 1786, moved the capital to Muscat. Hamad was followed in 1792 by his uncle Sultan who aligned with the British and allowed the British East India Company to establish a trading station. Sultan's son Salem briefly ruled alongside his brother Sa'id beginning in 1804, but assented to the rule of his brother in 1806. Sa'id bin Sultan established a second capital in Zanzibar, where many members of the family still live, though not all are Omani citizens (most hold Tanzanian citizenship).[3]

The modern Al Said line of the royal family began with Sa'id's son Turki, who came to power in 1871 following a protracted struggle within the ruling family. The struggle resulted in the split of Zanzibar and Muscat as separate centres of Al Said control, and the payment of an annual 'Zanzibar Subsidy' of 40,000 Mother Theresa Dollars from Majid bin Sa'id in Zanzibar to Thuwaini bin Sa'id in Muscat. Payments began in 1873 after Britain forced the signing of an anti-slavery treaty.[4] When Britain demanded both sultans sign the treaty, the Zanzibar sultan complained it would reduce revenue and make payment to the sultan in Muscat a large financial burden. Britain agreed to pay the subsidy to the Muscat sultan on the Zanzibar sultan's behalf to offset this cost. This payment, however, quickly took on the form of patronage. When it became clear that this patronage was the subsidy's major objective, the British continued support through an 'arms traffic subsidy', which began in 1921. The subsidy was officially given as compensation for the construction of a British arms warehouse. As the political resident at the time reveals, however, 'the real reason for the regrant of these subsidies was the impending financial collapse of the Sultan's administration'. The Sultan was granted Rs. 100,000 to 'prevent the financial collapse of the Muscat State'.[5] Unlike Kuwait's rulers who could rely on merchants for income – albeit at the price of granting them political power – Oman's leaders still relied on British financial support for survival well into the twentieth century.

Preconditions to State Building in Oman

The history of Oman before state building is a story characterised by sophisticated patterns of political manoeuvering. Ruling family feuds pitted brothers against each other and alliance systems were both complex and subject to rapid change. Among Oman's residents, there were similarly sophisticated albeit usually less conflictual mechanisms of politics. As in Kuwait, tribal groups governed themselves through kinship authority. In Oman, however, these groups existed among and within a framework of Omani towns and villages where settled tribal groups shared land and water. The centre of Omani power has changed numerous times since the 1600s but moved to Muscat in 1783 under Sultan Hamad bin Sa'id.

Preconditions in the Centre

Muscat, like Kuwait City, was a Gulf port city filled with merchant families who played an important role in regional trade. Muscat is now Oman's capital city but was historically a small secluded port. The area's sharp rocky coastline provided the town with excellent defence against a maritime attack.[6] Two forts overlooking the water built by the Portuguese in the 1500s helped considerably in this regard. However, due to the danger of running a ship into these rocks, most maritime trade occurred (and occurs today) in the adjacent town of Mutrah.

Water Access

Before state building, Muscat was a small port city where ships could pick up drinking water before exiting the Gulf of Oman en route to India or Yemen.[7] The town's water originated in one of approximately twenty springs in the area or in wells.[8] Much of it came into Muscat via canals, channels and pipelines. The water was used for the irrigation of twelve or so farms in the area, but was also used in gardens and in the buildings and forts in Muscat.[9] In the early twentieth century, Sultan Sa'id bin Taymur owned some of the date trees in the nearby village of Ruwi watered from nearby wells, the fruits of which were often sold in the market at Mutrah.[10] Water was also stored in reservoirs and transported via pipeline to a distribution point near Mutrah souk where it was put into buckets or goatskin bags and sold to locals. While prices fluctuated, a record from 1871 notes that during a drought the price rose to ten fils, indicating that the price was usually lower.[11] Such a system for water distribution existed in Muscat until 1955.[12]

Kinship groups lived together in and around Muscat. Merchant families like the Ajam and Lawati lived in specific (and gated) areas of the city. The Lawati, for example, were based in neighbourhoods of Muscat and Mutrah but later branched out to Sur al-Lawatia.[13] However, it does not appear that kinship was the basis of resource access with regards to water. Other items, such as marriage and divorce, religious occurrences, and speakers in the community, were (and are) managed in Muscat's Shi'a families by committees comprised of family members. As with the tribes and families of the interior, each family had a sheikh who was appointed by the government and reported to the *wali*. While originally the sheikhs had direct relationships with the Sultan himself, the *wali* system put some distance between the sheikh and Oman's leadership.[14]

Authority in the Centre

Within Muscat, large merchant families were often overseen by a sheikh or family patriarch. This leader had a direct relationship with the Sultan, and there was little bureaucracy in between them.[15] The Sultan ruled not as the head of a bureaucratic state but as the leader of a ruling family.

In addition to urban families, the Sultan also maintained relations with tribes in Oman's interior, whose leadership would periodically visit seeking 'gifts' in the form of money or guns. Tribal contact was not always friendly. In 1895, a group of tribes led by Ali bin Saleh al-Harithi breached Muscat's walls and forced the Sultan to seek refuge in Fort Jalali. Only after being paid off did the tribes leave, and even then they looted and burned buildings on their way out.[16] By the early 1900s, Muscat consisted of al-'Alam Palace and several large houses in which members of the royal family, major families, and senior governing officials lived. There were also several mosques which represented Sunni, Shi'a and Ibadhi Islamic practices.[17] This diversity reflected the cosmopolitan aspect of life in Muscat, bolstered by its function as a regional water depot for international shipping routes. In the neighbouring town of Mutrah, the souk was also regional crossroads for goods exchange. A British report from 1911 notes fourteen languages that could be overheard in the souk's shops and covered corridors, including Swahili, Turkish and Gujrati.[18]

Preconditions in Non-urban Areas

Like the Al Sabah, the power of the Al Said ruling family was based partially on its ability to garner the loyalty of non-urban tribes.[19] Patronage was an important part of this process. Oman's tribes have their origins in Yemen (the Qahtani confederation) and Saudi Arabia (the 'Adnani confederation). Disputes between tribes were common given limited resources in the Omani desert. In addition to being divided by origin, Oman's tribes were organised into two large confederations – the Ghafiri and Hinawi. Early British histories of Oman attribute the split to the Qahtani/'Adnani division, but in fact it emerged in the eighteenth century during conflict over succession to the Ya'ruba Imamate.[20] Generally speaking, the Hinawi – groups aligned with the Bani Hina – tended to be Ibadhi Muslims, while the Ghafiri – who were in turn aligned with the Bani Ghafir – had a plurality of orthodox Sunnis and Wahabis.[21] Ibadhism is related to the *khariji* Islamic tradition emphasising the equal eligibility of all Muslims to lead the *ummah*.[22] However, these identities were fluid and it was not unheard of for a tribe to switch from one confederation to another based on political circumstances.[23] That is to say, these identities were not particularly sticky ones. Peterson notes that, 'if the inhabitants of the upper part of a valley or town were Ghafiri, then the populace of the lower part of the valley or town would generally be Hinawi. Tribes with traditional feuds generally chose opposite sides.'[24] The Ghafiri and Hinawi confederations were not themselves kinship identities. However, divisions between the confederations fell along tribal lines.

Periodically, tribes came to visit the Sultan seeking mediation. In 1905, for example, the Siabiyin, Rahbiyin and Nedabiyin asked the Sultan to arrange a truce between them after they were unable to reach an agreement among themselves.[25] In other cases the tribes would seek more than good council – they sought gifts, mediation, or some other payoff. If the Sultan refused to pay, he risked these tribes invading the capital. Sometimes, the Sultan could not convince the tribes to hold off, and they did in fact invade. Sultan Faisal bin Turki, for example, faced an 1893 rebellion by Hinawi tribesmen.[26] The sums of money in question in tribal negotiations were not large. In 1891, for example, a set of Ghafiri tribes raided an al-Harth tribal settlement in the eastern Sharkiah region. Tribes in the Sharkiah at the time were aligned with the Sultan, and so Sheikh Saleh of the al-Harth appealed to the Sultan for mediation. The compensation for property looted in the raid was $1,800 dollars.[27]

Comparable to Kuwait, while the Sultan mediated disputes between tribes, he did not have strong control over the tribes or their territories. Tribes would respond to unsatisfactory policy from Muscat by blocking mountain roads and passages. This infrastructure was basic at best, but critical for trade and transportation between the coast and the interior. In 1913, tribes in the interior rebelled openly against Sultan Faisal bin Turki and continued the rebellion against his successor and son, Taymur bin Faisal. The Sultan's limited resources and the alliance of Ghafiri and Hinawi tribes allowed the tribes to continue the rebellion.[28] As Britain's Deputy Political Resident in the Persian Gulf, A. P. Trevor, wrote wistfully in 1919, 'Omani tribes may remain as a hinterland – no man can control them.'[29]

The dispute was resolved seven years later with the Seeb Agreement of 1920. The agreement, named for the town of Seeb to the west of Muscat where it was signed, created two separate states: Muscat and Oman. Oman was placed under the control of Imam Mohammed bin Abdulla al Khalili. The Imam was supported by the Harthi Sheikh Isa bin Salih who led the Hinawi confederation at the time, and Sheikh Sulaiman bin Hamyar who led the Ghafiris. Muscat remained under the control of the Sultan, Taymur bin Faisal Al Said.[30] Five years later (in 1925), Taymur signed an agreement with D'Arcy Exploration Company Limited to search for oil. The contract stipulated that the Sultan would receive half-yearly royalties on any oil produced in commercial quantities. While the expedition was unsuccessful, it lay the groundwork for future expeditions that eventually led to success.[31]

Water Access

Oman's fresh water supply comes from the mountains. However, the date and lemon groves of the Sultanate's villages nestled in the valleys, where the land was flat, and where the mountains offered protection to the village inhabitants. In some cases, a well (*zaygra*) could meet some of the water needs of these villages and towns. However, tapping into other sources proved vital. Annual rainfall in Oman amounts to twenty millimetres in the desert but three hundred millimetres in the mountains.[32] In order to bring water to the village, its affluent tribal leaders sponsored the construction of irrigation tunnels called *aflaj*. Unlike dirt irrigation ditches in Kuwait, the *aflaj* ran underground and were constructed from stones or clay (*sarooj*). *Aflaj* is an Arabic word which means 'divisions', referring to the various channels (*qanat*) which brought water to the farms of the village.[33] The oldest *aflaj* are estimated to be 2,500 years old, and five of them are UNESCO World Heritage Sites.[34] In 2003, 3,017 of Oman's 4,112 *aflaj* were still active.[35] As Rabi and others point out, this access to water was of 'critical significance'.[36]

There were three kinds of *aflaj* in Oman. The *ghaili aflaj* ran above ground from *wadis* to open channels. *Da'udi aflaj* ran underground and connected a well to farms. *'Aini aflaj* ran from natural springs to the farms.[37] From these water sources, the *falaj* channel ran into the village to an uncovered section called *al-shari'a* where all inhabitants of the village could obtain clean drinking water and wash dishes and clothes. This section was located at the head of the system because it was where the water was cleanest and most suitable for drinking.[38] The channel then ran, covered, into the mosque where it was used for the ritual washing before prayer. From there, the channel ran through the residences of members of the tribe whose sheikh had sponsored the *falaj* system. Finally, it split into smaller channels that ran through the farms of the village's inhabitants.[39]

The water that the *falaj* brought to the village was a vital limited resource in Oman's arid environment. Omanis in these villages created a cap-and-trade system to manage this water supply. The unit by which water from a *falaj* is distributed is called an *athar*. The *athar* is not a unit of volume, but rather a unit of time, roughly thirty to forty minutes.[40] The *athar* gives its owner the right to divert the water flow from the main *aflaj* channel to his groves for a specified amount of time. A farmer could purchase an *athar* or pay an annual fee for it.[41] *Athar* could also be passed as an inheritance from a renter to members of his family upon his death.[42] This time was measured in some villages using the positions of the sun and stars. In others, it was measured using a water clock in which a small vessel would take one *athar*'s worth of time to fall to the bottom of a bowl of water.[43] The divisions of *athars* could be extremely precise. In the interior city of Bahla, for example, a person could own a segment of time as small as a quarter of a minute.[44]

Aflaj were often funded by a local tribal sheikh. Thus, some of the water distribution advantaged members of a certain tribe in the town or village.[45] For example, the *aflaj* channel would often run just outside the houses of members of the sheikh's tribe, giving them easier and more access to water than non-tribe members.[46] Such behaviours seem on the surface to be consistent with patronage politics and were to some extent just that. However, the sheikh funded water distribution infrastructure for the entire village, not just for his tribe. He was motivated not by purely economic considerations but also by 'responsibility according to tradition' to provide access to water for the village's inhabitants. Traditional norms governed the management of and access to water among the farmers who utilised the *aflaj* as well.[47]

Water access involved mediating interactions not only within tribes but across them. Cities like Ibra in Oman's interior had two separate kinship communities, each belonging to different lineages. Since these different kinship groups needed to coordinate for each member to obtain water, cities and villages required structures that operated along different lines than kinship.

Authority in Non-urban Areas

Administration of the *aflaj* required the creation of a small bureaucracy. The person who oversees the *falaj* system is called the *wakil* (literally, an 'agent' or 'representative'). The *wakil* received training through the oral transmission of knowledge from elders.[48] He managed the process of distributing water and mediated conflict between farmers. While a sheikh retained political oversight over the *aflaj*, the *wakil* was usually the most powerful actor overseeing the *falaj* system. In fact, a *wakil* could force a sheikh to pay his duty on the *aflaj*.[49]

Smaller *aflaj* systems have only a *wakil*, but larger systems have additional administrators to keep track of the allocation and auction of water rights, maintain the *aflaj* infrastructure, and resolve disputes that emerge surrounding the *aflaj*. In these larger systems, the *wakil* has a deputy called an *arif* who is in charge of timing irrigation and sometimes auctions the *athar*.[50] The auctioning of these *athar* is also overseen by a *khatab*, or recorder, who keeps track of the sale price, farmer, and time of day or night the water should be diverted to the farmer's field.[51] In addition, the *wakil* oversees a *qabidh* who acts as a treasurer for the *aflaj*, controlling its income and updating the *falaj* transaction book.[52] Across *aflaj* systems, the physical maintenance of the *aflaj* was performed by a *bayadir* or labourer.[53] While these positions were bureaucratic, each of them was staffed by a member of the local kinship structure.

Often, disputes over *aflaj* systems were handled locally. The *wakil* of one *falaj* would speak to the *wakil* of another *falaj*.[54] In these discussions, the *wakil* was more than a technical supervisor. He was also a sort of politician who represented the interests of his constituents. His authority was vested in his role as head of the *aflaj* rather than his personal gravitas. In other words, he was a bureaucratic representative for that *aflaj* system. While a *wakil* and his *falaj* system were independent of the national government, some situations required mediation by higher-level parties. *Walis*, or provincial governors, were appointed by the Sultan to mediate local disputes, including those arising between different *falaj* systems. For example, a *wali* might be asked to mediate in a case where one village used a water source but another village's *falaj* system influenced that source.[55]

Proto-bureaucracy made these disputes more easily manageable for the *wali*. The *wakil* of the *falaj* was the head of a proto-bureaucracy rather than the head of a kinship hierarchy. Thus, the *wali*, who had jurisdiction over the province and people within it, was mediating between leaders of bureaucratic authority institutions rather than tribes. To be sure, tribal mediation was a crucial part of a *wali*'s job. However, his management of proto-bureaucratic conflicts created a local/national relationship based on bureaucratic authority. Even prior to state building in Oman, building blocks of a national bureaucratic government existed. The origins of this governance were not in the *wali* who, again, mediated tribal and bureaucratic disputes. Rather, they were in the proto-bureaucratic management of vital limited resources by Oman's settled kinship groups.

This interaction differs starkly, furthermore, from patterns of cooperation in Kuwait between the centre and non-urban areas. Because no proto-bureaucracies existed among the nomadic kinship groups of Kuwait, local leadership was kinship-based. Unlike Oman, national-level leadership in Kuwait had no bureaucratic intermediary prior to state building. The starting conditions for governing these otherwise similar kinship-based societies differed in this critical way.

It is important to note that the *aflaj* system was relevant for administering some migratory populations in Oman as well. Omani *bedu* had tribal regions (*diyar*) like their Kuwaiti counterparts, but also made use of the *aflaj* system in certain cases. *Bedu* in Oman were not only nomadic, as the term *bedu* tends to connote. Many were in fact seasonally migratory.[56] In the winter, they lived by the coast and were involved in fishing. When the summer months made the coastal area too hot and humid, these *bedu* would migrate inland. They rented land and *falaj* water for two to four months in the interior's town and villages. These transactions could be mediated by the *wakil*, but could also be a private transaction with members of the town or village. While the *bedu* also made use of wells and springs, the *aflaj* were connected to urban centres in which these populations traded goats, sheep and camels for dates, lemons or vegetables.[57] Thus the proto-bureaucracies could extend to administer temporary kinship-based settlement as well as the town or village itself.

Oman's *aflaj* system made sedentary irrigation possible in an arid climate, which in turn facilitated the creation of settlements. Oman's government could then administer these settlements using a system of *walis* who reported back to the central government. They could also leverage the *aflaj* to coerce local populations. In November 1900, for example, Saiyid Sa'id-bin-Ibrahim Qais blocked the irrigation canals at Awahi to extract payment from the local population.[58]

Aflaj proto-bureaucracies created a social and political stability that extended beyond access to water. They were an important link between governance of resource administration specifically, and kinship-based societies more broadly. Grandmaison points out that 'lineal independence is counterbalanced by the community obligations stemming from the irrigation system . . . only the management of water counteracts this isolation'.[59] In other words, management of the *aflaj* system created stable political interaction between kinship groups that extended beyond the water management issues. This management superseded kinship authority, and was not only sufficient but also necessary to political interaction free from major conflict within Oman's towns and villages. Wilkinson points out that while many functions of *aflaj* management can be managed via kinship authority, 'tribalism can prove highly destructive once these conventions break down'.[60] The proto-bureaucratic management of water distribution created a stable basis for bureaucratic administration by reducing the occurrence of serious kinship-based conflict. They did not eliminate kinship authority among tribal groups, but rather existed as a supra-tribal institution. Thus, proto-bureaucracies created very different preconditions for state building in Oman than the norm-based governance of kinship groups in Kuwait.

Impetus for Government Outreach to Kinship Groups

While the Sultan had long-established ties with kinship groups, Western influence proved a key factor in kinship group outreach related to state building in Oman. Sultan Taymur bin Faisal abdicated in 1932, leaving Muscat in the hands of his son Sa'id bin Taymur. The British made a show of faith in Sa'id bin Taymur and after considerable internal discussion, continued the Zanzibar subsidy to the Sultan with the intent of 'keeping the Sultan of Muscat sweet'.[61] However, the British soon grew frustrated over difficulties surrounding oil exploration. In 1937, Petroleum Concessions Limited paid the Sultan in exchange for an oil exploratory concession in Muscat and Dhofar. This payment allowed the Sultan to continue to pay off tribes and keep himself in their good graces.[62] However, the British found the Sultan otherwise reluctant to pursue relations with these tribes that would open up oil exploration. Some tribes were willing to negotiate but most were reluctant.[63] Having previously fought with these tribes, Sa'id bin Taymur considered such outreach to be 'beneath his dignity'.[64] A 1953 British telegram complained about the Sultan's foot-dragging, noting, 'we much doubt his ability to establish, with his own resources, his authority over all Muscat and Oman against the wishes of the tribes'.[65]

Despite having financial means, the Sultan also showed little interest in creating a fully bureaucratic state with modern infrastructure. In 1946,

British engineering consultants designed plans for water pipes in Muscat, Mutrah and Sur. The Sultan rejected these plans as being too expensive.[66] By the 1950s, British reports noted the lack of a bureaucratic state as a major obstacle to Omani development and British oil exports. 'The Sultan's main error', they diagnosed, was 'not so much in building up his authority at the expense of . . . the sheikhs, but in his failure to develop a proper administrative machine as the necessary corollary to central government'.[67] In other words, while the Sultan had the capacity to create bureaucratic infrastructure, he lacked the interest and perhaps the incentive to do so. Kinship relations with the tribes were sufficient for him to maintain power, even though in the long term they were unlikely to advance the state overall.

In 1963 a tribal rebellion against Sa'id broke out in Oman's southern province of Dhofar. The rebellion was led by the Dhofar Liberation Front (DLF) under the auspices of Mussalam bin Nafl and Yusuf bin Alawi bin Adbullah who later became Oman's Minister Responsible for Foreign Affairs. The DLF, which also appealed to Marxist ideals, became the Popular Front for the Liberation of the Occupied Arabian Gulf (PFLOAG) in 1968. This rebellion in the south and tribal violence in the north put Sa'id bin Taymur under considerable pressure, although he benefitted from the support of Britain and Iran in fighting the PFLOAG.

Frustrated by this state of affairs, Britain set its sights on the Sultan's son, Qaboos bin Sa'id. Qaboos was born in November 1940 as the only son of Sa'id bin Taymur. He was educated in Salalah, and later studied in England as well. At age twenty, he entered the Royal Military Academy at Sandhurst and upon graduating joined the British Army of the Rhine in Germany for one year. This education and experience, along with his position in the royal lineage, made him a direct threat to Sa'id's rule. Upon his return to Oman in 1966, Qaboos was placed under house arrest and isolated from government affairs. However, faced with the prospect of a sultan who was dragging his feet on development and deeply entangled in conflicts with tribal groups to the north and Marxist rebels to the south, Britain sought to help Qaboos take power.

On 23 July 1970, Qaboos deposed Sa'id bin Taymur in a *coup d'état*. Out of a desire to avoid the appearance of colonial interference, Britain denied heavy involvement in the overthrow. However, archival documents suggest officials instructed British special forces in Oman to intervene if the coup appeared to be failing.[68] Faced with the rebellion in Dhofar and the need to create assent to his newly established rule, Sultan Qaboos moved quickly to modernise Oman and contrast his rule with that of his father's.

State Capacity

The sudden *coup d'état*, though not announced within Oman until three days after it happened, had profound implications for the country's state-building process. As in Kuwait, this process began first with infrastructure, continued next with the expansion of bureaucratic authority, and benefitted finally from nationalism. However, kinship authority's political salience in Oman manifested itself differently than in Kuwait by the end of the state-building process. This difference is rooted in patterns of access to vital limited resources.

Oman saw rapid economic development following the ascent of Sultan Qaboos in 1970. Towns that had no telephones, indoor plumbing or electricity suddenly received all three. Oman extended national networks and created infrastructure for its settled population. As a result, Omanis became increasingly dependent on the government for social services and jobs.[69] This approach differed from Kuwait, which built new infrastructure in non-urban areas and moved populations onto it.

While Oman's rapid development is a demonstration of its capacity for control of resources, it was not a function of state capacity alone. When Sultan Qaboos came to power, he faced challenges to his assent to rule. Only by successfully navigating the political landscape could the Sultan achieve success. His ability to unify an Omani state was by no means a foregone conclusion, and no amount of state capacity would itself have been sufficient to address the challenges he faced. That being said, Sultan Qaboos was constrained by pre-existing patterns of resource access among Oman's settled kinship groups.

Stage One: Infrastructure

Oman's sparse desert climate made water a vital limited resource. Oases in the desert were one source of water for nomadic groups. As with Kuwait, tribal groups established territorial *diyar* to allocate these resources. Farmers sometimes also used wells to obtain water. Yet for the towns and villages of Oman's non-urban interior, a larger scale *falaj* system more efficiently brought water from aquifers and other water sources into a village. The villages themselves were comprised of mud-brick houses, fields, a mosque, and a public gathering space known as a *sibla*. Many villages were also home to a fort, which provided defence during various wars and tribal conflicts.

Following the 1970 coup, Oman initiated a major infrastructure building project which diminished kinship authority in non-urban areas. The aims of this project were threefold. First, it was aimed at creating rapid development that would benefit Oman's citizens given decades of slow growth under Sa'id bin Taymur. Second, it was intended to create the basis for state control of non-urban areas. Finally, it was intended to create an Andersonian 'imagined community' by designing infrastructure in ways that invoked Omani nationalist imagery. Kuwait and Qatar's state-building experience shared some of these goals, although its manifestation was different. Kuwait and Qatar developed as soon as the state had capacity to do so. Omani state building, in contrast, lagged because of the political decisions of Sa'id bin Taymur. Kuwait, Qatar and Oman created bureaucracy for the establishment of state bureaucratic control. However, whereas Kuwait and Qatar created infrastructure and moved non-urban populations onto it, Oman built infrastructure where people already lived. In certain cases, this meant moving from mud-brick housing on one side of a stream or river to modern housing on the other side. Yet the location of the village or town stayed in the same non-urban area it had been prior to state building.[70] Finally, while infrastructure in Kuwait and Qatar was designed to create national unity through patronage politics and government–subject interaction, in Oman it was designed to create uniform 'Omani-ness' and invoke what Weber refers to as 'the eternal yesterday'.[71] In other words, the state used infrastructure to construct a national historical narrative emphasising unity by appealing to common symbols of Oman's feudal past.

In the early 1970s, Oman's government sponsored a set of surveys and research projects to inventory Oman's water assets and determine where more needed to be built. The resulting five-year plan called for 'large scale irrigation projects' that required modern equipment.[72] The government moved quickly to lay water pipes and install other infrastructure for water provision. This infrastructure building expanded out to rural areas, but began in urban areas. The process of infrastructure building, therefore, involved the extension of infrastructure networks in the capital to non-urban areas. Oman's government also began trucking water to non-urban areas of the state. This water was free, and it was stored in large plastic water tanks in the village or town.[73] Omanis who had previously relied on the *aflaj* for water could now make use of this new water source provided by the government. Omanis living in towns and villages often considered this drinking water superior to local sources.[74] The symbolic value of this water is an indication of its deeper purpose. By providing water via truck, Oman's government was able to gain control over access to one of the state's most vital limited resources while simultaneously co-opting the power of *aflaj* proto-bureaucracies.

In the wake of nationalised water provision, traditional community knowledge of the *aflaj* system has decreased but not disappeared entirely.[75] Ultimately, the Omani government did not destroy proto-bureaucracies altogether. In theory, it would have been possible to send officials from Muscat to oversee local water politics, or to hold local elections for the leadership of the proto-bureaucracy. While such initiatives would have been rather inefficient, the capacity existed to do so. Oman's reason for keeping proto-bureaucracies, however, went beyond efficiency. Officials within the proto-bureaucracy were embedded in the local tribal structure as individuals, and they were trusted by the community. Critically, their position as 'proto-bureaucrats' was based on technical knowledge of the management of *aflaj*, but their identity as individuals was embedded within the tribal politics of the town. While generated by pre-state Oman, the system was made to fit new patterns of national governance in the Sultanate. More importantly, they were a bridge between kinship authority and bureaucratic authority. Oman's government maintained decentralised authority over the *aflaj*, but this authority was distinctly bureaucratic.

The *aflaj* continued to be a source of drinking water in Oman into the 1980s, and still represent a main source of irrigation water. The government's management of this system exemplifies the extension of infrastructure and bureaucratic governance in Oman to make the government the primary source of aid. As an Omani government official working on *aflaj* affairs explained, 'The aflaj are historic, traditional, and efficient. People don't like to change.' Sultan Qaboos also reportedly took a personal interest in the *aflaj* system and its preservation.[76] As such, the *aflaj* represent the instrumentalisation of traditional forms of authority by the bureaucratic state in Oman.

Oman's government points out that 'It is a mix of people and government that keep the *aflaj* running.'[77] While Oman's government makes a great effort to establish a presence in each town and city, it has not completely co-opted the integrity of the local *aflaj* bureaucracy and its affairs.[78] For example, well after state building in Oman, there was no national standardisation for the length of time of an *athar* across the various *aflaj* systems.[79] While some farms in Oman now use an individual well, others still use a public *falaj*, drawing on water as a shared community resource.[80] The overall management of the *aflaj* in Oman represent instrumentalised kinship authority and remain in place within the framework of the contemporary bureaucratic Omani state.

The state developed housing infrastructure in addition to water infrastructure. The importing of machinery and parts also jumped from OMR (Omani Rials) 232,000 to OMR 1,799,000. From 1970 to 1972, the import of cement to Oman increased from OMR 125,000 to OMR 576,000. This cement allowed for the construction of houses, hospitals, ministries and schools.[81] Telephone lines first built between Muscat and Mutrah in 1908 were extended into non-urban areas.[82] As a result of these extensions, non-urban villages were no longer isolated hamlets. Instead, they because part of a greater interconnected Omani population.

Stage Two: Bureaucratic Authority

Proto-bureaucratic management of the *aflaj* in Oman was a starkly different means of resource access than existed in Kuwait. While Kuwait's non-urban populations competed for access to water, Oman's non-urban groups cooperated, using the proto-bureaucracy to allocate water, oversee the trade of water rights, and resolve disputes between members of the village. Oman's expanded infrastructure served as the basis for the extension of bureaucratic authority as well. The way this extension of authority took place was shaped, however, by pre-existing cooperative patterns of resource access.

Specifically, bureaucratic authority in Oman instrumentalised kinship authority by embedding it within the bureaucratic state. Individuals whose power had originally come from kinship authority became bureaucratic officials. As such, the patronage networks they oversaw became instrumentalised by the state for the distribution of resources.

Housing Authority

Oman's Ministry of Land Affairs was established in 1972 and tasked by royal decree in 1975 with the distribution, registration, and arbitration of disputes surrounding land and land claims in the Sultanate.[83] The Sultan's objective with this and similar decrees was to build assent to rule from the population and gain government control over resources. One major element of this plan was modernising Oman's physical infrastructure. Before 1970, settled Omanis lived in mud-brick houses that were prone to damage. These houses generally encircled the house of the local leader and were in turn encircled by agricultural fields. After state building, Omanis moved into cement houses funded and built by the government. These houses came with running water, electricity and air conditioning. Each was provided by Oman's central government, solidifying government control over these resources and bureaucratic authority over those living in the houses equipped with them.

In addition, the government improved road infrastructure connecting these houses with each other and with services in the town or village. Before the coup, roads in Oman belonged to whomever could control them. Tribes would frequently block roads during disputes with each other and with the Sultan.[84] Oman's new modern highways and paved roads were built by the government. They were an assertion of government authority in areas through which they ran and proved difficult to block even if tribes had wanted to do so.

Roads also created new physical divisions in towns and villages, marking borders between neighbourhoods that were the work of government planners rather than tribes. These neighbourhoods consisted of houses built by families who had moved to larger plots of land and suburbs outside the town. That being said, not all neighbourhoods were inhabited by members of the same kinship group.[85] State building in Oman did not require the same kind of disruption of kinship authority that Kuwait's leaders sought. Families could keep their previous living configurations, but these configurations would be redesignated as bureaucratic residential divisions. Furthermore, their houses would be powered by electricity created by the government, and supplied with water from either government desalination or *aflaj*, which were in turn eventually administered through bureaucratic authority.

Water and Electricity

The *aflaj* system was a useful institution for Oman's central government. Since it was cooperation based, it was a system of allocating resources that had buy-in from the population. Since it was bureaucratic, Oman's government could easily embed the *aflaj* system into the broader national governance system. The government also provided water via a national network of pipes. Most houses in the Muscat region were connected to this network by 1973. The provision of water in non-urban areas was tied into a sense of progress. Omanis were happy to receive more water and similar amenities, and also believed this government provision to be part of a modernisation process. Many preferred 'government water' to that which they could access via the *aflaj*.[86] Thus, Oman's government did not need to alter existing kinship authority, but rather subsume it within a larger apparatus. When government water became available, kinship authority as it related to the *aflaj* became more marginalised in a larger bureaucratic system of water provision.

Oman's government also provided electricity via a series of grids throughout the country. Electricity production in Oman spiked from thirty-six megawatts in 1974 to seventy-seven megawatts by 1997.[87] With this new power, Oman's government could provide climate control and better lighting in houses. It could also provide street lights on highways and areas with major traffic. At the same time, electric lines did more than provide power. They also connected villages, towns and cities throughout Oman to government-controlled grids. By expanding this electricity infrastructure, Oman's government was also able to expand its bureaucratic reach.

Educational Authority

Education in Oman was another major government priority following the 1970 coup. At the time, only three formal schools existed in Oman, educating about 900 male students. Furthermore, 66 per cent of Omanis were illiterate.[88] Between 1970 and 1976, Oman built 200 schools and educated

65,000 pupils.[89] Attendance and textbooks were free, and the government provided transportation and boarding for students who lived in settlements far from the school. Girls were also able to attend school, albeit at different times of the day than boys.[90]

In addition to creating a generation of literate Omanis with skills that were useful for employment and civic participation, schools allowed the government to create contact with the upcoming generation of Omanis and shape their understandings of bureaucratic authority and national identity. Students learned about Sultan Qaboos and his national vision for Oman as part of classroom instruction. They also wore common uniforms that emphasised a common national identity. Whereas before state building, most instruction had been informal and vocational, Oman's new education system was designed to create a common basis of knowledge and a national identity that marginalised kinship identity in the Sultanate or otherwise embedded it into the bureaucratic state.

Citizenship Authority

While proto-bureaucracies were a crucial means of extending the state's bureaucracy to embed and instrumentalise kinship authority, they were not a replacement for a traditional kinship-based system. Tribal sheikhs in non-urban areas still held political power with which the state needed to contend. One method of doing so would have been the Kuwaiti approach – to continue paying off the sheikhs, as Omani leaders had done in the past. Oman had the state capacity to do so, as pre-state relations between sultans and tribes suggest. However, this approach would have risked exacerbating social divisions at a time when the Sultanate was working to form a unified state. It also would not have strengthened the bureaucratic power of a state whose leader was still in the process of establishing sovereignty. Linking proto-bureaucracies into a national governance structure, in contrast, offered a way to administer a unified Omani population.

Citizenship was an important way in which Oman's government delineated this unified population that fell under the bureaucratic authority of the state. Oman's 1983 citizenship law (RD 3/83) granted citizenship to those who had lived in Oman twenty years or more or were married to an Omani. Foreign women were allowed citizenship upon marrying an Omani after five years of living in the Sultanate. Children of naturalised Omani men were granted citizenship, though adult children of naturalised men needed to apply separately for citizenship.[91] In 2014, Oman issued a new citizenship law (RD 38/14) which tightened restrictions on spouses obtaining citizenship. It required the marriage between non-Omanis and Omanis to be certified by the Ministry of Interior. A non-Omani husband was also required to have fathered a son from an Omani wife. The law also outlined provisions for widowed or divorced women to obtain citizenship. Finally, it shifted the decision process on citizenship from courts to the Ministry of Interior, consolidating government authority over the granting of citizenship.[92] While Kuwait's citizenship law used the years 1899 and later 1920 as cutoff points for citizenship (years when tribal groups were settled in Kuwait City), Oman's law specifies a period of time during which one must have resided in the country. It stipulates residence within Oman's territory or relationship to a citizen as a precondition rather than kinship affiliation. While non-members of kinship groups can become Omani citizens, it is likely that any Omani with citizenship from birth will be a kinship group member. The easiest way to obtain Omani citizenship is to be born to an Omani father, or Omani mother if the father was Omani but later became stateless. While similar *jus sanguinis* bureaucratic provisions exist widely outside kinship-based societies, in the Omani context they are likely to largely encompass members of the Sultanate's kinship groups. As such, Oman's citizenship laws, while bureaucratic, embed kinship within their provisions.

In addition, Oman embedded kinship authority in the bureaucratic institutions it used to govern these populations. Before state building, sheikhs held kinship authority over kinship group members. During state building, Oman's government embedded sheikhs themselves into the bureaucratic apparatus of the state. As Valeri notes, this process was a critical step in Omani state building that was based on 'the incorporation of so-called "traditional" values into the state apparatus'.[93] In contrast to Kuwait, where sheikhs had a close but informal relationship with the government, sheikhs in Oman were given official neighbourhood designations and were employed by the Ministry of Interior.[94] Such an arrangement formalised territorial jurisdictions – a crucial component of bureaucratic governance. The Ministry also appointed *sheikh rashids* who presided over districts created by the Ministry itself. *Sheikh rashids* existed as part of tribal hierarchies before Oman's government, but during state building were subsumed into Oman's bureaucratic authority. At the end of state building, they fell under Oman's Directorate of Tribal Affairs within the Ministry of Interior, which also appointed the sheikh's replacement with local consensus and paid him an annual salary.[95] Using this system of sheikhs, Oman's government was able to incorporate kinship authority into the bureaucratic state by reframing the authority of local leaders in bureaucratic terms. Such arrangements also contributed to a tribalisation of Omani identity. Oman's adoption of a kinship-based bureaucratic governance strategy incentivised families not necessarily structured along tribal lines to adopt stronger tribal affinities.

Oman is a larger state than Kuwait and Qatar and as such required a physically larger bureaucratic apparatus. However, the decision to embed kinship group leaders into bureaucratic institutions was not solely a factor of country size. Kuwait, Qatar and Oman all had sufficient state capacity to extend bureaucracy as they wished and were home to hundreds of tribal groups with sophisticated patterns of interaction. Tribal leaders in both states had access to their leaders and to the patronage these relationships provided. Nor was it solely a factor of Oman's desire for a modern state. Kuwait, Qatar and Oman invested significant resources in creating modern infrastructure and bureaucratic governance. Rather, the difference in pre-state resource access patterns explains why Kuwait and Qatar's leadership perpetuated kinship's political salience while Oman was able to embed kinship politics into the state's bureaucratic apparatus.

Oman's government used infrastructure to extend bureaucratic authority from Muscat into non-urban areas of the state. It also created buy-in on the part of Omanis to bureaucratic versus kinship authority. Kinship authority did not disappear entirely in Oman during state building. Rather, it was subsumed and embedded into the state's bureaucratic apparatus by using infrastructure to gain control of the means of resource access. Cooperative patterns of resource access prior to state building made this process possible.

Stage Three: Nationalism

Nationalism was and remains a central aspect of Omani statecraft. Given the decentralisation and diversity of the country, Oman's Sultan required a successful unifying idiom of nationalism after the 1970 coup. Whereas in Kuwait this idiom had been temporal, in Oman nationalism was of a more territorial nature. Whereas Kuwait had defined its people's claim to national ownership based on their timing of settlement, Oman based its claim on the common heritage of people throughout Omani territory. Kinship authority was referenced with regard to Oman's past, but downplayed as part of Oman's contemporary identity. This downplaying of kinship authority as part of Oman's heritage made the success of this idiom possible.

After 1970, Oman's national idiom was tied inextricably to Sultan Qaboos. As in many authoritarian states, Omani nationalism frames the head of state as the nation's vanguard. For example, the national anthem opened with the line: 'Oh Lord, protect for us His Majesty the Sultan', and includes the exultation 'Be happy, Qaboos has come, with the blessing of Heaven.' Interviewees for this project across age, gender and sect lines, when asked about their hopes for Oman's future, almost unanimously replied that they prayed 'for the health of the Sultan'. Any Omani born after the late 1960s knew no other head of state.

The Sultan, however, was not put into power through a process of consensus-based succession. Rather, he overthrew his father in a coup. This ascent to power posed the challenge of creating national assent to his leadership, especially given domestic rebellions and dissatisfaction with his father, Sa'id bin Taymur's rule. Patronage and state development were important aspects of this buy-in but nationalism played an important role in enhancing it.

Given the military nature of the coup, Qaboos linked Oman's feudal past to a modern nationalist narrative to situate the overthrow of his father in a longer historical context. Villages in Oman often came under attack from competing tribal groups. Oman's politics before state building involved conflict between two major confederations, the Ghafiri and Hinawi. While not based in kinship, and while groups were known to switch confederations from time to time, these divisions were the basis of conflict for which Oman's residents needed to be prepared. In addition, conflicts between the Imam and the Sultan, and conflicts within the Al Busaidi family prompted defence preparations. Oman's status as a maritime power and its interaction with Western colonial governments also introduced the need for defence. Oman's royal palace, Qasr al-'Alm, is nestled between two Portuguese forts, Mirani and Jalali. Emphasising this feudal history and framing it as evidence of the nobility of Oman's character and fighting spirit allowed the Sultan to frame his coup as part of a longer history culminating in his victorious leadership.

Oman's government set out to create visual reminders of this history. Forts in cities like Nizwa, Rustaq and Bahla across Oman's interior were restored, standing guard over the cities they had once protected. Even in smaller cities like Izki, guard towers with crenelations remain intact on the hillsides. As Limbert points out, Oman's government 'encouraged fort imagery . . . to appear as features of office buildings, private homes, mosques, bus stops, telephone booths, and even water tanks'.[96] At the entrance to many cities and towns, the government constructed gates with these crenelations as well. Gates also appeared in the centre of major roundabouts. Muscat has a gate over the highway entering the city, and Old Muscat's gate is the site of a national museum.

Both inside and outside the capital, these gates were more than decoration. They served as national symbols and projected government presence and authority in the territory ruled by a decentralised but bureaucratic Omani state. Omanis who travelled only rarely to Muscat now had a constant reminder of the national government and Oman's national history. The presence of these gates in most towns also created a sense of the Andersonian 'imagined community', in which Omanis felt a sense of affinity to other towns with similar nationalist symbols. These symbols created a sense that

Omanis across the Sultanate were connected by virtue of common participation in the Omani nation.

These gates and crenelations followed a territorial idiom of nationalism – one in which physical space and the use of symbols within it create a shared sense of identity. Gates and crenelations are more than just symbols. They exist in a physical space. The physical presence of these symbols in a given territory indicated that the area was part of the larger Omani state. Since Oman extended infrastructure to its population rather than, as Kuwait had done, moving the population onto infrastructure, territory proved a more effective idiom than chronology as a basis for nationalist claims. It is true that Oman, like Kuwait, used historical imagery that made reference to a common imagined past. However, Omani nationalism constructed these more expressly physical and territorial manifestations to communicate its national narrative.

The *falaj* system itself was a key part of Oman's nationalist idiom. As a structure existing in a physical space, it also invoked a sense of territorially based national identity. As Omani government officials point out, there are cultural and heritage-based motivations for maintaining the *aflaj*, even as Oman has vastly expanded its capacity to provide water to its citizens. The government avoided changing the *aflaj* system, in part, to create a sense of an ongoing connection between Oman's land and its people.[97] As *aflaj* exist throughout Oman, they also contribute to a sense of an imagined community. A member of one village using one *falaj* would be reminded of Omanis in villages across the country making use of a similar system.

Another unifying element of Omani nationalism was dress. Omani women were originally excluded from the workforce and a national dress for them was not mandated. Men and boys in the government or in school, however, were required to wear specific clothing. This dress was not required in the private sector, which was originally the domain of wealthy Omanis. However, as the private sector expanded in Oman, traditional dress became more commonly worn across employment sectors in Oman.[98] For men, the official dress is a *dishdasha* (robe) whose design differs from others in the Gulf region. Altering significantly the design of this *dishdasha* has always been frowned upon and was specifically prohibited in 2015 by Oman's Ministry of Commerce and Identity.[99] Tailors can be fined for doing so and those who wear different *dishdashas* can reportedly face jail time. The Ministry of Commerce and Industry monitors social media for photographs of altered *dishdashas* and has conducted inspections of companies where employees wear *dishdashas*.[100]

The regulation of dress in Oman was not purely aesthetic. Rather, it was to create a sense of national 'same-ness' where divisions had existed before. National dress created a 'typical' male Omani which itself entrenched the idea of an Omani nation. Wide differences still existed in terms of head dress, sandals, or other elements of dress. Yet these differences did not necessarily connote an *identity*. While some accounts speculate that the traditional *masaar* head dress is an indication of a man's tribal affiliation, there is no evidence that suggests linkages between particular designs and particular tribal groups.

Schools were also an important tool of nationalism. In addition to their role in creating mass education, they were also a space where Omani boys came together wearing the *dishdasha* and learning Oman's national curriculum. In addition to their role as a meeting space, schools were an important driver of literacy in Oman. In 1970, only 33 per cent of Omani adults were literate. By 1990, the rate was 55 per cent, and by 2010 it was 87.2 per cent.[101] Literacy allowed for the spread of a national narrative through textbooks and classroom instruction.[102] It also created opportunities for mixing between youth from different communities in the same town or village. Since these schools were regulated by the Ministry of Education, they also represented the extension of national-level bureaucracy to non-urban areas.

Higher education was a part of Oman's national idiom as well. The national university, Sultan Qaboos University, drew students from all across the country. Founded in November 1986, the university has also been co-educational for the duration of its existence. Primary and secondary schools, in contrast, were historically gender segregated. Since the university draws students from all over the country, it serves as a unifying experience for many Omanis. These students are often forced to navigate regional differences among colleagues in their dormitories.[103] This experience, however, exposes Omanis at a relatively young age to a broad regional cross section of Oman's population. The effect is that being 'Omani' is based on the shared experience of those living in Omani territory, rather than the temporal question of whose family arrived before whose.

A temporal framing of nationalism would not have been successful in Oman. Because kinship groups cooperated for resources, they had less incentive to rely on the Sultanate before state building. Merchants in Muscat had an important relationship with the Sultan, but Oman's population in general was less reliant on the Sultan for security than Kuwait's population's reliance on the Emir. Before state building, Oman's Sultan mediated disputes and made payouts to Oman's well-established and often settled tribes, but did not have the same kind of long-term dependence as Kuwait's emirs on his population. Since many of these groups were already settled, they were also more subject to the Sultan's authority and coercion. In addition, since Qaboos' rise to power happened suddenly, the process of family alignment happened quickly in Oman as opposed to the decades-long process in Kuwait. Furthermore, as the Sultan's priority following the coup was unity, dividing the population by the timing of their alliance with him would have done little good.

Conclusion

State building in Oman created a decentralised bureaucratic state that instrumentalised kinship authority. Local leaders' kinship authority was first downplayed and later embedded into the government as it expanded infrastructure and connected localities to a centralised bureaucracy. That some of these leaders were members of kinship groups before state building made it easier for Oman's government to reframe positions carrying kinship authority in bureaucratic terms. As such, kinship was embedded into the state's governing apparatus and downplayed in Oman's national idiom.

Oman's cooperative access to resources shaped these patterns of state building. Non-urban populations established proto-bureaucracies to manage access to water. During state building, Oman's government brought these proto-bureaucracies into the state's bureaucratic apparatus. It extended infrastructure and improved living conditions for the population *in situ*, rather than moving them onto new infrastructure. It gave sheikhs an official position in government bureaucracies and used infrastructure as a basis for projecting government authority. Oman's nationalist idiom was territorial and based on the common historic nobility of the people in its territory. It brought different populations together under this common banner and erected physical symbols of a common 'Omani-ness'. This nationalist idiom enhanced buy-in by Oman's population to the government's state-building project.

While Oman subsumed kinship authority into the state, Kuwait and Qatar's kinship politics remained largely independent of the state apparatus. Oman's cooperative access to resources incentivised creation of a proto-bureaucratic form of authority, whereas Kuwait and Qatar's competitive access heightened the importance of kinship ties. While kinship authority was salient in Kuwait, Qatar and Oman before state building, processes of state building shaped by resource access led to different outcomes in the political salience of kinship authority after state building. These differences emerged despite the fact that these states had sufficient state capacity to impose certain means of governance. They also appeared despite a similar pattern of state building – first creating infrastructure, then using that infrastructure to gain control over access to resources via bureaucratic authority, and finally enhancing buy-in to that authority with a nationalist idiom. As a result of these differences, the political salience of kinship differs between the countries.

Notes

1. 'The Al bu Said dynasty in Arabia and East Africa by R. Said-Ruete', *Records of Oman 1867–1960, Volume I*, ed. R. Bailey (Cambridge, UK: Cambridge Archive Editions, 1992): 39.
2. The timeline presented here reflects only the kinship relations between Oman's subsequent rulers and not the complex and often contentious politics within the family that led to each leader assuming his role.
3. Interview, al-Khuweir, Oman, 31 March 2014.
4. Robert Geran Landen, *Oman Since 1856: Disruptive Modernization in a Traditional Arab Society* (Princeton, NJ: Princeton University Press, 1967): 209.
5. 'The Hon'ble Lt-Col. A.P. Trevor C.S.I. C.I.E., Political Resident in the Persian Gulf, Bushire. 19th May 1921, (R/15/6/188)', *Records of Oman 1867–1960, Volume 7*, 16–17, 33.
6. A watch tower at Ruwi, at which roads from the interior converged before leading into Mutrah and Muscat, helped defend against attacks from the interior. See '"Gazetteer of Arabia Vol. II" [1600] (679/688)', British Library: India Office Records and Private Papers, IOR/L/MIL/17/16/2/2, in *Qatar Digital Library*, http://www.qdl.qa/en/archive/81055/vdc_100023727635.0x00004e.
7. John Peterson, *Historical Muscat: An Illustrated Guide and Gazetteer* (Leiden, The Netherlands: Brill, 2006): 2, 98.
8. Peterson, *Historical Muscat*, 114.
9. Peterson, *Historical Muscat*, 33, 100–1.
10. '"Gazetteer of Arabia Vol. II" [1600] (679/688)', *Qatar Digital Library*, http://www.qdl.qa/en/archive/81055/vdc_100023727635.0x00004e.
11. '"History of the imâms and seyyids of 'Omân by Salîl-ibn-Razîk, from A.D. 661-1856; translated from the original Arabic, and edited with notes, appendices, and an introduction, continuing the history down to 1870, by George Percy Badger, F.R.G.S., late chaplain in the Presidency of Bombay" [212] (373/612)', British Library: Printed Collections, Arab.D.490, in *Qatar Digital Library*, http://www.qdl.qa/en/archive/81055/vdc_100023697836.0x0000ae.
12. Peterson, *Historical Muscat*, 56.
13. Interview, Ramal Boshar, Oman, 28 March 2014.
14. Interview, Ramal Boshar, Oman, 28 March 2014.
15. Interview, Ramal Boshar, Oman, 28 March 2014.
16. Peterson, *Historical Muscat*, 14.
17. Peterson, *Historical Muscat*, 19.
18. J. E. Peterson, 'Oman's Diverse Society: Northern Oman', *Middle East Journal* 58 no. 1 (Winter 2004): 34.
19. For more on the history of Oman's tribes, see John C. Wilkinson, *The Imamate Tradition of Oman* (Cambridge, UK: Cambridge University Press, 2009).
20. J. E. Peterson, 'Tribes and Politics in Eastern Arabia', *Middle East Journal* 31 no. 3 (Summer 1977): 305; J. E. Peterson, 'Oman: al-Ghafiriyah and al-Hinawiyah Tribal Confederations', *Arabian Peninsula Background Note*, No. APBN-001, 2003.

21. 'Notes on the Tribes of the Sultanate of Muscat and Oman, 1951 [R/15/6/245]', *Records of Oman 1867–1960, Volume 1*, xcvii.
22. Uzi Rabi, 'The Sultanate of Oman: Between Tribalism and National Unity', in Uzi Rabi (ed.), *Tribes and States in a Changing Middle East* (Oxford, UK: Oxford University Press, 2016): 81.
23. 'Annual Report on the Administration of the Persian Gulf Political Residency and Muscat Political Agency for the Year 1880–81', *Persian Gulf Administration Reports, Volume II*, ed. Penelope Tuson (Cambridge, UK: Cambridge Archive Editions, 1989): 29.
24. Peterson, 'Tribes and Politics in Eastern Arabia', 305. For a listing of Ghafiri and Hinawi tribes in Oman, see John Gordon Lorimer, *Gazetteer of the Persian Gulf, Oman and Central Arabia, Volume 9* (Cambridge, UK: Cambridge Archive Editions, 1986): 1391–411.
25. 'Diary of the Persian Gulf Political Residency for the week ending 22nd October 1905', *Political Diaries of the Arab World: Persian Gulf 1904–1965, Volume 1*, ed. Robert L. Jarman (Cambridge, UK: Cambridge Archive Editions, 1998): 192.
26. 'Administration Report of the Persian Gulf Political Residency for the Year 1913', *Persian Gulf Administration Reports, Volume VII*, 103.
27. 'Administration Report of the Persian Gulf Political Residency and Muscat Political Agency for 1891–92', *Persian Gulf Administration Reports, Volume IV*, 17.
28. 'Administration Report for the Persian Gulf Political Residency for the Year 1917', *Persian Gulf Administration Reports, Volume VII*, 41.
29. 'Administration Report of the Persian Gulf Political Residency for the Year 1919', *Persian Gulf Administration Reports, Volume VII*, 56.
30. 'Administration Report for the Muscat Agency for the Year 1921', *Persian Gulf Administration Reports, Volume VIII*, 53–4; 'Notes on the Tribes of the Sultanate of Muscat an Oman, 1951 [R/15/6/245]', *Records of Oman 1867–1960, Volume 1*, xciii.
31. 'Agreement Between Saiyid Taymur bin Faisal, C.S.E., Sultan of Muscat and Oman and the D'arly Explomation Company Limited, 1925 [R/15/6/24 1925]', *Records of Oman 1867–1960, Volume 7*, 208.
32. Mandana E. Limbert, *In the Time of Oil: Piety, Memory, and Social Life in an Omani Town* (Stanford, CA: Stanford University Press, 2010): 117–18.
33. The *qanat* system in Iran bears resemblances to the Omani system.
34. '*Aflaj* Irrigation Systems of Oman', *UNESCO*, 2019, https://whc.unesco.org/en/list/1207.
35. Abdullah al-Ghafri, Takashi Inoue and Tetuaki Nagasawa, 'Irrigation Scheduling of *Aflaj* of Oman: Methods and Modernization', in Z. Adeel (ed.), *Sustainable Management of Marginal Drylands: Applications of Indigenous Knowledge for Coastal Drylands – Proceedings of a Joint UNU-UNESCO-ICARDO International Workshop, Alexandria, Egypt, 21–25 September 2002* (Tokyo, Japan: United Nations University, 2002): 2.
36. Uzi Rabi, *The Emergence of States in a Tribal Society: Oman Under Sa'id bin Taymur 1932–1970* (Brighton, UK: Sussex Academic Press, 2006): 13.

37. Al-Ghafri *et al.*, 'Irrigation Scheduling of *Aflaj* of Oman', 3.

38. The water was not always clean. For example, the cholera epidemic in Oman in the late 1800s spread in part because dead bodies in the *aflaj* were contaminating the drinking water. See Persian Gulf Administration Reports 1883/84 – 1904/05 [229r] (462/602), British Library: India Office Records and Private Papers, IOR/R/15/1/709, in *Qatar Digital Library*, http://www.qdl.qa/en/archive/81055/vdc_100023373227.0x00003f.

39. Interview, 19 February 2015 [location undisclosed for subject's well-being].

40. Interview, Nizwa, Oman, 17 March 2014; Limbert, *In the Time of Oil*, 124. The volume of water in the *aflaj* changes over time based on rainfall for that season, so dividing shares by time was a more practical solution. However, there is a *falaj* in Lizuh that does use water volume as the basis for dividing shares.

41. Interview, Washington, DC, 24 June 2014.

42. Ahmed Salem al-Marshoudi, 'Water Institutional Arrangements of Falaj Al Daris in the Sultanate of Oman', *International Journal of Social Sciences and Management* 5 no. 1 (2018): 39.

43. See Harriet Nash and Dionisius A. Agius, 'Use of the Stars in Agriculture in Oman', *Journal of Semitic Studies* 56 no. 1 (2011): 167–82; al-Ghafri *et al.*, 'Irrigation Scheduling of *Aflaj* of Oman', 6.

44. Limbert, *In the Time of Oil*, 124.

45. Wilkinson, *The Imamate Tradition of Oman*, 26.

46. Interview, 19 February 2015.

47. Grace Remmington, 'Transforming Tradition: The Aflaj and Changing Role of Traditional Knowledge Systems for Collective Water Management', *Journal of Arid Environments* 151 (2018): 136; see W. R. Norman, W. H. Shayya, A. S. al-Ghafri and I. R. McCann, 'Aflaj Irrigation and On-farm Water Management in Northern Oman', *Irrigation and Drainage Systems* 12 (1998): 44.

48. Al-Marshoudi, 'Water Institutional Arrangements', 35.

49. Interview, Nizwa, Oman, 17 March 2014.

50. Al-Marshoudi, 'Water Institutional Arrangements', 36. In Bahla, the *arif* is paid for each auction by the Ministry of Religious Endowments, and making a profit was traditionally prohibited. See Limbert, *In the Time of Oil*, 124–5.

51. Al-Marshoudi, 'Water Institutional Arrangements', 37–8.

52. Al-Ghafri *et al.*, 'Irrigation Scheduling of *Aflaj* of Oman', 2–3. See also J. C. Wilkinson, *Water and Tribal Settlement in South-east Arabia: A Study of the Aflaj of Oman* (Oxford, UK: Clarendon Press, 1977): 113, 120.

53. Remmington, 'Transforming Tradition', 138.

54. Interview, al-Khuweir, Oman, 19 March 2014.

55. Interview, Nizwa, Oman, 17 March 2014.

56. Some Omanis also identity a category of mountain bedouin, or *shiwawi* who live in Northern Oman and have a semi-nomadic lifestyle. Interview, Medinat Sultan Qaboos, Oman, 18 March 2014.

57. Interview, Nizwa, Oman, 17 March 2014.

58. 'Part II – Administration Report of the Maskat Political Agency for the Year 1900–1901', *Persian Gulf Administration Reports, Volume V*, 15.

59. Colette Le Cour Grandmaison, 'Spatial Organization, Tribal Groupings, and Kinship in Ibra', *Journal of Oman Studies* 3 no. 2 (1977): 105.

60. Wilkinson, *The Imamate Tradition of Oman*, 38.

61. 'Letter to His Highness Saiyid Said bin Taymur Sultan of Muscat and Oman, 9th August 1932 [R/15/6/188 1932]', *Records of Oman 1867–1960, Volume 7*, 33; 'Note of a Meeting at the India Office on 12th February, 1946 [R/15/6/387 1946]', *Records of Oman 1867–1960, Volume 7*, 87.

62. 'Administration Report of the Political Agency, Muscat, for the year 1938', *Persian Gulf Administration Reports, Volume X*, 38.

63. 'Notes on the Tribes of the Sultanate of Muscat and Oman, 1951, R/15/6/245', *Records of Oman 1867–1960, Volume 1*, xciv.

64. 'Despatch No. 46, British Residency Bahrain, 14th April, 1951', *Records of Oman 1867–1960, Volume 8*, 181.

65. 'Telegram No. 123 of October 23, 1953', *Records of Oman 1867–1960, Volume 8*, 423.

66. 'Historical Summary of Events in the Persian Gulf Shaikhdoms and the Sultanate of Muscat and Oman, 1928–1953 [96v] (197/222)', British Library: India Office Records and Private Papers, IOR/R/15/1/731(1) in *Qatar Digital Library*, 1953, https://www.qdl.qa/en/archive/81055/vdc_100023415995.0x0000c6.

67. '(1943) British Residency, Bahrain, December 29, 1960', R. Bailey, CMG, *Records of Oman, 1961–1965: 1961*, ed. A. Burdett (Cambridge, UK: Cambridge Archive Editions, 1997): 8.

68. Jeremy Jones and Nicholas Ridout, *A History of Modern Oman* (Cambridge, UK: Cambridge University Press, 2015): 145–6; Thomas R. Mockaitis, *British Counterinsurgency in the Post-Imperial Era* (New York, NY: Manchester University Press, 1995): 74–5; Abdel Razzaq Takriti, 'The 1970 Coup in Oman Reconsidered', *Journal of Arabian Studies: Arabia, the Gulf, and the Red Sea* 3 no. 2 (2013): 155–73.

69. Uzi Rabi, 'The Sultanate of Oman: Between Tribalism and National Unity', in Uzi Rabi (ed.), *Tribes and States in a Changing Middle East* (Oxford, UK: Oxford University Press, 2016): 79.

70. Saleh al Shaibany, 'Oman's Historic Homes Under Threat', *The National*, 11 January 2010, http://www.thenational.ae/news/world/middle-east/omans-historic-homes-under-threat.

71. Max Weber, *Politics as a Vocation*, trans. H. H. Gerth and C. Wright Mills (Philadelphia, PA: Fortress Press, 1972).

72. Limbert, *In the Time of Oil*, 118–19.

73. Interview, 19 February 2015.

74. Limbert, *In the Time of Oil*, 127.

75. Remmington, 'Transforming Tradition', 136, 139.

76. Interview, al-Khuweir, Oman, 19 March 2014.

77. Interview, al-Khuweir, Oman, 19 March 2014.
78. M. S. al-Kalbani and M. F. Price, 'Sustainable *Aflaj* Water Management in Al Jabal Al Akhdar, Sultanate of Oman', *Water Resources Management* 8 (2015): 28.
79. Al-Ghafri *et al.*, 'Irrigation Scheduling of *Aflaj* of Oman', 15.
80. Al-Marshoudi, 'Water Institutional Arrangements', 33.
81. Limbert, *In the Time of Oil*, 118.
82. 'Political Diary of the Persian Gulf Residency for the Week Ending 13th (Received 21st) September 1908)', *Political Diaries of the Arab World: Persian Gulf 1904–1965, Volume 3*, 274.
83. 'History', *Sultanate of Oman Ministry of Housing*, https://eservices.housing.gov.om/eng/Pages/History.aspx (accessed 23 July 2018).
84. 'Administration Report of the Muscat Political Agency and Consulate for the Year 1890–91', *Persian Gulf Administration Reports, Volume IV*, 16, 17; 'Administration Report of the Political Agency, Muscat, for 1929', *Persian Gulf Administration Reports, Volume VIII*, 44.
85. Limbert, *In the Time of Oil*, 14.
86. Limbert, *In the Time of Oil*, 119, 127, 131.
87. Joseph A. Kechechian, 'A Vision of Oman: State of the Sultanate Speeches by Qaboos Bin Said, 1970–2006', *Middle East Policy Council* 15 no. 4 (Winter 2008): 117.
88. Maryam Khan, 'From Access to Success: The Story of Oman's School Education System', *Muscat Daily*, 18 November 2013, https://muscatdaily.com/Archive/Oman/From-access-to-success-The-story-of-Oman-s-school-education-system-2pri.
89. Marc Valeri, *Oman: Politics and Society in the Qaboos State* (New York, NY: Columbia University Press, 2009): 84.
90. Interview, Washington, DC, 24 June 2014.
91. 'Oman: Omani Citizenship Law (Repealed)', *Gulf Labour Markets, Migration, and Population (GLMM) Programme*, http://gulfmigration.eu/oman-omani-citizenship-law-repealed/ (accessed 25 July 2018).
92. 'Royal Decree No 38/2014: Promulgating the Omani Citizenship Law', *Official Gazette*, No 1066, http://www.refworld.org/pdfid/58dcfc444.pdf.
93. Valeri, *Oman: Politics and Society*, 72.
94. Limbert, *In the Time of Oil*, 39.
95. Valeri, *Oman: Politics and Society*, 156–7.
96. Limbert, *In the Time of Oil*, 22.
97. Interview, al-Khuweir, Oman, 19 March 2014.
98. Interview, al-Khuweir, Oman, 10 December 2013.
99. The prohibition is given in Ministerial Decision 70/2015. See Tariq Ziad Al Haremi, 'Ministry Approves Five Omani Dishdasha Designs', *Times of Oman*, 15 January 2017, https://timesofoman.com/article/100598.
100. 'MOCI Warns Against Altering Traditional Omani Attire', *Muscat Daily*, 3 July 2016, http://www.muscatdaily.com/Archive/Oman/MoCI-warns-against-altering-traditional-Omani-attire-4r4b.

101. Omani Ministry of Education and The World Bank, *Education in Oman: The Drive for Equality, Volume 2* (Muscat, Oman: Omani Ministry of Education and The World Bank, 2013): 33; 'Oman', *UNESCO*, 2016, http://en.unesco.org/countries/oman.
102. See Keith Darden and Harris Mylonas, 'Threats to Territorial Integrity, National Mass Schooling, and Linguistic Commonality', *Comparative Political Studies* 49 no. 11 (2015): 1446–79.
103. Scott Weiner, 'The Muscat Commute: A Young Generation's Journey Between Tradition and Modernity', *Arab Gulf States Institute in Washington*, 18 June 2015, http://www.agsiw.org/the-muscat-commute-a-young-generations-journey-between-tradition-and-modernity/.

7

KINSHIP SALIENCE AFTER STATE BUILDING IN KUWAIT, QATAR AND OMAN

Kinship salience varies according to patterns of access to vital limited resources. At the end of state building, it determines the means of access to power and resources in a state and can compel behaviour by members of those groups. Kinship authority can have either governing salience as in the case of Kuwait and Qatar, or instrumentalised salience as in the case of Oman. The differentiation between the governing and instrumentalised political salience of kinship authority is based on kinship authority's (1) relationship with the state and (2) its ability to compel action by kinship group members. When vital resource access is competitive before state building, kinship authority will have governing salience. In such cases, kinship groups use bureaucracy as a source of resources and access to power, marginalising the bureaucracy's ability to exert bureaucratic authority. When vital resource access is cooperative, kinship authority will have instrumentalised salience. The state in such cases co-opts kinship authority, using kinship networks as a means of patronage distribution and marginalising kinship groups as governing entities.

Salience is a way of conceptualising the political effects of kinship authority as a dependent variable. Despite its frequent usage among political scientists, it can be a difficult term to define and prone to conceptual stretching.[1] In political science, the concept appeared originally in survey research on voter preferences. However, even for such studies the term was fraught with ambiguity. It referred to where voters place an issue on a ranked list, but could account neither for changes over time, nor the possibility that voters do not literally hold fixed ranked preferences in their minds. Generally, salience

seems to connote that something is 'important' in a particularly prominent way. Yet while both 'importance' and 'prominence' are components of
salience, Wlezian notes that 'prominence is not completely orthogonal to
importance; it is different'.[2] For the purposes of this book, salience refers to
the extent that kinship authority matters in some politically relevant sense.
It is important, but in a particular way that is observable to individuals and
institutions within a society. To be useful for political science, however, discussions of salience require us to understand what salience, both governing
and instrumentalised, looks like in an empirical context.

This chapter clarifies, defines and operationalises the concept of kinship
salience. It provides explanations for differentiating clearly between governing
and instrumentalised salience. For each, it provides uniquely observable outcomes that are exclusive to each category of salience and are highly unlikely
to be driven by causal factors other than salience. This conceptualisation of
salience serves as the basis for evaluating kinship authority in Kuwait, Qatar
and Oman at the end of each country's state-building period.

Kinship Salience

Kinship authority has varying outcomes of political salience at the end of
state building. These differences are important because they determine the
basic governance mechanisms of the state. That some states have governing
kinship salience while others have instrumentalised kinship salience is not
merely a distinction without a difference. States are fundamentally bureaucratic entities. However, differences in the salience of kinship determine how
the state administers its population, how it allocates state resources, and
how it maintains the assent of its subjects to rule. Existing explanations cannot convincingly account for variation in these outcomes, which occur in
a multitude of states around the world where kinship authority has political salience. Empirically, kinship authority is not an oddity of state politics.
Theories of the state grounded in Western assumptions of state building are
thus seriously limited if they cannot account for kinship authority.

In addition to the explicitly political state functions mentioned above,
kinship authority can also have social salience. For example, it can determine
relative status between kinship groups or decorum between two individuals
in a social setting. However, social salience is different to political salience
and exogenous to the scope of the current work, which focuses on political
salience. Political salience refers specifically to the activation of kinship hierarchies that provide access to power and resources.

The 'political salience of kinship authority' means, first, the extent to
which it governs functions otherwise conducted by the state and, second,

the extent to which it compels political behaviour by members of kinship groups. The first criterion involves the extent to which kinship authority uses state bureaucracy and its functions of governance as a source of resources and access to power. States build a bureaucracy to administer and govern entities within their borders, including kinship groups. However, where kinship has governing salience, kinship groups use bureaucracy as a source of resources and access to power and, in so doing, marginalise the bureaucracy's ability to exercise bureaucratic authority. The state's bureaucracy becomes a patronage distribution network for kinship groups, and the state is unable to alter this situation without seriously destabilising the political order. In contrast, where kinship has instrumentalised salience, bureaucracy co-opts kinship hierarchies as a means of patronage distribution and marginalises kinship groups as governing entities. Kinship groups become embedded in the state's bureaucratic apparatus as a means of exerting control over the population. Kinship groups are unable to challenge the state's sovereignty in this regard.

The second component of kinship authority is not governmental but rather individual. Kinship salience is a function of kinship authority's ability to compel members of kinship groups to behave in certain ways. These behaviours relate explicitly to political outcomes involving the distribution of power and resources. Where kinship has governing salience, kinship authority can compel members of kinship groups to act against their personal wishes. Where it has instrumentalised salience, kinship authority may have some influence but ultimately does not play the decisive role in a kinship group member's decision in political matters.

Operationalisation

Both components of kinship salience have a set of discrete, observable and falsifiable outcomes. These outcomes will also serve as a framework for the empirical analysis found in the subsequent chapter of this book.

With regard to instrumentalisation of state bureaucracy, there are seven relevant indicators:

1. Are kinship group leaders government officials?
2. Are tribes officially recognised or registered with the state?
3. Does the government try to stop tribal primaries and, if so, is it successful?
4. Are public deliberative bodies kinship-based?
5. Is personal status (*wasta*) very important for obtaining resources and political access?

6. Who is the primary arbiter of disputes between kinship groups or kinship group members?
7. Do kinship group members approach kinship group leaders or bureaucratic officials first for help?

With regard to the strength of kinship authority, there are three relevant indicators:

1. How strongly is group 'purity' emphasised among kinship groups?
2. How strongly do social sanctions on behaviour generated by kinship authority compel kinship group member behaviour?
3. How strongly are dating and marriage behaviours constrained by kinship authority?

For the latter set of indicators, interview research can provide evidence that an individual felt constrained by kinship authority as well as the preponderance of social norms set by kinship authority. In particular, behaviours considered *'aib* (forbidden) as well as those that negatively affect *sum'a* (personal reputation) are of interest. Previous scholarship on the cases in question also provides useful data. These indicators can be coded as 'governing salience' when there is evidence of both individual compellence by kinship authority and a strong and pervasive social norm set by kinship authority. If one or both of these conditions are lacking, the indicator may be coded as 'instrumentalised salience'. Ultimately, the compellence must be strong enough to shape behaviour and it must actually affect a wide number of kinship-group members.

It bears mention that even in states where kinship has instrumentalised salience, kinship groups still play an important social and political role. However, their political importance in such cases is grounded in their instrumentalisation by the state. In other words, kinship groups still matter in such cases, but they matter in a fundamentally different way than in cases where kinship has governing salience.

Though they fall outside the scope of the current study, cases exist where kinship salience disappears entirely after state building. These include cases where kinship authority actively challenges state bureaucracy, where maintaining constant state supremacy over kinship authority would be more costly than demolishing it altogether, and where the state's ideological claim to authority precludes the use of kinship authority. In such cases, kinship may still exist in the state after state building but would retain social rather than political salience.

Table 7.1 Indicators of kinship salience

Operationalisation	Indicators	Governing Salience	Instrumentalised Salience
Instrumentalisation			
	Are kinship group leaders gov't officials?	No	Yes
	Are tribes registered with the state?	No	Yes
	Does the gov't try, and succeed, in stopping tribal primaries?	No	Yes
	Are public deliberative bodies kinship based?	Yes	No
	Is *wasta* very important for obtaining resources and access?	Yes	No
	Primary arbiter of inter/intra-group disputes	Kinship Group	State
	First line of help for personal problems	Kinship Group	State
Constraint on kinship group member behaviour			
	Extent to which group 'purity' is emphasised.	High	Low
	Extent to which social sanctions generated by kinship authority constrain behaviour.	High	Low
	Extent to which dating and marriage are constrained by kinship authority.	High	Low

Using the concept of salience as outlined above, the following section uses empirical evidence to analyse the nature of kinship salience on Kuwait, Qatar and Oman. What emerges is a clear distinction between states where kinship authority has governing salience (Kuwait and Qatar) versus instrumentalised salience (Oman).

Governing Kinship Salience in Kuwait after State Building

Competitive access to vital limited resources in Kuwait among nomadic non-urban populations incentivised the government to reach out directly to kinship groups. The patronage arrangements created by this outreach endured as the state created infrastructure. This was because the super-sticky nature of kinship was both difficult to change and provided a useful means of distributing patronage to non-urban populations. Kuwait moved non-urban populations onto infrastructure that it had created, but kinship authority remained strong. While the finding that urbanisation can enhance kinship ties has existed since the early 1960s, it is significant that these ties not only endure but retain political salience.[3] When Kuwait used this infrastructure as a basis of extending bureaucratic authority, it was mediated by pre-existing kinship authority among the population. Given these constraints, Kuwait introduced a temporal idiom of nationalism in order to encourage buy-in to its state-building project.

In Kuwait, kinship authority has governing salience. It exists in parallel to bureaucratic authority, especially as it relates to tribal politics and elections. Kinship authority is used to distribute patronage in Kuwait's government, including among the royal family, in government ministries, and between parliamentarians and their constituents. Kinship authority is also important in Kuwaiti society, particularly within the *diwaniya* system. Finally, the politics of marriage in Kuwait are regulated by kinship. Even when kinship group members want certain kinds of marriages, kinship authority often compels them to act contrary to these desires. Each of these points illustrates that, at the end of the state-building period in Kuwait, the kinship authority has governing salience.

Kinship Group Leaders

Kinship has governing salience when kinship group leaders are not government officials but rather carry power rooted in kinship authority. While Kuwait's leaders have longstanding and ongoing relationships with tribal sheikhs and leaders of influential merchant families, these family leaders are not government officials. Members of influential families are represented across Kuwait's government, but not as leaders of these families per se.

Tribal sheikhs are not bureaucratic officials in Kuwait's government. However, they have relationships with senior members of government, including the Emir himself. When problems arise between members of the tribe and the government, the sheikh acts as an intermediary between them, but his authority is rooted in kinship versus the state's bureaucracy. A sheikh can settle unrest within tribal groups, and bring tribal concerns to the government. In fact, tribe members often prefer sheikhs not to take on a formal bureaucratic role. Sheikhs often fail when they run for parliament in Kuwait because they are more valuable to their constituents as vanguards of kinship authority.[4] Tribal sheikhs also have influence over members of parliament who come from their tribe. One influential tribal sheikh in Kuwait explained, '[If] I see a fault with one of my tribal MPs . . . I'll go to the head of the faction and say to him "Do you accept what's happening with . . . your representative?"'[5] In such a case, the sheikh leverages kinship authority in an attempt to sway the bureaucratic politics of the state. A different influential sheikh claimed that his relationship with MPs is tribal, and that they do not discuss government business. However, he later noted that MPs sometimes approach him to request favours. This relationship suggests a system in which tribal sheikhs play a key role as kinship authorities that exists apart from the bureaucratic state.[6]

Legal Status of Tribes

While many government advisory bodies include members of Kuwait's major tribes, there is no legal registry of these tribes. Kuwaiti citizenship is based on when an individual's ancestors arrived in Kuwait rather than whether one has a tribal affiliation. While some tribal residents of Kuwait are stateless *bidoon*, other members of that same tribe do have Kuwaiti citizenship.

Tribal Primaries

Tribes in Kuwait also hold primaries for parliamentary elections. While these primaries are officially illegal, they are widespread. Bureaucratically developed laws about primaries, in other words, are insufficient to prevent kinship groups from organising them for political gain. Tribal primaries originally happened with assent of the government, which wanted tribal candidates to balance out merchant family representation in the parliament.[7] While they were outlawed in 1998, these tribal primaries have continued, including during the 2020 COVID-19 pandemic. One civil society leader in Kuwait noted that in the 2013 parliamentary elections, there were fifty-five tribal primaries. Of these, five were prosecuted.[8] In 2016, several tribes held primaries for the November parliamentary elections. Not only were the primaries not kept secret, their results were posted on social media and news websites.[9] Tribes were creative, however, about how these events were advertised. The Shammar tribe held a 'chess contest', and the Ajman organised a 'karate tournament', in which the best 'player' was voted upon by attendees from the tribe.[10] Many final ranked lists of candidates were posted on Twitter. While the government monitors social media and had full knowledge of these illegal primaries' activities, it did not intervene in them. In fact, when the Kuwaiti police arrested eight members of the Mutair tribe in March 2008 for organising a tribal primary, it led to demonstrations that turned violent.[11]

Tribal primaries incentivise individual members of a given tribe or family to rally around a particular candidate in Kuwait's national election. In return, the candidate is more likely to address tribal interests.[12] Tribal support has been an important aspect of the ruling family's strategy to remain in power. Strong historical support from tribal candidates has balanced against opposition from Kuwait City's merchant families. While Kuwait enjoys many aspects of democratic governance, parallel kinship authority structures facilitate the preservation of the al-Sabah family's leadership.[13]

Even among *hadhar*, electoral politics – particularly campaigns – are the purview of the family:

> Interviewee: Usually the families run the whole thing. The campaign. The person's family, and usually whoever's aligned with that family comes. And needs to – like you tell your friends, you tell other people you know, or families you're associated with to come.[14]

While certain *hadhar* groups associate based on ideological 'blocs', these family-based campaigns have the effect of extending kinship authority into the state, since those elected to parliament are supported by their families. In return, there is an expectation that these elected officials will provide for the needs of the family members who elected them. A former minister of parliament who ran as part of an ideological bloc faced difficulty after refusing to do so. The minister explained, 'Upon election, many people asked for favours and I didn't grant them. I lost a lot of support for that . . . When I ran in 2012 . . . members of the family made sure I wouldn't win.'[15]

Public Deliberative Bodies

Citizens of Kuwait deliberate and conduct discourse during weekly family gatherings called *diwaniyas*. The *diwaniya* itself is a room in a house used specifically for receiving guests. The (traditionally male) gathering inside the room is called a *diwaniya* as well. The size of the room depends on the size and status of the family. Some *diwaniyas* are the size of a large bedroom while others easily can seat 100 people. Affluent families have, in recent years, built their own free-standing *diwaniyas* separate from the family house. Traditionally, however, the weekly *diwaniyas* are held at a senior male family member's house.

Any man may attend any weekly *diwaniya* in Kuwait and social codes dictate that he must be given hospitality – usually tea, coffee and dates, but sometimes a full dinner as well. Usually, however, *diwaniya* attendees are male family members and the husbands, brothers and close cousins of female family members. This gathering contrasts to weekly family visits, or *zuaras*, which are held at a grandmother's (sometimes a grandfather's) house and involve a meal shared between men, women and children. The *zuara* is less formal and not as explicitly political, but many Kuwaitis block off an evening of their week to attend the family *zuara*, and men often discuss *diwaniya* politics there in the presence of the family's women.[16]

Seating at a *diwaniya* is often by status, with senior family members as hosts at one end of the room, and lower status or younger attendees seated further away. Junior attendees are taciturn and usually do not speak unless spoken to. Attendance at *diwaniyas* is considered good family politics, though many Kuwaitis no longer attend them regularly.[17] Among those who do, however, it is not uncommon for a man to attend three to five *diwaniyas* in a given night, making a quick appearance at each.

Because its purpose is to incentivise association and strong family ties, the *diwaniya* is an important kinship-based political institution in Kuwait. Since Kuwait's first parliamentary elections in 1962, election campaigns have taken place in *diwaniyas*, with candidates lining up outside them and entering one by one to give stump speeches and answer questions about their political platform.[18] It was also customary for the Emir to visit *diwaniyas* during holidays, and foreign diplomats visit the *diwaniyas* of influential families as well.

The *diwaniya* is an important arena for feedback to government policies. Since *diwaniya* attendees are usually among family and always in a private space, the tone of the discourse is more honest and open than in the public sphere. This openness reaches a peak during election season, when candidates visit the *diwaniya* to give stump speeches and answer audience questions.[19] Visits to *diwaniyas* by Kuwaiti government officials, including the Emir, are intended to gauge public opinion and provide a crucial mechanism for feedback. When feedback breaks down, *diwaniyas* can also be the gathering site for demonstrations. Activists choose *diwaniyas* as meeting sites because they know the police are reluctant to enter the private home to break up the gathering.[20] Despite legal closures of *diwaniyas* during the 2020 COVID-19 pandemic, some remained open.[21]

Kinship authority in Kuwait's *diwaniyas* creates a protected space where the bureaucratic authority of the state can govern in limited ways at best. *Diwaniyas* are subject to lower restrictions on speech, free association, and electoral politics – all of which the bureaucratic state tries to regulate. They are sites where kinship authority regulates these areas of governance rather than bureaucratic authority, and thus has governing salience.

Personal Status

Wasta (personal status) is a central feature of Kuwaiti politics and patronage extends to the highest levels of governance. Relations between members of the al-Sabah ruling family often determine access to power and resources. As a former British ambassador wrote, in 1969, the Al Sabah are a 'network of family influence, fortified by marriage, which operates behind the scenes . . . they fill the main policy making offices of the states and . . . ensure that no one is able to oppose their will without their knowledge'.[22] While individual members may advance their own interests, the family makes major governance decisions by consensus. These include appointing a crown prince and opening the parliament.[23] Marriages between the al-Sabah and other families often had political significance. For example, Sheikh Jaber al-Mubarak al-Hamad al-Sabah married women from the powerful Mutair tribe while Mohammed Shahrar, a Mutairi, was head of the Council of Ministers.[24] Such marriages created an alliance that disincentivised antagonism between the speaker and the royal family. Another example is Sheikh Jaber's son (Ahmed al-Jaber al-Sabah). He married Husa, daughter of Ibrahim bin Muhammed al-Jaber al-Ghanim, a prominent member of the influential Kuwaiti al-Ghanim family.[25] These marriages gave the royal family influence within these powerful kinship-based groups and disincentivised conflict. They also gave the al-Sabah influence in various branches of government.[26] The royal family deliberately placed its members in influential government positions. Today, members of the royal family receive monthly stipends and serve in leadership positions in Kuwait's government, and academic and private sectors.

Where kinship has governing salience, social welfare distribution occurs through kinship hierarchies rather than state-created bureaucracies. This is the case in Kuwait. Patronage is the basis of the Kuwaiti population's buy-in to the state. Yet despite the critical role patronage plays, much of it is handled by institutions of kinship authority versus bureaucratic authority. The increase in oil revenues in the 1960s 'gravely inflated the Civil Service and . . . contributed to the growth of disguised unemployment amongst Kuwaiti citizens'.[27] This meant that people were being hired not for their technical expertise but rather to prevent them from being unemployed and opposing the leadership as a result. Employment was a form of patronage. Britain's Ambassador to Kuwait put it bluntly in a 1969 report: 'Kuwait has maintained her independence so far by buying off her own people.'[28]

This bureaucracy-as-jobs programme continued after state building as well. It perpetuated kinship-based *wasta* because people could use their position within the bureaucracy to favour kin both inside and outside the organisation. The lack of bureaucratic expertise was not, practically, a barrier to entering the bureaucratic system and receiving a monthly paycheck. The use of kinship identity within such bureaucracies for access to resources is an indicator of the governing salience of kinship authority in Kuwait.

Government employment in a bureaucracy is a function we would expect bureaucratic authority to regulate. However, in Kuwait this authority competes with kinship authority in this governance space.

Kuwaitis' interactions with the government are often based on *wasta*. Despite official channels for job applications, Kuwait's ministries reflect the salience of kinship identity through informal nepotism and similar performative manifestations. Since these interactions are often off the record, interview evidence is useful in establishing the importance of *wasta* in Kuwait. *Wasta* in Kuwait often plays a central role in navigating around bureaucracy:

> Interviewee: All relations affect your personal interest. So you couldn't get anything done. You couldn't even maybe get into a hospital if you don't have *wasta*. If you're going to go into a government hospital, [or] get a job. Getting a job is all through *wasta*.[29]

While *wasta* can take many forms, kinship-based *wasta* is considered the best:

> Interviewee: Of course *wasta* from family is better than friends . . . Because family . . . you have more of a responsibility towards them. So it's very hard for you to say, 'no' or ignore them. Because you don't want to cut off relationships with your family. That will happen if you don't go through *wasta* with them. That's the best *wasta* that you can get.[30]

This sense of mutual obligation proves crucial for Kuwaitis looking for jobs or looking to circumvent an often entangled bureaucratic process.

> Interviewee: You either get an appointment ahead of everyone else or you don't based on . . . whether you have the right connections, whether you have people on the inside . . . you see a lot of *bedu* get away with tickets, for instance. They are related in some way with their captain or whatever . . . And so they talk to them and they get away with pretty much anything.[31]

Hadhar also experience similar preference based on family ties, as one *hadhar* Kuwaiti recounted, 'I got my driver's license – I passed my test and all, but still, because of *wasta*, the guy who was – when I was doing the test would tell me, "anything you need, let me know. I'll do it for you".'[32] Another explained, 'I had a tinted windshield. I was about to get by car impounded. [But] that's the beauty of our Kuwait. You can make a few phone calls and boom, your problem goes away.'[33] The interviewee continued that, because of the salience of kinship-based *wasta*, 'The worst job you can get in Kuwait is being in the law enforcement because it's the only job in Kuwait where you can't do your job . . . You arrested this guy . . . your brother calls you up and . . . you gotta let him go.'[34]

These kinship ties continue to be politically salient because they ensure resources and access for their members. Interviews confirm that the use of kinship ties is a preferred way to get this access. This kinship authority both subsumes bureaucratic procedures and replaces them.

Kinship ties also manifest themselves in the leadership of the Kuwait Oil Company. The company was founded 2 February 1934 and was the first company to discover commercially exploitable oil in Kuwait.[35] The Emir at the time, Sheikh Ahmed al-Jaber al-Sabah, put Kuwait's oil under the ownership of the bureaucratic state rather than the ruling family.[36] The Kuwait Oil Company is a subsidiary of the Kuwait Petroleum Corporation, a government-owned holding company which oversees all of Kuwait's oil operations. Despite this formal bureaucratic designation, the ruling family has created extensive ties to the Kuwait Oil Company whose oil revenues are a backbone of the Kuwaiti economy. One of Sheikh Ahmed's wives, Nura al-Tahus, whom he married in 1931, was the sister of Muhammed Al-Tahus, head guard of the Kuwait Oil Company.[37] Members of the royal family sit on the boards of Kuwait's oil companies. Per decree of the Ministry of Oil, Kuwait's Supreme Oil Council consists of the Prime Minister – a member of the royal family – and four ministers appointed by the Emir.[38] These embedded family members give the royal family important influence based on kinship authority.

Arbiter of Disputes

Kuwait has a judicial system which arbitrates criminal, civil and constitutional disputes. Judges are appointed by Emiri decree and the decisions of higher courts are usually respected, even when there is strong disagreement about the courts' decisions.[39] Kuwait's courts played a particularly prominent political role ruling on the constitutionality of a series of elections and dissolutions of parliament following protests in 2011.[40]

Neighbourhood disputes are often handled through a local *baladiya* council. Kuwait's fifty-six neighbourhood municipalities (*baladiyat*) came under the authority of the Ministry of Municipalities in 2005.[41] These municipalities, created in Kuwait's basic law of 1932, are responsible for sanitation, building licenses and development, among other functions. The municipality is financially independent of the ruler and is elected.[42] While *baladiyat* are run by local residents and are fairly bureaucratic, these residents often settled along kinship lines during state building. Thus, while informal, kinship can determine who is likely to be in leadership positions within the *baladiya*.

Finally, tribal sheikhs play an important role in arbitrating disputes between tribe members as well as between tribe members and the state. When protests broke out in 2011 in Kuwait, for example, the government engaged tribal sheikhs in order to quell the tribe members who were participating. The sheikhs acted as mediators who arbitrated this dispute, and the calming of protests suggests they were somewhat successful in this regard. On a more regular basis, tribal sheikhs mediate problems between members of different tribes. An influential tribal sheikh explained that if 'someone's relative kills someone from another tribe, the emir of the second tribe can mediate this problem . . . Sometimes the law doesn't settle the problems of the tribe.'[43] While there are legal systems that prosecute murder in Kuwait, a family may not file a civil suit should the family or the offender pay blood money (*dia*). The amount and payment of this money, however, would be negotiated by the family rather than through the state. Kinship group leaders might approach the father of the deceased to appeal to him to accept this money in order to settle the feud.[44]

First Source of Aid

In Kuwait, the immediate family is a primary source of aid. A Kuwaiti businessman explained, 'In the old days, even their children got married and had children and they also stayed in the grandfather's house. Now, not anymore . . . But always their parents support them. They support sometimes housing, buying a car, sometimes on a monthly basis or *ad hoc* basis.'[45] There is also an understanding in Kuwait that relatives must receive help before others. The same businessman described his support of family first as 'a commitment . . . I have to help them'.[46] A Shi'a businessman explained that having a kinship network in Kuwait provides protection: 'It makes you strong. In this society. Honestly, it makes you strong. Because you feel you have a family . . . "Don't touch him, he's my cousin."'[47] *Diwaniyas* can be useful for obtaining aid as well, a Kuwaiti university student explained. A Kuwaiti university student agreed that regular attendance at a *diwaniya* 'would help your ties with the family and if you need anything'.[48] Even in the event that a tribe member committed manslaughter against a member of a different tribe, he could appeal to a grandfather or uncle for *dakhil*, or protection from retaliation by that tribe.[49]

The Kuwaiti state provides considerable aid to citizens, but also distributes this aid along tribal patronage lines. A Kuwaiti researcher noted that 'before, conflicts were tribal and based on capturing from the other . . . Today conflicts have become about . . . who can obtain more from the state.'[50] *Hadhar* and *bedu* communities alike will agitate the state's ruling bargain when they see an opportunity for patronage. As a result, kinship group members often receive government aid that is mediated through tribal patronage networks.

The influence of kinship authority in Kuwait over members of kinship groups is strong. Even when members of kinship groups desire a certain behaviour, they are constrained by kinship authority. Interviewees, documents, and previous scholarship from Kuwait also detail the preponderance of social norms set by kinship authority.

Kinship Group Purity

Marriage in Kuwait is based heavily on kinship group status. Marriage between members of kinship groups and those outside the kinship network is strongly discouraged. A Kuwaiti university student from a major *hadhar* family, who is also a mother, explained,

> If you're going to marry from the labor class, that is a big no-no . . . If you're going to marry Asian [expatriates] . . . it's not right. That's how they think it is . . . [My son] can marry whoever he wants. But the consequences that – he's gonna suffer, from my family. He's gonna suffer.[51]

Family status in Kuwait is based on a combination of three elements. Most important is the affluence or the political influence of the family. The second, and strongly impacting the first, is the length of time the family been established in Kuwait. The third and final consideration is the purity of the family line.[52] Many Kuwaiti families prefer that a potential spouse come from a 'pure' (*asl*) line. 'Purity' refers to whether it is possible to trace back this individual's roots to a known family lineage. It is highly pejorative in Kuwait to refer to someone as *khikri*, or a mutt. Well-established families in Kuwait may also use the term *baysari* to refer to someone whose blood line is unknown. A merchant might even disown a son who marries a *baysari* woman.[53] This is because such marriages reflect not only on the couple, but on each's family as well. This stratification contrasts sharply with Oman, where according to one Omani political analyst, 'there isn't really a derogatory word for people with mixed lineage'.[54]

Role of Social Sanctions

Social sanctions imposed by kinship authority have strong influence in Kuwait. An individual's actions affect not only her personal reputation but that of her family and tribe as well. As a result, Kuwaitis are often limited by kinship authority in what they say. When asked how someone can protect their reputation in Kuwait, a female Kuwaiti student replied, 'You just basically have to keep your mouth shut.'[55] As described in Chapter 2, sanctioned behaviours in Arab Gulf countries are classified as *'aib*, or forbidden. The same student explained that if a member of a family engaged in *'aib* behaviours and gained a reputation for it, 'You wouldn't want to be associated from anyone with that family . . . anything vulgar is *'aib*. Anything not acceptable is *'aib*. Like revealing clothes. Basically anything you'll find that is vulgar or inappropriate.'[56] Kinship-based social sanctions therefore limit dress and personal expression. They also place limitations on associations between men and women. The gendered nature of these limitations is a cause of frustration for women: 'a girl cannot openly date but a guy can. It's counterproductive. I don't know how because his girlfriend is a girl.'[57] For men and women alike, what is considered *'aib* in Kuwait has changed over time. For example, it was traditionally *'aib* among some tribal families for a husband to discuss activities like shopping or going to dinner that he did with his wife. Today, such discussions are commonplace among less traditional tribe members. Additionally, while a child's bad behaviour used to reflect poorly on a family, the impact of this behaviour today is lesser than in the past.[58]

Kinship Authority's Influence over Dating and Marriage

When kinship has governing salience, kinship authority constrains the behaviour of kinship group members. Even when these members express preferences to disregard kinship authority, they will behave according to what kinship authority prescribes. For example, a Kuwaiti college student explained, 'I . . . asked my family before I majored . . . I said, "I wanna get into law", and they said "No, don't. You're not going to get into law." My aunts and all. Because they just don't like it.'[59]

Marriage is another example of the governing power of kinship authority in Kuwait. As one university student explained 'People marry based on family reputation. Reputation is a big thing in Kuwait.'[60] While marriage is in many ways a social institution, it has a distinctly political function as well, particularly in and among kinship groups. Kinship groups act as networks, and marriages are linkages between these networks. They obligate different kinship groups toward each other, and obligate individual members of kinship groups toward each other as well. Marriages are political, and not only among the ruling family. They are the basis for strong business ties between merchant families, and historically they stabilised alliances between tribes. Since marriage has these important political functions, kinship authority regulates it. The state also regulates it in that the Kuwaiti government gives a small grant to Kuwaitis who marry.[61]

As a marriage between a man and a woman is arranged, family members will make inquiries into the background of the prospective spouse's family. It is preferable that this individual come from a family with a relatively high status. This will give the couple – and the family – access to new resources and opportunities. It also preserves the exclusivity of high-status families, who only marry from within each other's ranks. A university student from a high-status family explained that when her cousin married a man from a lower-status family, 'she got a little backlash for that. Everyone was talking. "We don't usually take from that family, why is she taking this guy?"'[62]

Couples in Kuwait must take into account not only their personal reputation (*sum'a*) in a marriage but that of their family as well. A bad reputation can harm the family's ability to marry off other family members and could be a source of political embarrassment. Given the importance of kinship ties in many other aspects of Kuwaiti political life, marriage plays an important role in creating kinship relations that maintain political salience. Those who do not follow the norms of marriage face sanction, as one interviewee's father discovered from personal experience: 'My dad . . . was fixed to marry his cousin, but he didn't want to so he married someone else outside of the family without them knowing, and then they kicked him out of the family.'[63]

Since breaking the norms instituted by kinship authority can introduce instability in kinship group relations, families take pains to ensure these rules are followed. Sanctions like the one in this example are not only a signal to other groups that deviation from norms is an anomaly, but also to kinship group members. It signals to future marriage partners that failing to follow the norms of kinship authority face sanctions that are often severe. As one college student explained 'Here in Kuwait, there is no sense of sympathy for someone who attempted dishonoring the family.'[64] While challenging kinship authority in Kuwait is possible, it comes at the price of alienation or being ostracised from the group. Given the resources and opportunities a kinship group provides, this alienation carries a physical cost. The impact of this cost is that kinship group members are often compelled to act in certain ways by kinship authority even when their preference would be to act in a different way.

Kuwait's state-building patterns were based on competitive access to resources. Since the government was incentivised to reach out to individual kinship groups, the salience of kinship authority was preserved after state building. Evidence of kinship's governing salience manifests itself in two ways. First, it can carry out functions normally undertaken by states. In Kuwait, kinship authority is responsible for the distribution of patronage, which is critical to the Kuwaiti state. Tribal sheikhs in particular operate as tribal intermediaries who, despite lacking a formal government position, influence the distribution of state patronage and the policies of members of parliament. Families play a critical role in campaigns for parliament, from campaigning to primaries to elections. Kinship also allows Kuwaitis to circumvent bureaucracy when seeking employment in government ministries.

Kinship also affects politics in Kuwait separately from the state. *Diwaniyas* are a space for association between members of kinship groups and they keep kinship networks active. They provide a space for free political discussion and a site for political campaigning as well. While the *diwaniya* is a critical feedback mechanism for the government, it operates separately from the government and is a manifestation of kinship authority in that it shapes patterns of association, thought, and electoral politics in Kuwait.

Governing Salience in Qatar after State Building

Like Kuwait, kinship authority in Qatar has governing salience after state building. Kinship authority plays a major role in determining who in the country has access to power and state patronage, including government tenders. It has instrumentalised the bureaucratic state in order to provide these resources. Kinship authority also plays a strong role in dating and marriage in Qatar, with strong social sanctions for those who violate standards of appropriate behaviour.

Kinship Group Leaders

The Al Thani family is Qatar's ruling family and became as such with the help of support from tribes including the al-Murrah and al-Hawjer during the founding of the state.[65] Among the royal family, kinship has governing salience in Qatar. Both members of the royal Al Thani family and those who have married into the family enjoy special titles, positions and financial benefits.[66] The Al Thani also have strategic marriages with other ruling families in the Arab Gulf states. In 1957, Qatar's former ruler, Sheikh Ahmed bin Ali Al Thani, married Sheikha Mariam bint Rashid al-Maktum. Sheikha Mariam was the daughter of Rashid bin Said Al Maktum, the Sheikh of Dubai in the United Arab Emirates. When Sheikh Ahmed was deposed by his cousin Khalifa bin Hamad Al Thani in 1972, he fled to Dubai. He enjoyed safe haven there because of this marriage to the ruler's daughter. In addition to benefits that accrue to members of the royal family, members of the eighteen major tribes in Qatar serve in important positions in both the government and the army. These positions serve as an incentive for continued loyalty from kinship groups to the state.[67] At the same time, they give major kinship groups influence over the distribution of power and resources in Qatar's government.

Legal Status of Tribes

Qatar's government gives payouts to the leaders of tribal groups as a way of creating buy-in to the state's nationalist idiom and support for the Al Thani royal family. These payouts are crucial for the family's assent to rule. Citizens and tribal leaders can also appeal personally to the Emir, even in an otherwise bureaucratic Qatari state.[68]

Tribal Primaries

Elections and representative bodies in Qatar were designed to provide an outlet for tribal dissent and instrumentalise kinship authority within the state's bureaucratic apparatus. However, evidence suggests that the opposite occurred. Tribal groups tended to run and elect tribal candidates for office, and even at the municipal level, kinship affinity was a major driver of voting behaviour.[69] Elections in Qatar are infrequent and data on specific tribal primaries are difficult to come by, but available evidence suggests that kinship politics play a major role in deciding for whom to vote.[70] This suggests that patronage networks created by kinship authority instrumentalise the state's bureaucratic apparatus to obtain resources for kinship group members.

Public Deliberative Bodies

While Qatar does not have an extensive *diwaniya* system like Kuwait, many families have a gathering space (*majlis*) which serves as a forum for discussion and making decisions about individual and communal issues facing the family.[71] Like the *diwaniya*, the *majlis* is in a designated room with traditional seating and decor, and guests are served coffee or tea and sweets. Mens' *majalis* (plural) are often physically separate from the rest of the house to prevent interaction between men attending the *majlis* and women who live in the house itself. Women also have *majalis* of their own, which are usually inside the house.[72] Attendance at the *majlis* is expected, and women may face sanction or disapproval from older members of their family if they do not attend. In addition, men's *majalis* tend to be more explicitly political that women's, although women often discuss pertinent social issues at the meetings.[73] Freer points out that, like in Kuwait, *majalis* in Qatar allow the government to gauge public reaction to its policies. Furthermore, Qatar's Emir has a weekly *majlis* to build consensus and assess public opinion regarding his policies.[74]

Qatar's legislature is called the Shura Council. Established on 1 May 1972, the Council consists of thirty-five members. While the Council is officially comprised of a mixture of elected members and Emiri appointees, the Emir can extend the existing Council's term if it is in the public's 'best interest'. This power has been invoked for years by Qatar's leaders. Al Thani ruling family members represent a portion of those appointed by the Emir to the Council, but the rest are from major tribal groups.[75] Zahlan points out that this inclusion represents an expansion of the inner circle of Al Thani leadership in order to build a stable governing coalition.[76] Changes to Qatar's demographics and politics are reflected in the Council's make-up as well. Women were first appointed to the Council in November 2017.[77]

Elections in Qatar are also highly tribal. A survey conducted after the 1999 municipal elections found that almost all respondents reported voting primarily according to tribal affiliation.[78] Electoral districts are often drawn along the lines of old tribal settlement patterns.[79] This voting pattern indicates that individuals in Qatar continue to benefit politically from their kinship ties. It also suggests that kinship authority remains strong in areas of state governance that are otherwise bureaucratic.

Personal Status

Personal status in the form of *wasta* is an integral part of Qatari life. Employment decisions – including employment in the government – are often a function of *wasta*. In addition, *wasta* is a part of bidding for government tenders despite the creation of an anti-corruption watchdog agency in 2011 designed to monitor abuse of power and funding in the government.[80] Using *wasta* to navigate the state bureaucracy is not only publicly discussed but upheld as a source of social prestige.[81] One Qatari man, writing about his difficulty certifying his marriage to a non-Qatari woman, describes using his grandfather's *wasta* with the Ministry of Interior to gain their approval for the certification.[82]

Arbiter of Disputes

Qatar's judicial system, part of the Ministry of Justice, is divided into *shari'a* courts, which deal with criminal and personal status issues for Muslims, and *'adalia* courts, which deal with felony and misdemeanor cases for non-Muslims according to Western legal traditions. *'Adalia* courts also deal with issues not addressed within the *shari'a* tradition.[83] Courts can order defendants to give blood payments for murder or manslaughter. At the same time, tribes and families continue to mediate internal disputes, often through the *majlis*.[84] While a bureaucratic system of arbitration exists, many decisions about kinship populations and their members are made according to kinship authority.

First Source of Aid

Social welfare laws passed in the 1960s provided vulnerable Qataris financial and housing support. These vulnerable populations included widows, divorcees, orphans, as well as low-income families.[85] These populations continued to receive services after the end of state building. At the same time, however, Qatar's large families and tribes provide social, financial and political support to their members.[86] The state is one participant in the process of aid provision alongside the family, rather than the sole actor.[87]

Kinship Group Purity

Kinship purity is emphasised in Qatar and marriages between certain families is encouraged. Roughly half of marriages in Qatar occur between members of the same tribe or family, and the purity of the bloodline is a motivating factor for these marriages.[88] Additionally, many young Qataris can name the families into which they will most likely be married.[89] Marriage between Qatari and non-Qatari citizens is very rare. Rather, marriages in Qatar usually take place within families or between families of a similar economic status.[90] Qataris have complained that the new styles of housing in the country make interactions with family and neighbours difficult. Yet these same individuals have worked hard to overcome these physical obstacles to family interaction.[91]

Role of Social Sanctions

Qatari woman face pressure to dress modestly in public. Asmi notes that this dress helps women to 'ensure that they maintain capital in the marriage market, largely by drawing on sources of kinship capital such as gender segregation and veiling'. In other words, a woman perceived generally as 'immodest' may be unable to marry a Qatari man because she does not conform to standards of appropriate behaviour delineated by kinship authority. Additionally, her immodest dress may reflect poorly on other members of her kinship group.[92] Similar harm may be incurred by the families of men who are particularly effeminate or members of the LGBTQIA+ community.[93]

Kinship Authority's Influence over Dating and Marriage

Growing up in Qatar, boys and girls are 'jokingly' paired off with each other, often planting a seed in each's head about making the other a future spouse. Upon reaching the age of marriage, engagement often happens quickly compared to contemporary Western timelines, and the family often takes the lead for arranging it. The couple then spends time together in public – behaviour sanctioned only for engaged and married couples. After marriage, they move in together.[94] This process maintains the governing salience of kinship identity by pairing men and women within the same group, preserving the exclusivity of resource access.

In Qatar, access to water resources was competitive prior to state building. These resources were distributed via kinship networks in a society where kinship authority had governing salience. As the state-building process took place, the creation of infrastructure and bureaucratic governance reaffirmed the political salience of kinship authority. Kinship has governing salience in the post state-building period in Qatar because of the competitive patterns of resource access that existed before state building.

Instrumentalised Kinship Salience in Oman after State Building

Throughout the 1990s, the Sultanate of Oman continued to see rapid economic development under the close supervision of Sultan Qaboos. The bureaucratic state continued to develop Oman's trade and tourism industries while kinship politics have remained embedded in the state itself. As compared to Kuwait, Oman saw little threat to its system of government or patronage throughout the 1990s. If anything, this neutrality and slow retreat from isolation would seem to favour more traditional means of politics since Oman was under less external pressure to embody more Western forms of governance. Nonetheless, Oman during this time period continued to use bureaucratic means of governance, while kinship authority retained instrumentalised salience.

The Sultanate continued to expand infrastructure during the 1990s. It also made strides in public health, improving hospital access for rural populations and creating a database of genetic disorders in the country.[95] In conjunction with the United States and the US–Omani joint commission, Oman built fisheries and schools providing both academic and technical education.[96] In 1996, the Sultan presented the *Basic Statutes of the State*, which is the closest document Oman has to a constitution. The document laid out basic rights, prevented conflicts of interest within the government, and outlined procedures for Qaboos' succession. Upon the ascent of Haitham bin Tareq, these procedures were scrapped in favour of a more monarchic model with the appointment of Haitham's son Dhi Yazan as Crown Prince.

In contrast to Kuwait, Oman had cooperative access to vital limited resources before state building. As a result, kinship after state building in Oman has instrumentalised salience, meaning that it is largely embedded into the state's bureaucratic apparatus and instrumentalised as a tool for state patronage. Cooperative access to vital limited resources in Oman among settled non-urban populations incentivised the creation of proto-bureaucracies. During state building, the government used these proto-bureaucracies as the basis for extending infrastructure. While Kuwait had built infrastructure first and moved nomadic populations onto this infrastructure second, Oman expanded infrastructure that existed where people already lived. Proto-bureaucracies were staffed by members of local kinship groups but their authority was bureaucratic. This allowed Oman's government to extend its bureaucratic authority, which replaced the old bureaucratic structure and expanded dramatically after the 1970 coup in ways that would obtain buy-in from non-urban populations. Oman introduced a territorial idiom of nationalism – one based on the use of common symbols to unite disparate regions of the Sultanate – in order to encourage buy-in to its state-building project.

As a result of these efforts, kinship authority has instrumentalised political salience in Oman. In this context, instrumentalised salience means two things. The first is that kinship groups will be embedded into the state's governing apparatus. Leadership of these groups will be formal members of the bureaucracy. As the start of this chapter shows, kinship groups exist independently of the state in Kuwait, and tribal sheikhs are not government officials. They exert influence from outside the bureaucratic system. Kinship-based *wasta* in Kuwait is extensive, well-documented, and discussed openly by multiple interviewees. In Oman, this openness is not the case. Kinship is embedded into the state apparatus using a series of official bureaucrats who mediate between these hierarchies and the state. Kinship authority, while existent, is less crucial to job placement in Oman's ministries than in Kuwait. *Wasta*, while incontrovertibly relevant in Oman, is emphasised to a lesser extent and is much more difficult to document in Oman than Kuwait and Qatar.

The second is that where kinship authority has instrumentalised salience, it will be limited in its ability to compel behaviour by kinship group members. In particular, states will be able to actually enforce laws that contradict kinship authority. In Kuwait, kinship authority often circumvents the laws and bureaucratic processes of the state and constrains the behaviour of group members. In Oman, this is much less frequently the case. The following analysis illustrates the instrumentalised political salience of kinship authority in Oman in light of the earlier section on Kuwait. It presents a side-by-side comparison of kinship authority after state building in both cases and shows that patterns of cooperative resource access before state building create an observably different level of salience than do patterns of competitive resource access.

Kinship Group Leaders

Oman's contemporary system of sheikhs is a creation of the bureaucratic state. During state building, the Sultan identified a need to balance the creation of a modern bureaucratic state with the traditional forms of authority to which Omanis were accustomed. The solution was a set of government officials whose name and duties *resembled* those of kinship group leaders, but who were official bureaucrats of the state. A local administrator, called a *sheikh rashid,* is a state official descended from a high-status family. As Valeri explains, 'he officiates in a geographical district . . . and no longer according to tribal or family criteria'. In the 1980s, the state also established a *sheikh qabila* (tribal sheikh) for Shi'a families in Oman.[97]

The creation of this 'neo-tribal' authority in Oman is evidence of the instrumentalised salience of kinship. Genuine kinship authority has been recast by the state in terms of an authority that resembles kinship authority, but is in fact bureaucratic in nature. This is a starkly different outcome from Kuwait, where kinship authority remains intact and independent from the state. In Kuwait, kinship authority governs in political spaces we would expect state bureaucratic authority to control. In Oman, kinship authority is reshaped and employed strategically by the state in these same spaces.

Legal Status of Tribes

Tribal lineage in Oman has been standardised by the government. The government legally mandates that individuals take three names: their given name, father's name, and family/tribal name. In addition, Oman's government provides official recognition to 216 recognised tribes, and membership in one of these tribes is certified by a *wali* or by a local sheikh. Thus, a sheikh appointed by virtue of kinship authority is given a bureaucratic role by Oman's government. Certification of tribal lineage is not merely a matter of identity in Oman. It was (and remains) the basis for obtaining a land permit or passport.[98] In this sense, the sheikh acts as an intermediary between kinship-based tribal groups and the bureaucratic state. However, unlike in Kuwait, his capacity is officially recognised by the bureaucratic apparatus.

While the state did not create kinship identities in Oman, its bureaucracy defines the scope of which identities are real in the legal-rational sense. Tribal sheikhs, who are also approved by the state's bureaucratic apparatus, play a key role. Their participation in certifying kinship lineage for official purposes is an act that reconfigures kinship authority in ways that ultimately bring more authority to the state. In Kuwait, tribal sheikhs are also intermediaries but they act outside the formal bureaucratic system.

Challenges to this standardisation process, furthermore, have been unsuccessful. In May 2006, the Omani Ministry of Interior's Committee for the Correction of Tribal Names and Titles decided that members of the al-Tuwaiya and the al-Khalifain tribes would adopt the last name Harthi on their identification documents. These included passports, ID cards, marriage contracts, and car registrations.[99] The Harthi are a strong tribe in Oman, but the Tuwaiya claimed that such a change implied they would be considered servants of the Harthi according to Oman's kinship traditions. They also rejected the alternative 'Awlad Tuwaiya.[100]

Tribe members responded by writing letters not to sheikhs but to fifteen officials including the mayors of Qabil and Ibra and the Minister of Interior. On 15 September 2007, Zina bin Khalfan al-Tuwaiya and Salem bin Khalfan al-Tuwaiya filed a lawsuit against the Minister of Interior demanding a reversal of the decision, but the court ruled that it lacked jurisdiction in the matter.[101] Salem al-Tuwaiya appealed the decision but was unsuccessful. He argued that this erasure of Tuwaiya identity represented discrimination against the tribe. Under this scrutiny, the government verbally revoked the order in December 2009. However, it continued to make such determinations.[102]

The al-Tuwaiya and al-Khalifain cases are highly illustrative of the instrumentalised salience of kinship in Oman. Given a conflict between tribal and bureaucratic authority, the bureaucracy ultimately triumphed. Even though the Tuwaiya and Khalifain tribes strongly oppose changing their members' last names, they have been forced to do so by the bureaucracy. The Omani state, while recognising the importance of tribes, continues to curate tribal identities through bureaucratic means. Additionally, rather than circumvent or ignore the government's determination, the tribes challenged it directly, and did so through the bureaucratic court system of the state.

Tribal Primaries

Tribal primaries in Oman are illegal but the law is often difficult to enforce. Communities in Mutrah are known to hold primaries, and they occur elsewhere as well. However, a civil society leader in Oman working on elections opined that primaries are 'not very forceful upon the tribe members to vote exactly within them – they are not considered as strong commitment as in Kuwait. [If you don't vote with the tribe, the repercussions are] mainly social . . . but no economic repercussions . . . just an unpleasant atmosphere'.[103] A former government official explained that northern tribal groups try to find the most qualified person within the tribe rather than the one with the most kinship authority.[104] In other cases, tribe does not affect voter choice. A local elected official in Muscat, for example, described running against several tribal candidates, but still winning the most votes in the electoral district. While such an outcome is not always the norm, it indicates that at least for certain districts in Oman, tribal affiliation is less important than other factors in elections. Prior to the 2011 elections, Oman's Grand Mufti issued a statement urging Omanis to 'look past' tribal identity when voting.[105]

Public Deliberative Bodies

Whereas the *diwaniya* in Kuwait is a family-owned meeting space, local public meeting spaces in Oman are administered by bureaucratic authorities. The *majlis*, a building in each town, is owned by the municipality (though they pre-date the creation of municipalities) and can be used for family occasions, town-hall style meetings, or political campaigning for the Majlis al-Shura. Neighbourhood and family gatherings, including mourning periods, also take place at the *sabla*, a meeting hall often next to a mosque.[106] Whereas these spaces in Kuwait tend to be the purview of kinship authority, in Oman they are administered by the bureaucratic state. The state intends to maintain control of these spaces for the foreseeable future. In May 2018, Oman's Public Prosecutor issued a decree against Omanis who were trying to establish tribal fora and gatherings.[107]

Family is important to Omanis, but the coercive power of kinship is different in Oman than in Kuwait. For some families, gatherings are often ad hoc, except for holidays and major life cycle events.[108] For others, including some Shi'a families, they are an occurrence each weekend called a *ramza*, at which the extended family gathers and eats together.[109] In neither case, however, is the meeting as formally political as in Kuwait.

Personal Status

At the top of the kinship system in Oman is the royal family, the Al Busaid. Following state building in Oman, members of the al-Said branch of the family were and continue to be represented at high levels of government, including in Oman's cabinet. Other prominent families are represented in the cabinet as well. The Sultan maintains a careful balance in his inner circle between different families, but also among different religious sects and the business community.

Unlike royal families in other Gulf states, members of the Al Busaid family do not receive special payouts from the government. 'Royalness' is concentrated among the small al-Said branch of the family itself. Patronage among the ruling family does not extend beyond this inner core. 'We don't have a close relationship to the ruling family', noted a member of the Al Busaidi tribe.[110] An Omani activist notes: 'Oman . . . has the least percentage of royal family members in leadership positions. I monitored Kuwait elections three times and three time I'm just amazed at how many royal family members there are.'[111] In addition, marriage outside the Al Busaid is not uncommon, and members are known to marry among a number of different families of varying status. These families include the Abri, Barwani, Harthi, Mahrooqi and Ziqwani families.[112] If kinship identity were politically salient, this is the opposite of what we would expect since kinship groups tend to limit the access of outside members. This limited exclusivity of the Al Busaid is one example of the instrumentalised political salience of kinship in Oman.

Some of Oman's tribes look down upon this extensive marriage outside the Al Busaid family, and the al-Said's framing themselves as 'above' the rest of the tribes. Importantly, this scorn does not undermine the political power of the family, which we might expect if kinship were politically salient.[113]

Assessing the extent of kinship-based *wasta* among the Al Busaid – a person's personal gravitas within a network of people – is difficult in Oman. The subject is a sensitive one, but it is slowly entering public discussion. One young member of the Al Busaid family claimed 'some family *wasta* exists but I haven't seen it. I've only heard about it.' Restricted discussion of kinship-based *wasta* suggests that family *wasta* is not as normalised and widely accepted as states with governing kinship salience like Kuwait and Qatar.[114]

Officially, kinship and family name play little to no role in government opportunities in Oman. Applications to Sultan Qaboos University (SQU) and bureaucratic government positions are evaluated mostly on qualifications rather than kinship ties.[115] Upon graduation, the Ministry of Higher Education grants a certificate that is the basis for employment.[116] The government also issues housing permits without regards to kinship. One interviewee explained, 'In the new modern cities . . . when the Ministry of Housing divides plots, they don't care that you're Balushi, Mukheini, [or] Saidi.'[117] Informally, however, kinship ties can sometimes make a difference. As one doctoral candidate at SQU put it: 'Kinship isn't necessary, but it can help.'[118] Another Omani stated, 'You can only be employed by these [the Ministry of Civil Service and the Ministry of Manpower]. But it still plays a role – your family and tribal ties.'[119] For this example in particular, it bears mention that the key factor is tribal affiliation versus personal ties between members of the same kinship group per se. This is a contrast with Kuwait where both elements matter. As another Omani put it, 'a last name is not enough. You also need influence.'[120] For example, while there are several families known for their business success (for example, the Bahwan, Barwani, Zawani and Zubair), not all members of the families are involved in business nor are they all wealthy.[121] Tribal names carry respect in Oman, but that respect does not always translate to political power as directly as it would in Kuwait. The use of kinship authority to circumvent bureaucratic authority happens in Oman, but it is not the norm to the same extent as in Kuwait. While Kuwaitis openly discuss the use of kinship ties to circumvent bureaucracy, Omanis are much less forthcoming on the topic. This indicates that kinship salience plays a different role in Oman, given that even discussing the use of kinship authority to circumvent bureaucracy is socially undesirable. Even taking into account Kuwait's more open political discourse, the willingness of its citizens to discuss using kinship to circumvent bureaucracy is significantly higher.

Arbiter of Disputes

Sheikhs have historically provided aid and arbitration to tribe members in Oman. Prior to 1970, many had personal relationships with the Sultan. Following the 1970 coup, however, *walis* gained power as arbiters of disputes. In addition, bureaucratic layers emerged that separated sheikhs from the Sultan.[122] Sheikhs were also appointed as *sheikh rashids*, making them government officials. As such, their kinship authority was instrumentalised by the state.

Walis govern in the Sultanate's provinces and serve as mediators between local communities and the national bureaucratic state. They also report to the Majlis al-Shura, Oman's lower legislative house. *Walis* as a governance mechanism pre-date the Omani state-building process, but continue to play a role as power-holders whose authority comes from the ruler rather than kinship. In contemporary Oman, *walis* are appointed by Oman's Ministry of Interior and represent the state's interests at the provincial level. Each *wali* in Oman serves a two- to five-year term, and usually governs in an area other than where he is originally from. This prevents accusations that the *wali* is biased in his decisions toward the tribe from which he originates or with whom his tribe is aligned. *Walis* are not appointed on the basis of kinship. However, in the past, *walis* from the royal family were appointed to start them on a political path – subject to promotion if they were successful.[123] As state officials, *walis* are involved with official visits to the province, elections and census activities.[124] *Walis* have advisers on the local tribal politics of their province, and they are accountable to the Ministry of Interior. Within their province, *walis* mediate disputes that cannot be resolved by local sheikhs. These sheikhs will mediate between aggrieved parties in the province but some parties will approach the *wali* should this mediation prove unsuccessful.[125] Traditionally, the role of the *wali*, in addition to enforcing law and order, was to be a point of contact between Oman's government and its tribes.[126] If the residents in a province were unhappy with the *wali* they could request that the Ministry of the Interior remove him from power.[127] Sheikhs could (and did) also appeal directly to the Sultan himself. They would make periodic visits and leave placated with gifts.

Walis represent another layer of the Omani bureaucratic system that embeds kinship authority. They embody certain functions of kinship authority, including mediation among and between kinship groups and their members. However, they play a bureaucratic role and are state officials. Kinship retains salience in Oman, but the system of *walis* demonstrates that kinship has instrumentalised salience, especially in comparison with Kuwait. Whereas Kuwait uses kinship group leaders themselves as intermediaries between kinship groups and the state, Oman uses a multi-layered bureaucracy where functions of kinship authority are embedded. This bureaucracy was a feature of the post-1970 Omani state. The granddaughter of a former sheikh from a Shi'a family in Muscat noted 'now, there are a few steps between the sheikh and His Highness [the Sultan]'.[128]

Kinship authority may regulate disputes over land or divorce in Oman. When such disputes arise, Omanis may approach a sheikh to resolve these issues. However, conflict resolution in Oman is based ultimately on bureaucratic authority. As a member of Muscat's Municipal Council pointed out, 'The government tries to appoint the most skilled people to set a precedence of not using tribe as a basis for eligibility for office . . . This is a formal structure. There are laws.'[129] While they are the words of a government official, this statement differs starkly from those of Kuwaitis who point out the strong influence of kinship authority in the country's governance.

First Source of Aid

Families remain an important source of aid for Omanis. However, as a result of bureaucracy and economic development, many Omanis live apart from their families in order to make a living. Oman's ministries are bureaucratic but, in some cases, feature informal patronage that flows along tribal lines. Ministers sometimes feel obligated to employ their relatives or give grants to certain tribes. Oman's cabinet also reflects members of most major families in Oman, though not all of these families are 'tribal'. While patronage politics are central in Kuwait, several interviewees noted that in Oman, kinship ties are helpful but not themselves sufficient.[130] An Omani political expert noted change over time, stating, 'now it's moved. In the past [kinship] was about survival.'[131]

In the modern Sultanate of Oman, *aflaj* are administered by the General Water Resources Management for Aflaj Affairs in the Ministry of Regional Municipalities and Water Resources. The role of the government is mostly technical and relates to upgrading and fixing *aflaj*. This function is highly bureaucratic. First, a *wakil* must request maintenance from the government via letter or an official form. Government engineers go to the *falaj* to assess its state and will report back to the government. This assessment is then entered into a government database and assigned an urgency of first, second or third priority. Given budget constraints, first priority items constitute the bulk of maintenance work, with some second priority issues being given attention. Often this work includes replacing *sarooj* (mud) with cement to make the *falaj* more durable. More recently, the government has been trying to assist local systems to manage the excess water of the *falaj*. At *Falaj Daris*, for example, the government worked on building storage tanks for the excess water that previously had drained into a *wadi* (dry riverbed).[132]

Despite their continued function however, the *aflaj* have become less important as a form of resource access. Oman's government not only provides fresh water but also creates it through a set of desalination plants administered at the national level. The Oman Power and Water Procurement Company (OPWP), owned by Oman's Ministry of Finance, was founded in 2005 to help contract these plants.[133] Desalinated water originally flowed to homes in Muscat following the 1970 coup. By 1973, most houses in Muscat were connected to the city's water distribution network.[134] Desalination plants, beginning with al-Ghubrah in 1976, increased the amount of available fresh water for Muscat and other rapidly expanding urban centres. Since that time, Oman has continued contracting and building these plants. Oman's government after 1970 also began providing free water via trucks that was stored in water tanks.[135] Consistent with other shifts from localised to nationalised access, Omanis living in towns and villages often considered this drinking water 'better' than local sources.[136] This preference for 'government water' is an indication of the population's acceptance of national-level bureaucratic authority.

Kinship Group Purity

Tribal purity is less important in Oman than in Kuwait. 'There isn't really a derogatory word for people with mixed lineage', noted one Omani expert.[137] The fact that Omanis place less emphasis on 'purity' speaks to the lesser exclusivity and importance of kinship as a means of access in Oman versus Kuwait.

Family affiliation matters to marriages, but usually because it signifies a potential spouse's status and reputation rather than political access per se.[138] While it is not impossible to marry someone from a different kinship group, an Omani political activist explained that marrying someone from a similar tribe 'makes your life a lot easier because . . . from a social perspective you will guarantee that you are socially comparable'.[139] Many young Omanis go to Muscat for university and settle there afterwards because of the economic opportunities. The city's distance from their hometowns also creates anonymity that translates to a weaker role for kinship authority. Educated women in Omani cities have apartments and cars, hang out in coffee shops or movie theatres, and most importantly, work alongside their male counterparts in offices.[140] This is a different kind of outcome, however, from the political utility that would characterise the governing salience of kinship identity in Kuwait.

Role of Social Sanctions

As in Kuwait, *'aib* is a means by which kinship authority regulates behaviour in Oman. In both Muscat and in Oman's interior, gender is a major dividing line for activities considered *'aib*. An Omani college student pointed out that '*'aib* is for men and women, but women more than men . . . A man can talk to girls. But a woman talking to a man is a big problem.'[141] That being said, Omanis from the interior who come to Muscat face less social sanction for engaging in behaviours considered *'aib*. This is to some extent the result of state bureaucracy. Because the state's bureaucratic apparatus extends to non-urban areas, there is adequate infrastructure to facilitate movement between the capital and other regions. Because application to universities is bureaucratic, students from the interior can come to study in Muscat. Because job hiring also tends to be bureaucratic, it is viable for someone with no family history in Muscat to find gainful employment there. Bureaucratic infrastructure creates the conditions for movement in the country and a mixing of different kinds of Omanis. The effect of both of these factors is that *'aib* is less stringently policed in the capital, although it is still policed to some extent. A young Omani woman in Muscat noted that her brother calls to check on her while she is out in public spaces.[142]

Gender segregation is common in Oman, but bureaucratic authority has also had a hand in enforcing it. Public schools are traditionally gender segregated after grade four, though both boys and girls now attend school in Oman.[143] While instruction at Sultan Qaboos University is co-ed, men and women live in separate buildings. There are separate men and women's areas in cafeterias on campus, and the University of Nizwa has separate dining halls for each. Both universities have separate men and women's sections in the library, with the book stacks in the centre of the building. Men and women work together in ministries, but have limited association with each other beyond official duties. Thus, while gender separation in Oman may originate in traditions of kinship authority, it too has been subsumed within the bureaucratic state.

Kinship Authority's Influence over Dating and Marriage

Marriage in Oman is traditionally a family affair. In the more traditional south, marriage within the tribe is common, and it is often arranged. Omanis were generally of the opinion that forced marriage in the country is extremely rare. However, children in the interior are sometimes told from a young age (between six and ten years old) that there is a certain person they will eventually marry.[144] In the north, families may arrange marriages, but Omani men and women in Muscat may meet each other through work or work-related social events.[145] Others meet through social media or common friends, meeting for the first time over coffee or dinner. Other meetings may also be arranged on an ad hoc basis at a local hotel or an apartment cleared of roommates for the evening.[146] If things go well between two marriage-minded

Omanis, the man would call or speak with the woman's mother, and then with her father to discuss the prospect of marriage.[147]

Marriage to non-Omanis requires a lengthy bureaucratic process and must be approved by the Ministry of Interior, Royal Oman Police, Ministry of Social Development, and the Ministry of Health. Omani women must obtain an opinion from authorities on the 'appropriateness' of an age difference between her and her non-Omani husband. Failure to follow all of these regulations is punishable by a minimum fine of OMR 2,000 and a ban on public sector work.[148]

Among tribes, members will pool their money together to raise a dowry so that a member of the tribe can marry his bride.[149] The wedding ceremony itself, called a *mulkah* (similar to the *milche* in Kuwait) takes place at a mosque among male friends and family. Women celebrate with the bride at a separate ceremony, which the groom later comes to in order to escort the bride home.[150] The amount of money given as a dowry is regulated by the social status of the family. A college student from Dhofar estimated a typical dowry at roughly $26,000 (OMR 10,000) but a dowry paid to a high-status family can exceed $90,000 (OMR 35,000).[151] The cost of marriage has historically been prohibitive in Oman. Many young men and women are prevented from marrying because of the high cost of a dowry and wedding ceremony prescribed by traditional kinship authority. However, the Omani government has responded to this need by organising group weddings at a fraction of the cost.[152] Thus Oman's bureaucratic authority is able to overcome the otherwise prohibitive tradition of lavish weddings based in kinship authority.

Notes

1. Giovanni Sartori, 'Concept Misinformation in Comparative Politics', *American Political Science Review* 64 no. 4 (1970): 1033–53.
2. Christopher Wlezien, 'On the Salience of Political Issues: The Problem with "Most Important Problem"', *Electoral Studies* 24 (2005): 557.
3. See Joan Aldous, 'Urbanization, the Extended Family, and Kinship Ties in West Africa', *Social Forces* 41 no. 1 (October 1962): 6–12.
4. Interview, Salmiya, Kuwait, 25 February 2014.
5. Interview, Sabah al-Salem, Kuwait, 6 January 2014.
6. Interview, Kuwait, 6 January 2014.
7. Jill Crystal, *Oil and Politics in the Gulf: Rulers and Merchants in Kuwait and Qatar* (Cambridge, UK: Cambridge University Press, 1990): 89.
8. Interview, [location undisclosed for interviewee's well-being], Kuwait, 24 December 2013.
9. https://twitter.com/h_k_alhumaidi/status/790729275196448769; https://twitter.com/aljjahra/status/790608892841590784.

10. https://twitter.com/alhayyani/status/789124507520958464.

11. 'Kuwait', *Freedom House*, 2009, https://freedomhouse.org/report/freedom-world/2009/kuwait.

12. See Kamal Eldin Osman Salih, 'Kuwait Primary (Tribal) Elections 1975–2008: An Evaluative Study', *British Journal of Middle Eastern Studies* 38 no. 2 (2011): 141–67.

13. Protests in 2011 included a strong tribal element. The seriousness with which Kuwait's government approached this swing from tribal support to tribal opposition is an indication of how fundamental it is to Kuwait's governance.

14. Interview, Salmiya, Kuwait, 13 March 2014.

15. Interview via telephone, 8 September 2013.

16. Interview, Salmiya, Kuwait, 25 November 2013; Interview, Salmiya, Kuwait, 18 December 2013; Interview, Salmiya, Kuwait, 13 March 2014.

17. When asked the interview question 'Do you attend weekly *diwaniyas*?' one of the most common responses from Kuwaiti men across age, class and background was 'I don't, but I should.'

18. 'Despatch No. 3, British Embassy, Kuwait (31 January, 1967)', in *Records of Kuwait, 1966–1971: 1967*, ed. Anita Burdett (Cambridge, UK: Cambridge University Press, 2003): 72; Interview, Salmiya, Kuwait, 6 January 2014.

19. Interview, Salmiya, Kuwait, 6 January 2014.

20. A raid on a *diwaniya* in 2011 was met with deep resentment by Kuwaitis. See Kristin Smith Diwan, 'The Politics of Transgression in Kuwait', *Foreign Policy*, 19 April 2013, http://foreignpolicy.com/2013/04/19/the-politics-of-transgression-in-kuwait/.

21. Abdullah Alkhonaini, 'Kuwait Goes to the Polls: Discussing the 2020 Parliamentary Elections', Online Speaker Panel, *London School of Economics*, 8 December 2020, https://www.lse.ac.uk/middle-east-centre/events/2020/kuwait-goes-to-the-polls.

22. 'S. Falle to British Embassy Kuwait, 1 December 1969 (26/5)', *Records of Kuwait 1966–1971: 1969*, 63–4.

23. Michael Herb, *All in the Family: Absolutism, Revolution, and Democracy in the Middle Eastern Monarchies* (Albany, NY: State University of New York Press, 1999): 33, 36.

24. Interview, Salmiya, Kuwait, 24 February 2014.

25. H. R. P. Dickson, *Kuwait and Her Neighbours* (London, UK: George Allen & Unwin, 1956): 41.

26. Crystal, *Oil and Politics in the Gulf*, 12.

27. 'First Five Year Development Plan 1967/8–1971/2', *Development Plans of the GCC States (Kuwait 1)* (Cambridge UK: Archive Editions, 1994): 5.

28. 'The Future of Kuwait. Mr. Falle to Mr. Stewart, 27 May 1969', *Records of Kuwait, 1966–1971: 1969*, 30.

29. Interview, Salmiya, Kuwait, 6 March 2014.

30. Interview, Salmiya, Kuwait, 6 March 2014.

31. Interview, Salmiya, Kuwait, 21 November 2013.

32. Identity withheld due to the sensitivity of the interview content. The phenomenon of passing license tests based on *wasta* was confirmed in off-the-record conversations with other Kuwaitis.

33. Interview, Salmiya, Kuwait, 5 December 2013.

34. Interview, Salmiya, Kuwait, 5 December 2013.

35. Mary Ann Tetreault, *The Kuwait Petroleum Corporation and the Economics of the New World Order* (Westport, CT: Quantum Books, 1995): 2.

36. 'Kuwait: The Internal Situation. Mr. Arthur to Mr. Stewart (6 January, 1969)', *Records of Kuwait, 1966–1971: 1969*, 73.

37. Alan Rush, *Al-Sabah: History and Genealogy of Kuwait's Ruling Family, 1752–1987* (Atlantic Highlands, NJ: Ithaca Press, 1987): 58.

38. 'Decree for Establishing the Supreme Petroleum Council (26 August, 1974)', *Ministry of Oil, State of Kuwait*, http://www.moo.gov.kw/About-Us/Ministry-Decrees/Decree-for-Establishing-the-Supreme-Petroleum-Coun.aspx.

39. 'Judicial System of Kuwait', *Abdul Razzaq Abdullah & Partners*, http://www.arazzaqlaw.com/judicial-system-of-kuwait/.

40. Kristian Coates Ulrichsen, 'Politics and Opposition in Kuwait: Continuity and Change', *Journal of Arabian Studies* 4 no. 2 (2014): 214–30.

41. Interview, Hawally, Kuwait, 24 December 2013.

42. Crystal, *Oil and Politics in the Gulf*, 46.

43. Interview, Sabah al-Nasr, Kuwait, 19 February 2014.

44. Interview, Jahra, Kuwait, 12 January 2014.

45. Interview, Salmiya, Kuwait, 6 January 2014.

46. Interview, Salmiya, Kuwait, 6 January 2014.

47. Interview, Shuweikh, Kuwait, 6 March 2014.

48. Interview, Salmiya, Kuwait, 6 March 2014.

49. Interview, Jahra, Kuwait, 12 January 2014.

50. Interview, Salmiya, Kuwait, 30 December 2013.

51. Interview, Salmiya, Kuwait, 13 March 2014.

52. A family that is long-established in Kuwait but is not affluent or influential would be of a lower status than a family which arrived later but achieved financial and political success. Specific examples are withheld here due to the sensitivity of family status in Kuwait.

53. Interview, Jahra, Kuwait, 12 January 2014.

54. Interview, Qurum, Oman, 1 April 2014.

55. Interview, Salmiya, Kuwait, 13 March 2014.

56. Interview, Salmiya, Kuwait, 13 March 2014.

57. Interview, Salmiya, Kuwait, 13 March 2014.

58. Interview, Jahra, Kuwait, 5 March 2014.

59. Interview, Salmiya, Kuwait, 6 March 2014.

60. Interview, Salmiya, Kuwait, 5 December 2013.

61. In 2015, this grant was 2,000 KD, or about $6,600. See B. Izzak, 'Lawmakers Reject Proposed Measures to Reduce Welfare – New Anti-Corruption Law to

be Approved on Jan 12', *Kuwait Times*, 27 December 2015, http://news.kuwait-times.net/website/lawmakers-reject-proposed-measures-to-reduce-welfare/.

62. Interview, Salmiya, Kuwait, 6 March 2014.

63. Interview, Salmiya, Kuwait, 13 March 2014.

64. Interview, Salmiya, Kuwait, 25 November 2013.

65. Fromherz offers a detailed list of major Qatari tribes and tribal histories.

66. Allen J. Fromherz, *Qatar: A Modern History, Updated Edition* (Washington, DC: Georgetown University Press, 2017): 134.

67. Al-Shawi, 'Political Influences of Tribes', 22–3.

68. Fromherz, *Qatar* (2017), 32.

69. Crystal, *Oil and Politics in the Gulf*, 50.

70. See Rehunama Asmi, 'Finding a Place to Sit: How Qatari Women Combine Cultural and Kinship Capital in the Home Majlis', *Anthropology of the Middle East* 11 no. 2 (Winter 2016): 21; 'Tribal Families in Qatar', *Harvard Divinity School Religious Liberty Project*, https://rlp.hds.harvard.edu/faq/tribal-families-qatar.

71. 'Tribal Families in Qatar'.

72. Elsa Exarhu, 'The Majlis Culture in Qatar', *Qatar Tribute*, 12 October 2016, http://qatar-tribune.com/news-details/id/28164; 'Majlis, a Cultural and Social Space', *UNESCO Intangible Cultural Heritage*, 2015, https://ich.unesco.org/en/RL/majlis-a-cultural-and-social-space-01076.

73. Asmi, 'Finding a Place to Sit', 20, 25.

74. Courtney Freer, *Rentier Islam: The Influence of the Muslim Brotherhood in Gulf Monarchies*, (Oxford, UK: Oxford University Press, 2018): 117.

75. 'Decision of the Emir of the State of Qatar Number 62 in the Year 2004 Renewing the Membership of Some Members of the Shura Council and Appointment of New Members to the Council', *Al-Meezan Qatar Legal Portal*, 15 February 2005, http://www.almeezan.qa/LawView.aspx?LawID=5565&language=ar&opt (Arabic).

76. See Rosemarie Said Zahlan, *The Creation of Qatar* (Lanham, MD: Rowman and Littlefield Publishers, 1979).

77. 'Qatar Appoints Four Women to Shura Council', *Al-Jazeera*, 9 November 2017, https://www.aljazeera.com/news/2017/11/qatar-appoints-women-shura-coun-cil-171109165044169.html.

78. Fromherz, *Qatar* (2017), 140.

79. Fromherz, *Qatar* (2017), 176.

80. Shane McGinley, 'Qatar Sets up Corruption Watchdog for State Agencies', *Arabian Business*, 30 November 2011, https://www.arabianbusiness.com/qatar-sets-up-corruption-watchdog-for-state-agencies-432769.html.

81. Mohd Noorudeen, 'Wasta is Very Much a Part of Qatari Culture', *Qatar Living*, May 2017, https://www.qatarliving.com/life-qatar/posts/wasta-part-culture-qatar.

82. 'I'm Qatari, and I want to be able to decide for myself who I marry', *Doha News*, 8 November 2016, https://dohanews.co/im-qatari-want-able-decide-marry/.

83. A. Nizar Hamzeh, 'Qatar: The Duality of the Legal System', *Middle Eastern Studies* 30 no. 1 (January 1994): 82.

84. Fromherz, *Qatar* (2017), 21.

85. Suzi Mirgani, 'Strengthening the Family in Qatar: Challenges and Required Actions', *Georgetown University Qatar Center for International and Regional Studies*, May 2015, https://cirs.georgetown.edu/community-outreach/strengthening-family-qatar-challenges-and-required-actions.

86. A. Hadi Alshawi and Andrew Gardner, 'Tribalism, Identity, and Citizenship in Contemporary Qatar', *Anthropology of the Middle East* 8 no. 2 (Winter 2013): 56–7.

87. 'Promoting QNV 2030's Vision of a Good Society: Towards a Social Policy for Qatar', *Social Affairs Department, General Secretariat for Development Planning*, May 2009: 7.

88. Geoff Harkness and Rana Khaled, 'Modern Traditionalism: Consanguineous Marriage in Qatar', *Journal of Marriage and Family* 76 (June 2014): 587–8.

89. Sharon Nagy, 'Social and Spatial Process: An Ethnographic Study of Housing in Qatar', PhD dissertation, University of Pennsylvania, 1997: 47.

90. Abdallah Yousef al-Maliki, 'Public Administration in the State of Qatar: Origin, Development, Problems, and Current Directions', PhD dissertation, Golden Gate University, 1989: 50.

91. Nagy, 'Social and Spatial Process', 145.

92. Asmi, 'Finding a Place to Sit', 29.

93. Asmi, 'Finding a Place to Sit', 31.

94. Harkness and Khaled, 'Modern Traditionalism', 598–9.

95. Anna Rajab, 'Genetic Disorders in Oman', in Ahmad S. Teebi (ed.), *Genetic Disorders Among Arab Populations* (Oxford, UK: Oxford University Press, 1997): 476.

96. Calvin H. Allen and W. Lynn Rigsbee II, *Oman Under Qaboos: From Coup to Constitution, 1970–1996* (New York, NY: Routledge, 2013): 197.

97. Marc Valeri, *Oman: Politics and Society in the Qaboos State* (New York, NY: Columbia University Press, 2009): 156–7; Interview, Ramal Boshar, Oman, 28 March 2014.

98. Interview, al-Khuweir, Oman, 9 December 2013.

99. 'Report on Violations of the Minority Rights of the Al Tuwaiya People in Oman', *UN Office of the High Commissioner on Human Rights*, 2011, http://lib.ohchr.org/HRBodies/UPR/Documents/Session10/OM/TDF_TamkeenDevelopmentFoundation_eng.pdf.

100. 'Report on Violations of the Minority Rights of the Al Tuwaiya People in Oman'.

101. 'Administrative Court of Justice Rules it Lacks Jurisdiction', *altowayyah.blogpost.com*, 16 February 2008, https://altowayyah.blogspot.com/2008/02/blog-post.html.

102. Uzi Rabi, 'The Sultanate of Oman: Between Tribalism and National Unity', in Uzi Rabi (ed.), *Tribes and States in a Changing Middle East* (Oxford, UK: Oxford University Press, 2016): 92.

103. Interview, al-Khuweir, Oman, 9 December 2013.
104. Interview, Medinat Sultan Qaboos, 18 March 2014.
105. Rabi, 'The Sultanate of Oman', 92.
106. Interview, al-Khuweir, Oman, 29 December 2014; Mandana E. Limbert, *In the Time of Oil: Piety, Memory, and Social Life in an Omani Town* (Stanford, CA: Stanford University Press, 2010): 41.
107. 'Public Prosecution Issues Statement concerning Tribal Fora or Gatherings and this is the Text', *Atheer.com*, 8 May 2018, https://ath.re/2I7Z4Vm (Arabic).
108. Interview, German University of Technology, Oman, 28 March 2014.
109. Interview, al-Khuweir, Oman, 19 March 2013; Interview, Ramal Boshar, Oman, 28 March 2014; Interview, German University of Technology, 26 March 2014.
110. Interview, al-Khuweir, Oman, 31 March 2014.
111. Interview, al-Khuweir, Oman, 9 December 2013.
112. Interview, al-Khuweir, Oman, 31 March 2014.
113. Interview, Qurum, Oman, 1 April 2014.
114. The same interviewee was comfortable saying bribery existed in Oman among former officials, as well as for 'big projects' currently underway. We can thus infer that the interviewee's comments about kinship-based *wasta* are not tempered by reticence to discuss bribery or corruption overall.
115. Interview, al-Khuweir, Oman, 19 March 2014.
116. Interview, Sultan Qaboos University, Oman, 24 March 2014.
117. Interview, al-Khuweir, Oman, 21 March 2014.
118. Interview, Sultan Qaboos University, Oman, 24 March 2014.
119. Interview, al-Khuweir, Oman, 9 December 2013.
120. Interview, Qurum, Oman, 1 April 2014.
121. Interview, German University of Technology, Oman, 26 March 2014.
122. Interview, Ramal Boshar, Oman, 28 March 2014.
123. Interview, Medinat Sultan Qaboos, Oman, 18 March 2014.
124. Interview, al-Khuweir, Oman, 29 December 2014.
125. Interview, Washington, DC, 24 June 2014. In addition to *wilayat*, Oman established municipal councils for eleven provinces in Oman in 2011. See Sultan's Decree No. 116/2011, Promulgates Municipal Councils Law (2011), https://www.mmc.gov.om/Pages.aspx?PAID=3&MID=13&PGID=8.
126. Interview, al-Khuweir, Oman, 29 December 2014.
127. Interview, Medinat Sultan Qaboos, Oman, 18 March 2014.
128. Interview, Ramal Boshar, Oman, 28 March 2014.
129. Interview, Ramal Boshar, Oman, 28 March 2014.
130. Interview, Qurum, Oman, 1 April 2014.
131. Interview, Medinat Sultan Qaboos, Oman, 18 March 2014.
132. Interview, Nizwa, Oman, 17 March 2014. The Ministry has also tried to specify that UNESCO sites should be fixed with traditional mud and stone rather than cement to preserve their historic composition.
133. OPWP is owned by the Electricity Holding Company of the Oman Oil Company, owned in turn by Oman's Ministry of Finance. The Ministry of Finance

itself has a 0.01 per cent stake in OPWP. See 'Introduction to OPWP', *Oman-PRP.com*, http://www.omanpwp.com/About.aspx#1opwp.

134. Limbert, *In the Time of Oil*, 119.

135. Interview 29, Oman, 19 February 2015.

136. Limbert, *In the Time of Oil*, 127.

137. Interview, Qurum, Oman, 1 April 2014.

138. Interview, Sultan Qaboos University, Oman, 24 March 2014; Interview, Ramal Boshar, Oman, 28 March 2014.

139. Interview, al-Khuweir, Oman, 9 December 2013.

140. In the interior, Omanis often prefer that women work with other women. Interview, Ramal Boshar, Oman, 28 March 2014.

141. Interview, Qurum, Oman, 30 March 2014.

142. Interview, Qurum, Oman, 30 March 2014.

143. Interview, Washington, DC, 24 June 2014; Interview, al-Khuweir, Oman, 31 March 2014.

144. Interview, Ruwi, Oman, 16 March 2014.

145. Interview, Qurum, Oman, 30 March 2014.

146. Interview, Medinat Sultan Qaboos, Oman, 18 March 2014.

147. Interview, al-Khuweir, Oman, 31 March 2014.

148. 'Fines, Jail for Illegal Marriages in Oman', *Times of Oman*, 16 July 2018, https://timesofoman.com/article/138251/Oman/340-marriage-law-violations-recorded-in-Oman-last-year.

149. Interview, Sultan Qaboos University, Oman, 24 March 2014.

150. Stephanie Dahle, 'Weddings in Oman: Traditional and Modern', *Forbes*, 22 February 2011, http://www.forbes.com/sites/stephaniedahle/2011/02/22/weddings-in-oman-traditional-and-modern/#4efb04a53ef3.

151. Khalid M. al-Azri, *Social and Gender Inequality in Oman: The Power of Religious and Political Tradition* (New York, NY: Routledge, 2013): 78; Interview, Sultan Qaboos University, Oman, 24 March 2014.

152. 'Forty-Nine Couple Enter Wedlock at Group Wedding Held in Al Khaboura', *Times Of Oman*, 22 June 2013, http://timesofoman.com/article/19113/Oman?page=-43.

8

KINSHIP AFTER STATE BUILDING

The end of state building in Kuwait, Qatar and Oman was followed by decades of political shifts. Changes in leadership, regional conflicts, globalisation, and the 2011 Arab uprisings changed the context of kinship politics in the Gulf region. Taking some of these changes into account helps emphasise the continuing importance of pre-state conditions in modern states. These changes have implications for our understanding of kinship during state building as well, since they speak to the nature of 'salience' as a concept. Finally, they provide an important context to the model of state building presented here. While the model's scope may end when state building does, the states themselves do not. Examining what happens in these states following state building is an important indication of the continuing relevance of kinship salience as an aspect of statecraft.

Kuwait

Kuwait's basic governing bargain remained intact after the end of state building and kinship continues to have governing salience. However, political changes following state building have created new political contexts in which this salience manifests itself. In particular, the Gulf War, Kuwait's Orange reform movement, and protests in 2011 have posed new challenges to the state as it seeks to navigate the governing salience of kinship authority in the country.

During the 1970s and 80s, the Kuwaiti state increased bureaucratic control as a result of political pressures from abroad and from within. At the time, Kuwait's leadership faced several threats. For example, politicians at the time understood a wave of pan-Arab nationalism in the region to be incompatible with – and thus a threat to – monarchic rule. The British shared these sentiments. A British diplomat opined in 1970 that 'Kuwait is ideally made for a lightning *coup*', and Ambassador A. J. Wilton wrote in 1971 that 'military *coups* are so fashionable that their occurrence [in Kuwait] must almost be regarded as a matter of time'.[1]

Kuwait also faced security threats in the aftermath of the Iran–Iraq war. Due to its support for Iraq, Kuwait faced backlash from radical Shi'a groups throughout the 1980s. In 1983, attackers linked to the Shi'a Islamic Dawa party conducted a truck-ramming attack at the US Embassy that killed five people, in addition to attacks at the French Embassy injuring five, Shuaiba Petrochemical plant, the Kuwait International Airport control tower killing one, the Electricity Control centre, and a residence of workers for the Raytheon Corporation. In 1985, a radical Shi'a group called Islamic Holy War rammed a bomb-laden car into the motorcade of Emir Jaber al-Ahmed on 25 May. The Emir survived the attack but the royal family was shaken.[2] In response to these attacks, Kuwait initiated security crackdowns that included roadblocks, rounding up foreign workers, and permission for those at the checkpoint to shoot those who refused to be searched. These crackdowns limited civil liberties and freedoms that Kuwait's merchant families had ensured previously for the state. The loyalty of tribal groups, however, helped insulate the royal family from merchant push-back as a result of these policies. The crackdowns also indicated the royal family's insecurity with the ruling bargain it had struck with these merchants and tribal groups alike. This insecurity shows that the governing salience of kinship authority in Kuwait was not entirely the design of the state. Given the chance, Kuwait's leadership made a grab for greater power and a renegotiation of power relations in the state. Kuwait's leadership would be tested to the maximum a few years later, however, with the Iraqi invasion and occupation of Kuwait.

The Gulf War

The Iraqi invasion of Kuwait on 2 August 1990 was a critical juncture in Kuwaiti history whose effects ripple well into the twenty-first century. After roughly two years of increasing tensions between Iraq and Kuwait following the end of the Iraq–Iran war in 1988, a deeply indebted Iraq took military action against its weaker southern neighbour. Kuwait's military was not on alert at the time and was unable to defend the country from being overrun. In only four hours, Iraq's military and air force took over and occupied Kuwait, including the royal residence at Dasman Palace. Kuwait's royal family had fled to Saudi Arabia with the exception of the Emir's brother Fahad, who remained at the palace and was shot and killed in the Iraqi assault. Kuwait remained under occupation until January 1991 when an international coalition liberated Kuwait, extinguished the fires Iraq's military had set at Kuwait's oil fields, and facilitated the return of the Al Sabah to power.

The Iraqi occupation of Kuwait had three major effects on kinship politics in Kuwait. First, it created a legitimacy challenge for the Al Sabah, who had fled the country during the invasion. Informal conversations with Kuwaitis indicate that the Al Sabah face criticism decades later for the decision to leave while roughly 250,000 Kuwaitis remained in the country.[3] In addition, the combination of economic recession in the 1980s and the cost of recovery from the occupation left Kuwait with high unemployment and a budget deficit of billions of dollars that lasted well into the 1990s.[4] One means the family used to re-establish legitimacy upon their return was to target Kuwait's stateless *bidoon* tribes. Between 130,000 and 160,000 *bidoon* who had fled to Saudi Arabia were denied re-entry to Kuwait following the end of the Gulf War. While *bidoon* had participated in anti-Iraq activities during the occupation, those who had been employed by the government prior to the date of the Iraqi invasion were dismissed from their jobs. They were also denied residency permits that the state gave to others living in the country. In addition, the *bidoon* were indicted collectively for participation in the Popular Army, an Iraqi militia group that few *bidoon* actually joined.[5] Since 1991, Kuwait's government has issued 900 'security blocks' which prevent *bidoon* from obtaining citizenship on the grounds that they allegedly collaborated with Iraq.[6] These actions by Kuwait's government reduced the number of kinship group members to whom it was obligated. They also sent a signal reaffirming the 'Kuwaiti-ness' of kinship groups who continued to receive patronage from the state.

The Al Sabah's exile and subsequent return to power also brought intra-family conflict to the surface. The Emir at the time, Jaber al-Ahmed, was extremely distressed during the invasion and subsequent liberation. The Crown Prince, Saad al-Abdullah, stepped up to handle security coordination with the US and Saudi Arabia and took charge of the temporary government following liberation.[7] However, Saad was from the Salem branch of the Al Sabah while Jaber was so-called for his grandfather, for whom the Jaber branch of the family is named. The contrast between Jaber and Saad exacerbated divisions between branches of the family.

The second effect of the Gulf War on kinship was that the royal family was put under pressure by Kuwaitis as well as international actors to respect political freedoms. The government's decision in exile to institute three months of martial law upon its return was met with criticism. In addition, there was pressure to professionalise the government rather than having a system based on kinship ties.[8] However, the government's crisis of legitimacy made it averse to any major changes. Its dependence on kinship-based ties for leadership ultimately outweighed the cost of pressure to implement major reforms.

Finally, Kuwaitis who remained in place under Iraqi occupation maintained their kinship networks. Their resistance actions during the occupation also served as the groundwork for participation in politics and public life afterwards. When parliament was reopened in 1992, these groups had been continuously organising and associating. The result was a stronger and more sophisticated tribal constituency in Kuwait's parliament. Tribal constituents growing up in the 1990s were also privy to increased access to information and closer contact with their urban *hadhar* counterparts. While their parents and grandparents had lived in tents, the young generation of tribal Kuwaitis lived in houses and attended public schools with *hadhar*, although there was informal segregation among them in the schoolyard:

> Interviewee: They used to be in groups. Literally. You'd see them sitting as a group. This is the Awazim. When you'd say hi . . . 'Hi Awazim,' you know? . . . You have the Ajman there, you have the Mutran. All of them were in groups.[9]

A combination of greater exposure, a sense of national ownership in Kuwait, and frustration over old ways of politics set the stage for protests in 2011. These protests continue to have important reverberations in Kuwaiti politics.

2011 Protests in Kuwait: The Orange Movement and Electoral Politics Demonstrations

Scholars continue to debate the extent to which protests that began in December 2010 in Tunisia 'diffused' throughout the Middle East. However, Kuwaitis generally consider these protests as distinct from those that took place in Kuwait during the same time period. In many ways, they were a follow on from Kuwait's Orange Movement in 2006. This movement, comprised mainly of young educated activists, called for electoral reform and an end to corruption in Kuwait's government. These protests in the downtown area of Kuwait City, as Kuwaitis point out, called for reform and the resignation of corrupt officials, not the fall of the regime. In addition, the strong tribal politics upon which the 2011 protests in Kuwait were grounded bear little resemblance to those in Tunisia or Egypt. Public protests, while uncommon in Kuwait, have occurred in the past, and have continued after 2011 as well.

The 2011 protests in Kuwait began after a celebration of the twentieth anniversary of Kuwait's liberation from Iraq. To commemorate the occasion,

Kuwait's Emir announced a government payout of 1,000 KD to every citizen and a grant guaranteeing their free access to essential food items for a year. This grant was the largest in Kuwait's history.[10] However, it excluded the stateless *bidoon*, who protested on 19 February 2011. Demonstrations in Kuwait escalated through the summer and autumn of 2011 after news of a corruption scandal involving sixteen MPs who allegedly took bribes in return for supporting government policies.[11] The *bidoon* were joined by youth and tribal opposition movements who called for the resignation of Prime Minister Nasser al-Sabah (a nephew of the Emir). Leaders of the Kuwait Democratic Front, including Ahmed al-Khatib, Jasem al-Qatami and Abdullah al-Nibari, also supported the protest, including through the liberal *al-Talia* newspaper. Protesters gathered in al-Erada Square and on Gulf Road, which runs along the southern edge of Kuwait Bay. These protests were met with force and, in some cases, protesters were detained.[12] On 16 November 2011, a group of protesters and prominent MPs forced their way into parliament and demanded the Prime Minister step down. In response to this public pressure, Sheikh Nasser was forced to resign on 28 November 2011.

The 2011 protests had lingering political effects in Kuwait. Two of the MPs who participated in the storming of parliament, Jamaan al-Harbash and Waleed Tabtabaie, were re-elected in 2016, but sentenced to jail time in 2017 (and a reduced sentence in 2018) after which they fled the country. In October 2018, Kuwait's parliament voted to grant them immunity and allowed both to return to Kuwait and remain in parliament. However, in December 2018 the Constitutional Court ruled that article 16 of the parliament's bylaws was unconstitutional, claiming that parliament lacked the authority to grant such immunity. As a way to avoid a constitutional crisis, the parliament voted to remove Harbash and Tabtabaie in January 2019.[13]

Tribal and Islamist opposition candidates gained a majority in the February 2012 parliamentary elections, winning thirty-four of the parliament's fifty seats with 60 per cent voter turnout. However, Kuwait's Constitutional Court ruled these elections invalid in a surprise July 2012 decision. As a result, the December 2011 parliament was re-instituted, but failed to achieve a quorum when it tried to convene twice in the summer of 2012 due to MP boycotts. The government then asking the Constitutional Court to rule on the validity of amendments to the electoral law that would redraw Kuwait's electoral districts. On 25 September 2012, the court rejected the proposed changes.[14] On 7 October 2012, the Emir dissolved parliament once again. On 19 October, he decreed that each Kuwaiti would have one vote for minister of parliament in the upcoming elections, rather than the four they had enjoyed up until that point.[15]

The dissolution of parliament and change to a one-person one-vote system had deep political effects for kinship-based groups in Kuwait. When kinship group members had enjoyed four votes, they could cast one for the candidate chosen by the tribe or family, and the other three for different candidates they preferred. A reduction to one vote, however, meant that this diversified voting scheme was no longer possible. Tribes and families would be under increased pressure to convince members to use their one vote on the chosen candidate. The shift to one vote, in other words, changed fundamentally the political incentives of kinship group members. It increased the difficulty kinship groups faced to maintain a united voting constituency.

One of the leaders of the demonstrations was an MP named Musallem al-Barrak. Al-Barrak was a member of the Mutair tribe, but had established himself through working in Kuwait's *baladiyas* (municipalities) and labour unions. His background was tribal, but his influence came as a result of membership in non-kinship-based associations. Al-Barrak was elected to the Kuwaiti parliament for the first time in 1996. In both that year and in 2012, he set records for the highest number of votes received by a candidate in elections. However, during the protests against electoral changes, al-Barrak made a speech that was interpreted as insulting the Emir, a violation of Kuwaiti law. Al-Barrak was arrested, released on bail, and sentenced to two years in prison in 2015.[16]

The sentence not only sent a message to others who would challenge the leadership itself, but also removed al-Barrak temporarily from the political playing field, giving the royal family time to manage the discontent within Kuwaiti society. At the same time, it angered members of al-Barrak's tribe, the Mutair. They felt that the government's decision to target al-Barrack was discriminatory against tribal Kuwaitis like the Mutair that he represented. They also believed it was based on guilt by association between al-Barrak and the oppositional figure Sheikh Ahmed al-Fahd al-Sabah.

To quell the protests, Kuwait's Emir and senior members of the ruling family reached out personally to prominent tribal leaders. Rather than using bureaucratic means, they appealed to the power of kinship authority. Their objective was to secure an end to the electoral boycott and in the process, break the opposition coalition. These efforts were ultimately successful. Several tribal sheikhs met personally with the Emir in October 2012. Following the meeting, they spoke out against the protests and issued statements of support for the Emir.[17]

Al-Barrak, however, remained in prison. In 2016, snap elections announced in October but held in November ensured that al-Barrak could not run for parliament since he remained in jail. A July 2016 law directed at al-Barrak also excluded anyone convicted of insulting the Emir from holding a seat in parliament. Nonetheless, opposition MPs captured almost half of the parliament's seats and held a series of grillings of cabinet members during parliament sessions. The pressure of these grillings, which included multiple interrogations of Prime Minister Jaber al-Mubarak al-Sabah, led to a cabinet reshuffle in October 2017. However, grillings persisted following the reshuffle.

The demonstrations and the tone of political rhetoric surrounding them are examples of how the governing salience of kinship authority has continued to exist in Kuwait. When existing manifestations of kinship authority were challenged via changes to the electoral system, members of tribal groups banded together to resist these changes. The government, though holding bureaucratic authority in the state, was forced to respond. At stake in the conflict was not only preservation of benefits to the tribe but the system of benefits provision itself. After a dip in oil prices in 2015 kept state patronage limited, these negotiations remained an ongoing facet of Kuwaiti politics and those in other states where kinship has governing salience. Kuwaiti interviewees, when asked their hopes for Kuwait's future, mentioned frequently the issue of corruption and government reform as the most important issues facing the country.

Qatar

Leadership Transitions in the Al Thani Family

Emir Ahmad bin Ali Al Thani ruled Qatar from 1960 until 1972 when he was deposed by his cousin Khalifa Al Thani. Kinship politics played strongly in this deposition. Khalifa's father Hamad bin Abdullah had died in 1948 when Khalifa was only sixteen. Ahmad, Khalifa's cousin, was made ruler but attempted to shift succession from Khalifa to his own son Abdelaziz. Khalifa seized power in 1972 on the grounds that Ahmad's plan for succession violated a 1949 agreement specifying Khalifa as successor.[18] As Emir, Khalifa played a deeply involved role in the modernisation and development of Qatar, involving himself closely in many aspects of state building and consolidating control over the state's financial resources.[19] Under his rule, the size of Qatar's military increased and Qatar began offering citizens public housing incentives and pensions. Qatar University, established in 1973, provided public education as well as a pipeline to jobs in the Qatari government bureaucracy.[20] The jump in oil prices between 1975 and 1985 also helped to greatly expand Qatar's bureaucracy. While Qatar's government had 10,250 employees in 1974, this number expanded to 29,329 by 1984.[21]

During his reign, Khalifa delegated his son Hamad as his successor, angering Ahmad and his family who claimed the two branches of the Al Thani family had concluded a deal to alternate power between them. Rather than leave the succession question open following his death, Khalifa groomed his son for leadership, allowing him to appoint a cabinet and run Qatar's daily affairs.[22] By the time he was forced to abdicate on 27 June 1995, Khalifa had ensured that the fate he had enacted on Ahmad would not be returned in kind.

Hamad bin Khalifa began his rule in 1995 but had consolidated power throughout the 1990s through cabinet reshuffles and the sidelining of potential successors. To prevent threats to his rule, he instituted a new constitution in 2003 which guaranteed that only his sons could succeed him as Emir.[23] Similarly to Sultan Qaboos, Hamad used his training at Sandhurst to swiftly tamp down a 1996 counter-coup led by Hamad bin Jasem, the chief of police at the time.[24] Rumours about Saudi and Emirati support for the coup have fed animosity between Qatar and its regional neighbours. Kinship politics during the coup continue to impact Qatari domestic politics as well. One subset of the al-Murrah tribe, the al-Ghufran, supported the Emir, and as a result were persecuted following the change in leadership.[25] In 2004, a decree from the Ministry of Interior stripped 5,266 people of Qatari citizenship and was targeted at supporters of the former Emir. Qatar argued that these individuals were Saudi, not Qatari citizens.[26] The government also began deportation proceedings against those affected.[27] The al-Ghafir tribe continues to advocate in international fora, including the UNHCR, for Qatar to grant them citizenship, and Qatar continues to pursue the tribe. In 2017, Qatar revoked the citizenship of the sheikh of the al-Murrah tribe, Taleb bin Lahom bin Shreim.[28]

Qatar and the 2011 Protests

Qatar experienced little unrest during the 2011 Arab uprisings, and virtually no unified demands from its citizens. Its decades-long embrace of Muslim Brotherhood leaders, including controversial Egyptian Muslim Brotherhood theologian Yusuf al-Qaradawi, gave it connections to Islamist opposition movements throughout the region. These Brotherhood leaders in Qatar were accommodated with the unspoken understanding that they would not comment on Qatari politics, removing prospects of an Islamist-led opposition to the Qatari leadership.[29] Qatar also gave support to pro-democracy actors in Egypt and Tunisia, and weapons and training to opposition militias in Libya.[30] These measures aligned Qatar's government with opposition movements rather than the leaderships that had drawn the ire of Arab publics across the Middle East. In 2011, it also announced that elections for the Shura Council would be held in 2013 as a means of encouraging citizen participation in politics through official channels. These elections, which had been postponed in 2008, were again postponed until October 2021.

In June 2013, King Hamad abdicated in favour of his son Tamim bin Hamad. Tamim had long been the heir apparent though the timing of the transition had not been foreseen, especially given that Tamim was only thirty-three at the time. Fromherz analyses the transition as an attempt to reduce internal political discord and foster confidence in Tamim's rule through a peaceful transition of power.[31]

Sheikh Tamim and the Gulf Crisis of 2017

Sheikh Tamim oversaw a Qatar which continued its rise to regional prominence despite isolation by Saudi Arabia and its allies. In March 2014, Saudi Arabia, the United Arab Emirates, Bahrain and Egypt withdrew their ambassadors from Qatar. In Syria's bloody domestic conflict, many Gulf countries, including Qatar, invested heavily in opposition militias. Qatar's support for groups antagonistic to its regional allies further exacerbated tensions. In May 2017, the Qatar News Agency was hacked by unknown entities, which Qatar and other governments suspected were linked with the UAE. The hackers posted fake quotations from Sheikh Tamim, which were carried on Saudi and Emirate media minutes after they were posted with well-prepared commentators ready to offer their anti-Qatar analysis. Days later, leaked emails between the Emirate Ambassador to the United States appeared on the Al Jazeera network, whose international headquarters are in Doha.[32] Saudi Arabia and its allies considered the leaks a retaliation and a provocation by a state a fraction of its size attempting to embarrass the Kingdom. It responded by escalating the situation.

Between 5 and 6 June 2017, Saudi Arabia, the UAE, Yemen, Egypt, the Maldives and Bahrain announced they were cutting ties with Qatar. Saudi Arabia closed its border with Qatar and, in August 2018, announced the construction of a canal to turn the country into an island rather than a peninsula. Qatar Airways flights were not permitted to fly in the airspace of many Arabian Peninsula countries and Saudi Arabia pressured banks in the Kingdom not to trade in Qatari riyals. On 1 January 2018, Qatar announced that it would leave the Organization of Petroleum Exporting Countries.[33] The fracture remained until January 2021, when Saudi Arabia and its allies agreed to lift restrictions on Qatar's access to joint maritime borders and regional airspace at a Gulf Cooperation Council (GCC) summit in al-Ula. Saudi Arabia announced soon thereafter that it would re-open its embassy in Doha.[34]

Oman

Oman throughout the 1990s was less isolated than it had been under Sa'id bin Taymur.[35] Its strong relationship with Britain remained an important aspect of its foreign policy. However, Oman maintained neutrality and was reluctant to push for greater integration among the states of the GCC, founded in 1981. As a country which produced less oil and had less security capabilities than its neighbours, Oman often advocated for its self-interest as opposed to greater integration among the GCC states. This integration would have favoured stronger states like Saudi Arabia, rather than Oman.[36] Despite reticence over GCC integration, however, Oman pursued bilateral relations with historic partners like the United Arab Emirates and India. It also maintained close ties with Iran, serving as a regional (and eventually international) mediator. Oman also pursued relations with Israel, leading to a 1994 meeting between Sultan Qaboos and Prime Minister Yitzhak Rabin, and a meeting with Prime Minister Shimon Peres in 1996, and with Prime Minister Binyamin Netanyahu in 2018.

2011 Protests in Oman

On 17 January 2011, roughly 200 Omanis protested rising commodity prices and government corruption outside the Ministry of Housing. These demonstrations were followed by other small protests over subsequent days. After organising on social media, the first of a series of 'Green Marches' took place on 8 February, with a second ten days later on 18 February. The latter culminated in the handing over of a petition to the Diwan of the Royal Court. Similar to Kuwait, the protests targeted corrupt government officials rather than the head of state himself.[37]

A few small protests continued in Muscat as well as the northern city of Sohar, during which police killed two protestors.[38] Sultan Qaboos replaced the chief of police as well as six cabinet members in response to the protests.[39] However, these replacements came from influential families just as their predecessors had. In addition to the cabinet shuffle, the Sultan promised 50,000 new jobs, unemployment benefits, and a stipend for students. These concessions were targeted at youth protestors rather than particular kinship groups. The issue at stake, in other words, was not the tribal politics of the country but perceptions of corruption by the general public. Over time, the protestors' demands had shifted from being anti-corruption to targeting specific corrupt individual ministers. Whereas in Kuwait protestors has been upset with systems of kinship-based patronage (particularly those from which they did not benefit), Omanis were upset about individuals taking wealth for themselves. Protestors did not come from any particular kinship background, though protests tended to take place in cities rather than non-urban areas. The instrumentalised salience of kinship authority in Oman continued to manifest itself throughout these protests.

Interviewees in Oman identified two major hopes for the Sultanate's future. The first related to provision of basic welfare. Omanis called for more access to jobs and housing for citizens of the Sultanate. Many interviewees called for continuing to build up Oman's institutions of higher education, but given that many of them were themselves enrolled in such institutions, this viewpoint may well have been overrepresented among them compared to the general population. Omanis also called for greater international recognition of the country and its contributions. While Oman's critical role in brokering the 2015 Iran nuclear deal helped raise its international profile, Omanis wished for more recognition and integration into international politics for a Sultanate known traditionally as 'the Hermit Kingdom'. Taken together, all of these statements reflect those made by citizens of a bureaucratic state. They do not appear to reflect an expectation that a kinship group should provide access or a solution for these needs. Even when low oil prices in the mid-2010s strained government resource provision in Oman, there is little evidence that the salience of kinship changed in a significant way. Rather, it retained instrumentalised political salience while the bureaucratic institutions of the state remained the preferred means of resources access and distribution.

Since the 2011 protests, Oman's government has continued its 'Omanisation' policy of replacing expatriates in the public and private sector with Omani employees. It has also invested heavily in its tourism economy in order to create jobs for Omanis. In addition, municipal elections in December 2016 provided an outlet for political frustrations. Turnover in these elections was high, indicating the ongoing nature of addressing Omani citizens' concerns.

Following a long battle with cancer, Sultan Qaboos died on 11 January 2020. His successor, the sixty-six-year-old Haitham bin Tareq Al Said (and Qaboos' first cousin) was appointed overnight in a highly orchestrated bid to ensure domestic stability and signal Oman's ongoing role as a mediator in the Gulf region. In the months following his succession, Sultan Haitham announced his intention to continue economic reforms and address unemployment in Oman, including announcing an end to water and electricity subsidies.[40] He also designated Oman's first Crown Prince, his son Dhi Yazan bin Haitham, further consolidating dynastic rule in the Sultanate.

Protests in Kuwait had a stronger familial element than those in Oman. These differences should be read as a reflection of pre-existing conditions rather than motivating factors for the protests themselves. Kinship politics did not cause the protests, but they are nonetheless reflected in the make-up of some major protest constituencies. At the same time, the political solutions to protestors' grievances across the region will require engagement with kinship groups, which are major players in their respective societies. Understanding how these groups interact differently with governments in different cases can provide important insights into how the effects of the 2011 protests will continue to shape politics in the Middle East, particularly after new rounds of protests in Algeria and Sudan in 2019 deposed heads of state in societies where kinship plays a political role as well.

Notes

1. 'Summary and despatch from Mr S. Falle, Kuwait, to Secretary of State for Foreign Affairs, London 30 April 1970, "Revolution in Kuwait: Why, How, When, and its Effect on our Interests"', *Records of Kuwait 1966–1971: 1970*, ed. Anita Burdett (Cambridge, UK: Cambridge Archive Editions, 2003): 15; 'Summary and despatch from Mr A. J. Wilton, HM Ambassador to Kuwait, to Secretary of State for Foreign Affairs, 14 March 1971, "Second Thoughts About Kuwait" [FCO 8/1655]', *Records of Kuwait 1966–1971: 1971*, 3.
2. 'Car Bomber Fails in Attempt to Kill Leader of Kuwait', *New York Times*, 26 May 1985, http://www.nytimes.com/1985/05/26/world/car-bomber-fails-in-attempt-to-kill-leader-of-kuwait.html.
3. Judith Miller, 'War in the Gulf: The Royal Family; Kuwait's Joy Tempered by Rift Over Absolutism', *New York Times*, 28 February 1991, http://www.nytimes.com/1991/02/28/world/war-in-the-gulf-the-royal-family-kuwait-s-joy-tempered-by-rift-over-absolutism.html.
4. Shafeeq Ghabra, 'Kuwait and the Dynamics of Socio-Economic Change', *Middle East Journal* 51 no. 3 (Summer 1997): 361.
5. 'The Bedoons of Kuwait: Citizens Without Citizenship', *Human Rights Watch*, August 1995, https://www.hrw.org/reports/1995/Kuwait.htm.
6. Claire Beaugrand, 'Biduns in the Face of Radicalization in Kuwait', *Arab Gulf States Institute in Washington*, 18 August 2015, http://www.agsiw.org/biduns-in-the-face-of-radicalization-in-kuwait/.
7. Miller, 'War in the Gulf'.
8. Miller, 'War in the Gulf'.
9. Interview, Salmiya, Kuwait, 6 March 2014.
10. 'Kuwaiti Ruler Grants $4 Bln, Free Food to Citizens', *al-Arabiya*, 17 January 2011, https://english.alarabiya.net/articles/2011/01/17/133805.html.
11. Kristian Coates Ulrichsen, 'Kuwait; Political Crisis at Critical Juncture', *BBC*, 23 October 2012, http://www.bbc.com/news/world-middle-east-20026581.
12. Sami Aboudi, 'Kuwait Protests Challenge Ruling Family', *Reuters*, 24 October 2012, https://www.reuters.com/article/us-kuwait-politics/kuwait-protests-challenge-ruling-family-idUSBRE89N0MS20121024.
13. 'Kuwait: National Assembly Announces Vacancy of Two Convicted MPs' Seats', *Asharq al-Awsat*, 31 January 2019, https://aawsat.com/english/home/

article/1570261/kuwait-national-assembly-announces-vacancy-two-convicted-mps-seats.

14. Ulrichsen, 'Kuwait'.

15. Ulrichsen, 'Kuwait'.

16. Habib Toumi, 'Kuwait's Highest Court Upholds Two-Year Jail for Al Barrak', *Gulf News*, 18 May 2015, http://gulfnews.com/news/gulf/kuwait/kuwait-s-highest-court-upholds-two-year-jail-for-al-barrak-1.1513094.

17. 'Tribal Leaders Re-Affirm Allegiance to HH Amir, Reject Violence', *Kuwait News Agency (KUNA)*, 21 October 2012, https://www.kuna.net.kw/ArticleDetails.aspx?id=2269731&Language=en.

18. Allen J. Fromherz, *Qatar: A Modern History, Updated Edition* (Washington, DC: Georgetown University Press, 2017): 79.

19. Fromherz, *Qatar* (2017), 78.

20. Fromherz, *Qatar* (2017), 80.

21. Abdallah Yousef Al-Maliki, 'Public Administration in the State of Qatar: Origin, Development, Problems, and Current Directions', PhD dissertation, Golden Gate University, 1989: 74–5.

22. 'Smooth Qatar Handover Rooted in Turbulent Past of "Father Emir"', *Reuters*, 3 July 2013, https://www.voanews.com/a/smooth-qatar-handover-rooted-in-turbulent-past-of-father-emir/1694301.html.

23. Mehran Kamrava, *Qatar: Small State, Big Politics* (Ithaca, NY: Cornell University Press, 2015): 117.

24. Fromherz, *Qatar* (2017), 85–6.

25. One account claims 119 members of the al-Ghufran were part of the counter-coup against Emir Hamad bin Khalifa. See 'Qatar', *Institute on Statelessness and Inclusion, Rights Realization Centre & Global Campaign for Equal Nationality Rights*, 4 October 2019, http://www.institutesi.org/UPR33_Qatar.pdf: 6.

26. 'Qatari Tribe Accuses Authorities of Systematic Repression', *Gulf News*, 18 September 2017, https://gulfnews.com/news/gulf/qatar/qatar-crisis/qatari-tribe-accuses-authorities-of-systematic-repression-1.2092012.

27. 'Human Rights Violations in Qatar: Al-Ghufran Family', *Arab Federation for Human Rights*, February 2018, http://arabfhr.org/wp-content/uploads/2018/03/Qatar-Ghufran-Feb-2018-Final.pdf: 5.

28. 'Head of al-Murrah Tribe Confirms Qatar Revokes Family's Citizenship', *al-Arabiya*, 14 September 2017, http://english.alarabiya.net/en/features/2017/09/14/Head-of-al-Marri-tribe-confirms-Qatar-revokes-family-s-citizenship.html.

29. Kristian Coates Ulrichsen, 'Qatar and the Arab Spring: Policy Drivers and Regional Implications', *Carnegie Endowment for International Peace*, 24 September 2014, https://carnegieendowment.org/2014/09/24/qatar-and-arab-spring-policy-drivers-and-regional-implications-pub-56723.

30. Shadi Hamid, 'There Aren't Protests in Qatar – So Why Did the Emir Just Announce Elections?', *The Atlantic*, 1 November 2011, https://www.theatlantic.com/international/archive/2011/11/there-arent-protests-in-qatar-so-why-did-the-emir-just-announce-elections/247661/.

31. Fromherz, *Qatar* (2017), 125.

32. David D. Kirkpatrick and Sheera Frankel, 'Hacking in Qatar Highlights a Shift Toward Espionage-for-Hire', *New York Times*, 8 June 2017, https://www.nytimes.com/2017/06/08/world/middleeast/qatar-cyberattack-espionage-for-hire.html.

33. Marc Champion, 'Qatar's Departure from OPEC Suggests Gulf Rights is Here to Stay', *Bloomberg*, 3 December 2018, https://www.bloomberg.com/news/articles/2018-12-03/qatar-s-departure-from-opec-suggests-gulf-rift-is-here-to-stay.

34. Agence France-Presse, 'Saudi FM Says Embassy to Reopen in Qatar Within Days', *Voice of America*, 16 January 2021, https://www.voanews.com/middle-east/saudi-fm-says-embassy-reopen-qatar-within-days.

35. For a description of politics in Oman during this time, see Uzi Rabi, *The Emergence of States in a Tribal Society: Oman Under Sa'id bin Taymur 1932–1970* (Brighton, UK: Sussex Academic Press, 2006).

36. Calvin H. Allen and W. Lynn Rigsbee II, *Oman Under Qaboos: From Coup to Constitution, 1970–1996* (New York, NY: Routledge, 2013): 187.

37. James Worral, 'Oman: The "Forgotten" Corner of the Arab Spring', *Middle East Policy Council* 19 no. 3 (Fall 2012): 98–115.

38. 'Oman Police Kill Two Protestors', *Reuters*, 27 February 2011, http://www.reuters.com/article/us-oman-protests-idUSTRE71Q0U420110227.

39. Saleh al-Shaibany, 'Sultan Qaboos Fires Oman's Police Chief', *The National*, 15 March 2011, http://www.thenational.ae/news/world/middle-east/sultan-qaboos-fires-omans-police-chief.

40. Tawfiq Nasrallah, 'Oman to Phase Out Water and Electricity Subsidies in 5 Years', *Gulf News*, 21 December 2020, https://gulfnews.com/world/gulf/oman/oman-to-phase-out-water-and-electricity-subsidies-in-5-years-1.1608504634277.

9

CONCLUSION:
KINSHIP POLITICS IN
COMPARATIVE PERSPECTIVE

While the cases presented in this book are Arab Gulf states, the underlying mechanisms of the model extend beyond these countries. Two examples in particular – Somaliland and Iran – provide empirical grounding to the model. They also illustrate the analytical leverage of the model in a real-world context, and one which extends beyond the Arab Gulf states.

Somaliland: Governing Salience after State Building

Somalia is a state outside the Gulf region, but one which meets the scope conditions of the analysis. In particular, the protectorate of British Somaliland fell under British colonial authority and eventually used infrastructure construction and the extension of bureaucracy as part of the state-building process. Furthermore, the protectorate was characterised by the imposition of impersonal governance, resulting from colonial establishment of a centralised government. Finally, kinship groups in British Somaliland were, albeit at the lower levels of organisation, based on common descent from real ancestors. These ties remained salient after the state-building process. The 'state-building' period in Somaliland, for the purposes of this shadow case, refers to the period between British colonialism in the 1930s through the disbandment of Siad Barre's Somali Revolutionary Socialist Party in 1976.

In Somaliland, access to water resources before state building was competitive. During state building, both the British and Somaliland governments attempted to impose bureaucratic initiatives, but kinship authority instrumentalised this bureaucracy. As a result, kinship authority after state building had governing salience.

Somaliland before State Building

Somaliland was ruled in the nineteenth century by a series of Sultans but eventually fell under the colonial control of Britain and Italy. British Somaliland was established in 1888 in the northern part of the territory. Throughout the 1880s, Italy signed a series of treaties with the Sultans in central and southern Somaliland, creating the protectorate of Italian Somaliland. In the Second World War, Britain occupied Italian Somaliland and, following the war, it fell under British military administration. In 1949, the United Nations granted Italy a trusteeship of Italian Somaliland under which Italy would prepare Somaliland for independence by 1960. On 1 July 1960, this trusteeship merged with British Somaliland to form an independent Somalia.

Access to water resources in British Somaliland before state building was competitive, particularly during the drought season. This scarcity posed a problem for both pastoral nomads and farmers living in the territory. During the rainy season, however, surface water was available and in the central Ogo region, deep wells provided sufficient resources for families and livestock alike.[1] Families in Somaliland were a unit of subsistence – they had herds consisting of sheep, goats and camels. These families were pastoral but lived together and cooperated to dig wells and meet other joint needs.[2] Control of grazing lands was a function of strength and the kinship group's ability to maintain its position against others.[3] The non-urban populations who inhabited these lands herded either sheep and goats, or camels. The camel-herding populations lived in what Lewis calls 'nomadic hamlets'. These hamlets contained between three and six nuclear families and were led by the eldest man of the majority family. Boys began learning camel husbandry at the age of seven or eight and continued to work with camels until marriage.[4]

Political kinship in Somaliland was usually based on patrilineal descent but in some cases was matrilineal as well.[5] As in the Gulf states, clans could also be comprised of a federation of kinship groups.[6] Kinship authority regulated relations between groups by enforcing norms and informal rules of behaviour. At a lower level, certain kinship groups committed to each other, via contract, to make a blood payment in the event the member of one group killed a member of another. At higher levels, elder councils mediated disputes in an ad hoc council called a *shir*. As the *shir* was an ad hoc assembly, it had no standing committees and was dissolved as soon as the dispute was resolved.[7] It constituted a set of unwritten laws and was motivated by the principle that individual liability was shared collectively among the kinship group.[8] As Samatar explains: 'Intra-Somali conflicts were resolved either through negotiation or at spearpoint.'[9] At larger inter-clan conferences, elders might be supported by advisors, but no permanent proto-bureaucratic structure existed.[10] Members of the *shir* drew authority and claimed expertise from their personal status rather than that given to them by the *shir*. In addition, an 'escort' system existed by which one kinship group's caravan could travel through an area controlled by another kinship group on its way to trade with coastal merchants. The caravan would be 'guided' by an escort (*abaan*), whose kinship status held leverage with those who controlled the area.[11]

Kinship authority before state building in Somaliland was the basis of a complex system of relations within and among kinship groups. As state building began, this system constrained the government's patterns of outreach in the form of infrastructure and bureaucratic governance. The result was that kinship salience retained governing salience in Somaliland after state building.

State Building in Somaliland

The British played a strong role in the building of infrastructure and imposition of bureaucratic governance in Somaliland. Despite their attempts to diminish kinship authority however, it ultimately instrumentalised bureaucratic authority. Competitive resource access constrained their ability to diminish kinship authority, which instead reasserted itself throughout the state-building process.

Stage One: Infrastructure

In the 1930s, the British began a programme of water boring and conservation to support pastoral populations in the colony. They also improved security and communication in non-urban areas. These improvements had the effect of rendering the kinship-based *abaan* escort system obsolete since traders could now conduct business in the interior itself and drive the herds they purchased to the coast.[12] The bureaucratic state gained control over access to vital limited resources and political access. Nonetheless, kinship groups still existed in the colony and managed their affairs through kinship authority.

Stage Two: Bureaucracy

Pre-existing kinship authority constrained two facets of British colonial development in Somaliland. First, the British divided political districts according to pre-existing clan territories. These delineations were a reflection of the kinship-based allocation of resources (territory and the water within these territories). Second, the British reached out to clan elders directly, signing treaties with many of them. While these elders often opposed colonial initiatives such as taxation of the pastoral population, many later became members of the British colonial administration, ensuring that state patronage was distributed in ways favourable to their clan.[13] Thus the kinship-based arrangements of resource allocation that pre-dated British state building reasserted themselves by instrumentalising bureaucratic authority.

Kinship authority in British Somaliland sometimes endured British attempts to diminish it. For example, the British tried to establish schools in which Somali would be the language of instruction. However, local opponents argued that this instruction would diminish the importance of Arabic, and more importantly, would reduce the status of non-Somali-speaking tribes. As a result of this opposition, the educational policy was never implemented. By the end of the 1930s, only one elementary school existed in the country.[14]

Stage Three: Nationalism

British and Italian Somaliland united to form the Somali Republic in 1960. In 1969, the Republic's president, Abdirashid Ali Shermarke, was killed by his bodyguard and Major General Mohamed Siad Barre became the leader of the independent Somali Democratic Republic. Barre governed on a principle of 'scientific socialism' in an attempt to diminish kinship authority. Nonetheless, he was constrained by strong clan opposition to his rule, including from his own clan.[15] In 1975, half of Barre's twenty-member Supreme Revolutionary Council (SRC) were from the same clan-family (Darood) as himself.[16] Despite his attempts to impose bureaucracy, kinship authority remained salient. Despite the ideas of scientific socialism, Barre governed through a cult of personality. Some at the time referred to Somaliland's government by the initials MOD, which stood for the names of the three clans from which Barre, his mother, and his son-in-law originated.[17] Despite attempts to create a secular form of nationalism, Barre was constrained by the strong influence of kinship groups in Somaliland.

Somalia after State Building

Expansion of the bureaucratic state in Somalia had mixed success. Following independence, Siad Barre began a programme of expanding public infrastructure in an attempt to build up the Somali state as a socialist society. Education opportunities grew alongside a literacy campaign. The government also oversaw the development of agricultural and fishing projects as the basis of economic growth, although this effort proved unsuccessful.[18]

Barre took an antagonistic approach toward kinship, eliminating codes allocating water, land and grazing rights to clans.[19] Effigies of 'tribalism' were burned and blood payments were made illegal.[20] Barre also ordered Somalis to address each other as 'comrade' rather than 'cousin', and forbade asking about clan affiliation. Somalis, however, circumvented this attempt to impose bureaucratic authority by asking each other about 'former' clan affiliation.[21] Barre himself continued to use kinship authority, manipulating his existing kinship ties and requesting personal favours from senior officials. Often, he gave preference to members of his own Darood clan.[22] Other political elites used kinship as a way to access state resources and as a patronage network.[23] Ultimately, Bradbury concludes that 'the kinship system remains an important feature of Somali social, political, and economic life despite more than forty years of state-building'.[24]

Despite attempts to degrade the political salience of kinship authority in Somalia, it remained a primary means for non-urban populations to access resources and political power. Competitive access to resources that existed prior to state building shaped outreach and state building by both the British colonial government and that of Siad Barre. As a result, kinship authority remained salient in the country following the state-building process.

Iran: Instrumentalised Salience after State Building

Access to vital limited resources in Iran was cooperative and state building instrumentalised the salience of kinship authority. As bureaucratic power expanded, rulers instrumentalised non-urban proto-bureaucracies, embedding them into the bureaucratic governing apparatus. Proto-bureaucratic institutions pre-dating state building were the basis of bureaucratic extension that instrumentalised kinship authority during the state-building period. Throughout a tumultuous state-building period marked by a series of coups and transitions of leadership – many initiated by Western states – authority over these institutions was decentralised but bureaucratic in nature. As a result, kinship authority today has instrumentalised political salience in Iran.

Iranian state building occurred under a heavy British influence. British interest in Persia was originally based on trade interests. However, in the twentieth century Britain intervened repeatedly and more directly in Iranian politics with an eye on the area's oil reserves. After a 1905 revolution which established a parliament and imposed a constitution on Persia's leader, Mozaffar ad-Din Shah, the British signed the Anglo-Russian convention of 1907. This agreement between Britain and Russia denied Persian autonomy over territory it had controlled for centuries. It also helped Britain solidify the monarchy's stability despite the objection of many Persians who sought a constitutional state. Tribes also played an important role in protecting the monarchy from these constitutionalists. While the monarchy reached out to these tribes for protection, the British also reached out to them in order to gain access to oil, going so far as to design plans for a tribal 'statelet' in the centre-south of Iran.[25]

Iran before State Building

Access to resources in Iran was cooperative. Water flowed to villages and towns via channels called *qanat*, which are the technological predecessor of the Omani *aflaj*.[26] While major cities, including the capital Tehran, obtained water from *qanat* until after the Second World War, the *qanat* have played a continuously important role in the political organisation of non-urban areas too.[27] The men in charge of constructing these *qanat* were known as *muqanni* and they passed down their skill set orally from father to son.[28] In addition to constructing *qanat*, the *muqanni* were also responsible for their cleaning and maintenance.[29]

The people in Iran's villages and towns were organised into a group called a *buneh*, a multi-family collective which allocated resources among themselves. Given limited resources, this collective approach allowed the different families of the *buneh* to benefit by pooling their resources. Administration of the *buneh* was proto-bureaucratic. Landowners chose a *sarBuneh* or *abyar* to manage the *buneh* with the help of an administrative staff of four or five assistants. The *sarBuneh* was responsible for distributing land, assigning crops to each farmer and coordinating irrigation of the farmland. In addition, the *muqanni* who built *qanat* were employed by the *sarBuneh* when their services were required.[30] Larger towns and villages employed a *mirab* to keep track of water shares, which were traded similarly to the *athar* in Oman. These officials were village members and their position was usually permanent.[31]

In 1921, the British helped engineer a coup that brought Reza Shah Pahlavi to the throne. Abrahamian notes that Reza Shah 'took over a country with a ramshackle administration and left it with a highly centralized state'.[32] Britain aided in this regard, throwing its support behind the new Shah during tribal rebellions in 1924 and 1929. With this British support, and through the creation of infrastructure, the Pahlavi state was able to extend its power into the periphery in order to disarm and settle tribes.[33]

Iran during State Building

Upon his rise to power, Reza Shah instituted bureaucratic governance. This process involved embedding existing proto-bureaucratic institutions into the state's governing apparatus. As a result of these changes, the bureaucratic state diminished, embedded and instrumentalised kinship authority.

Stage One: Infrastructure

Upon coming to power, Reza Shah divided Iran's eight provinces into fifteen, each with counties, municipalities and rural districts. Regional governors and town mayors were no longer semi-independent, but rather were appointed by the Interior Minister in consultation with the Shah.[34] The Shah also instituted a patronage system which offered jobs, salaries and pensions to workers and members of the military, which expanded rapidly under his rule.[35] The

Shah built up an army of over 100,000, began construction of a trans-Iranian railroad in 1927, and built thousands of miles of roads.[36] Revenues from oil royalties, tax delinquents, customs duties and consumer goods taxes funded these projects.[37] By creating this infrastructure, Iran's central government gained greater control over access to resources and influence in the country.

Stage Two: Bureaucracy

In 1932, Reza Shah instituted a programme to increase the power of bureaucracy and instrumentalise kinship authority. The programme allowed the government to claim eminent domain over private agricultural land in exchange for barren land or other compensation. It also allowed the government to claim water rights. Whereas in the past tribal fighting power had been important to the protection of the regime, the bureaucratic state's acquisition of military technology shifted power away from these kinship groups. The Shah also forcibly sedentarised nomadic tribes, and set out to 'disarm, pacify, conscript, and, in some cases, "civilize"' tribe members.[38] While these changes bred resentment among tribal populations, they were made possible by a bureaucratic state that embedded local proto-bureaucratic institutions into national state governance. With these measures, the Shah reduced the power and influence of tribal leaders by gaining control over access to vital limited resources.[39]

After a lack of sufficient support for the war effort, the British forced the Shah to abdicate in favour of his son, Mohammad Reza Pahlavi, in September 1941. After the elected Prime Minister, Mohammed Mossadegh, nationalised Iran's oil in 1951, Britain and the United States engineered a coup in 1953 in which Mossadegh was overthrown. In 1963, Mohammed Reza began a series of reforms known as the White Revolution, intended to strengthen the power of non-urban populations which supported the Pahlavi dynasty against urban upper-class families who were increasingly opposed to it. These reforms included the creation of a Department of Land Reform and land redistribution programmes. Non-urban groups now interacted with government officials in this department instead of local landlords.[40] These landlords were limited in terms of how much land they were permitted to own, though they could pass villages to close relatives. Non-urban Iranians had to join rural cooperatives managed by the Ministry of Agriculture and the Ministry of Rural Affairs. The reforms also reduced the number of people practicing a nomadic lifestyle in Iran.[41] Control of water resources also featured in the government's reforms. A 1968 law declared that water is 'national wealth and belongs to everyone', and put the government in charge of maintaining water infrastructure as well.[42]

Stage Three: Nationalism

Reza Shah based nationalism in Iran on an unbroken connection to ancient Persian civilisation. This helped shape an 'eternal yesterday' to which all Iranians could subscribe and with which they could identify. Reza Shah's brand of Iranian nationalism also emphasised secularism, which helped to build his assent to rule from the country's various religious groups. Given the diversity and size of Iran's populations – including its kinship groups – such a nationalist idiom was the most effective choice.

Iran after State Building

The weakening of kinship authority in Iran during the reign of Reza Shah coincided with the expansion of the bureaucratic state. While kinship remains important socially, political functions historically governed by kinship authority were instrumentalised by the state's bureaucracy.

Water access after the state-building period in Iran became the purview of the government. A 1983 law gave the Ministry of Energy responsibility for the distribution of water, although the Ministry delegates some authority to Regional Water Authorities to maintain local infrastructure.[43] Additionally, the Ministry of Agriculture oversees water distribution for domestic use and collects fees accordingly.[44] Similarly to Oman, management of local *qanat* is decentralised but ultimately bureaucratic.

This bureaucracy extends to other aspects of politics traditionally regulated by kinship authority. Marriage in Iran, for example, is not distinctly political. However, it does play an important social role. As with other societies examined in this project, marriage is a family affair requiring lengthy discussions between the kinship groups who are to be joined by the marriage.[45] However, similarly to Oman, Iran has been able to use bureaucratic authority in ways that allow kinship group members to circumvent traditional kinship practices, though religious conservatism limits the extent to which this is the case. The Family Protection Law of 1967, for example, extended new rights to women in marriages, restricted polygamy, and improved their custody rights.[46] In addition, government modernisation in Iran between the 1940s and 1970s increased the number of Iranian women with education and a job before marriage. These women, while just one subset of the population, face less economic and social pressure to adhere to the rules and norms of kinship authority. Bureaucratic authority in Iran creates these opportunities.

Because of cooperative access to resources before state building, Iran's government embedded proto-bureaucratic institutions into the national bureaucratic state. Its extension of infrastructure and bureaucratic governance during state building instrumentalised kinship authority. As a result, kinship authority after state building in Iran has instrumentalised political salience.

Conclusion

The Middle East is one of many regions where European powers intervened seeking influence and power. As such, colonialism features prominently in many accounts of state formation and its various facets in these regions. Given the substantial impacts European powers had on these regions, including the appointment of local leaders, such a focus is justifiable. However, while acknowledging the importance of European powers, it bears remembering that these regions were neither empty nor ungoverned beforehand. Rather, they were populated with local groups who governed themselves according to a complex set of rules, norms and practices rooted in traditional kinship authority.

Kinship politics are not a historical vestige or catch-all for explaining the political eccentricities of regions where they exist. Rather, kinship groups are an active part of regional politics that shape the behaviour of members of Arab Gulf societies, including their leadership. While small states with tribes and dynastic monarchies are often treated in social science as functionally equivalent, this book has shown that important differences exist among them. Variation in salience is not merely a distinction without a difference. It is an important indication of the incentive structures of these states. Where kinship authority has governing salience, governments and leaders will be more beholden to the patronage interests of tribal constituencies than in places where it has instrumentalised salience. These interests can shape major elements of state policy, including to whom a development contract is rewarded, which groups are represented in the security services, and who is hired by government ministries. Counter-terrorism efforts may also rely on understanding ties between armed groups and the tribes that support them. Kinship salience also shapes perceptions of corruption. While nepotism may be considered corrupt behaviour in states with instrumentalised kinship salience, it may be seen as more acceptable in states where it has governing salience – at least by kinship constituencies within the population.

A state's governance of its population is at the heart of comparative politics. Yet governance is more than state bureaucratic authority. Other forms of authority co-exist with the state, with kinship authority being one prominent example. Modelling kinship salience gives scholars a more accurate sense of how bureaucratic governance is articulated and limited by pre-state conditions. In addition, by reframing old insights from modernisation theory and state formation literature, we gain analytical leverage in scholarly discussions of patronage and ethnic identity. Considering kinship in the context of recent insights in the study of identity highlights important questions surrounding the political relevance of these identities. Kinship groups possess a unique identity trait – super-stickiness – that distinguishes them from other identity types. This unique trait constrains patterns of state building beyond the extent that a patronage network or electoral constituency would.

This book has explained, using process tracing through archival evidence and field interviews, why kinship authority is an important and stable facet of governance in contemporary states. Understanding how kinship authority operates is part and parcel of understanding the function of states themselves. It can take on the functions of governance often relegated to the bureaucratic state. Yet it does not always do so, and for reasons existing explanations have difficulty explaining. The process by which kinship authority and bureaucratic authority come to co-exist is a long one, shaped by conditions that pre-date the state itself. While traditionally, scholars have considered pre-state conditions somewhat irrelevant, this book has shown that they matter to important political outcomes.

Patterns of resource distribution and patterns of settlement are the building blocks of these pre-state conditions. When resource are dispersed throughout a territory, kinship groups tend to be nomadic. In contrast, when resources are concentrated, kinship groups tend to be settled. In both cases, interaction between kinship groups is regulated by norms and rules of behaviour generated by kinship authority.

Competitive and cooperative patterns of access to vital limited resources shape the political salience of kinship after state building. When resource access before state building is competitive, the ruler reaches out to individual kinship groups since no institution exists that would coordinate between them. This outreach has the effect of perpetuating the political salience of kinship identity, since membership in the group continues to provide benefits. Kinship authority in such cases will have governing salience because of the use during state building of kinship hierarchies and their leaders to move populations onto infrastructure and create buy-in to the state-building project. Kinship authority will administer functions of governance that the state may wish, but is unable, to administer. It will also continue to restrict the behaviour of kinship group members.

In contrast, when access to vital limited resources is cooperative prior to state building, kinship groups can form proto-bureaucracies to manage this access. Since proto-bureaucracies offer a bureaucratic means of resource access, kinship authority will be instrumentalised by the bureaucratic state as a means of patronage. Kinship authority will not administer aspects of governance that the state wishes to control. It will also have limited ability to constrain the behaviour of kinship group members. Either kinship authority will have limited power to impose sanctions in general, or its power to do so will be limited by laws imposed by the bureaucratic state. In such cases, kinship authority will have instrumentalised salience.

The difference between governing and instrumentalised salience illustrates that states with similar preconditions before state building can exhibit vastly different configurations of state–society relations. Where kinship authority has governing salience, traditional forms of governance endure alongside the contemporary state. Bureaucratic institutions are instrumentalised by kinship authority, which uses the bureaucracy to obtain resources and political access. Where kinship authority has instrumentalised salience, the state embeds kinship authority within a bureaucratic state that shapes and limits the political power it has. Interrogating these differences also speaks to shortcomings in our understandings of the state. While state capacity may explain some element of the state's engagement with kinship authority, it is ultimately insufficient to account for observable variation. This limitation speaks to the overemphasis scholars have placed on state-centric explanations of modernisation and state development. It is logical to examine state agency primarily in the context of state building. However, states do not undertake state building in a vacuum. Quite often, they contend with pre-existing forms of authority that also have a stake in the manifestation of state governance. Better understanding this process gives scholars important insights into not only how kinship groups achieve and maintain salience in bureaucratic states, but a more basic question of how states navigate the basic challenge of extending authority within their borders.

The findings also bridge between anthropology and political science as disciplines. They draw upon insights about how kinship shapes human interaction from anthropology as well as fieldwork from anthropologists. The book uses political science methods of systematic inquiry to situate these insights within a testable model. This interdisciplinary approach allows political scientists to study kinship groups on their own terms, using rigorous work from other scholarly sources as a foundation for this study. The usage of anthropology literature in a political science book also speaks to the utility of an interdisciplinary approach in political science toward discussions in the field already studied by other disciplines.

While we have examined a specific set of state-building experiences, others merit scholarly attention as well. The model presented here can serve as a useful starting point for considering these cases. Infrastructure, bureaucracy and nationalism are fundamental elements of state building, but they need not always occur in that order or in the ways specified in this book. Further research can examine different patterns of state building to further assess how durable the effects of pre-state conditions really are. It can also consider differences in access to vital limited resources. While water is a quintessential example of a vital limited resource, others may be different in the exact ways they are obtained and distributed. While the model presented here should be able to account for these vital limited resources, looking at arable land or a means for heating (firewood, oil) could uncover interesting insights about the mechanics of competitive and cooperative resource access.

Throughout the long – and sometimes painful – state-building process, local populations were not passive actors. Kinship groups were not merely co-opted or overpowered by the arrival of modern bureaucratic states. On the contrary, they played an active role in shaping their own destinies, albeit within the confines of power structures imposed from the top down. In the Arab Gulf region, it is a fallacy to think of the population as the helpless victims of colonialism. These populations had complex and sophisticated forms of politics that pre-dated the colonial period with elements that remain largely in place today. The result is a set of states in which populations were not passive victims of political forces beyond their control, but rather agents in perpetuating centuries-old systems of governance that they had built, refined and maintained on their own. As bureaucratic states continue to modernise and develop, the role of kinship authority in these states will likely be stable, durable and vital for the foreseeable future.

Notes

1. Abdi Ismail Samatar, *The State and Rural Transformation in Northern Somalia, 1884–1986* (Madison, WI: University of Wisconsin Press, 1989): 14.
2. Samatar, *The State and Rural Transformation*, 24.
3. I. M. Lewis, *Blood and Bone: The Call of Kinship in Somali Society* (Lawrenceville, NJ: The Red Sea Press, 1994): 23.
4. Lewis, *Blood and Bone*, 25.
5. Alice Hashim, 'Conflicting Identities in Somalia', *Peace Review* 9 no. 4 (1997): 528.
6. Samatar, *The State and Rural Transformation*, 25.
7. Samatar, *The State and Rural Transformation*, 26.
8. Gedamu Kalewongel Minale, 'How did Somaliland Emerge as a Stable and Peaceful Polity?', *International Commentary* 9 no. 34 (December 2013): 31.
9. Samatar, *The State and Rural Transformation*, 36.
10. Minale, 'How did Somaliland Emerge', 32.
11. Samatar, *The State and Rural Transformation*, 27.
12. Samatar, *The State and Rural Transformation*, 52–3.
13. Samatar, *The State and Rural Transformation*, 44, 57.
14. Samatar, *The State and Rural Transformation*, 49.
15. 'Maj. General Siad Barre', *Harvard Divinity School Religious Literacy Project*, https://rlp.hds.harvard.edu/faq/maj-general-siad-barre.
16. 'Siad Barre and Scientific Socialism', in Helen Chapin Metz (ed.), *Somalia: A Country Study* (Washington, DC: Government Press Office for the Library of Congress, 1992).
17. These were the Marechan, Ogaden and Dulbahante clans (see Metz, *Somalia*).

18. Nina J. Fitzgerald, *Somalia: Issues, History, and Bibliography* (Huntington, NY: Nova Science Publishers, 2002): 23–4.

19. Fitzgerald, *Somalia*, 23.

20. Mark Bradbury, *Becoming Somaliland* (London, UK: Progressio, 2008): 36.

21. Hashim, 'Conflicting Identities in Somalia', 531.

22. Fitzgerald, *Somalia*, 39.

23. Bradbury, *Becoming Somaliland*, 14.

24. Bradbury, *Becoming Somaliland*, 15.

25. Stephanie Cronin, *Tribal Politics in Iran: Rural Conflict and the New State, 1921–1941* (New York, NY: Routledge, 2007): 18–19.

26. For a detailed explanation of how *qanat* made their way to Oman from Persia, see Dale Lightfoot, 'The Origin and Diffusion of Qanats in Arabia: New Evidence from the Northern and Southern Peninsula', *The Geographical Journal* 166 no. 3 (2000): 221.

27. Paul Ward English, '*Qanats* and Lifeworlds in Iranian Plateau Villages', *Yale F&ES Bulletin* 103 (1998): 198.

28. Mohammad Reza Balali, Jozef Keulartz and Michiel Korthals, 'Reflexive Water Management in Arid Regions: The Case of Iran', *Environmental Values* 18 no. 1 (February 2009): 96.

29. Michael E. Bonine, 'From *Qanat* to *Kort*: Traditional Irrigation Terminology and Practices in Central Iran', *Iran* 20 (1982): 148.

30. Balali *et al.*, 'Reflexive Water Management in Arid Regions', 97–8.

31. Bonine, 'From *Qanat* to *Kort*', 157.

32. Ervand Abrahamian, *A History of Modern Iran* (Cambridge, UK: Cambridge University Press, 2008): 65.

33. Stephanie Cronin, *Armies and State Building in the Modern Middle East: Politics, Nationalism, and Military Reform* (New York, NY: I. B. Taurus, 2014): 124–5; Philip Carl Salzman, 'Tribes and Modern States: An Alternative Approach', in Uzi Rabi (ed.), *Tribes and States in a Changing Middle East* (Oxford, UK: Oxford University Press, 2016): 213.

34. Abrahamian, *A History of Modern Iran*, 71.

35. Abrahamian, *A History of Modern Iran*, 72.

36. Elton L. Daniel, *The History of Iran* (Westport, CT: Greenwood Press, 2001): 135.

37. Abrahamian, *A History of Modern Iran*, 67.

38. Abrahamian, *A History of Modern Iran*, 92.

39. Mohammad Gholi Majd, *Great Britain and Reza Shah: The Plunder of Iran, 1921–1941* (Gainesville, FL: University Press of Florida, 2001): 186.

40. James A. Bill, 'Modernization and Reform from Above: The Case of Iran', *The Journal of Politics* 32 no. 1 (February 1970): 32, 34.

41. Abrahamian, *A History of Modern Iran*, 131, 133.

42. Mehmood Ul Hassan, Asad Sarwar Qureshi and Nader Heydari, 'A Proposed Framework for Irrigation Management Transfer in Iran: Lessons from Asia and Iran', *International Water Management Institute Working Paper* 118 (2007): 7.

43. Hassan *et al.*, 'A Proposed Framework', 7–8.
44. 'Legislation on Use of Water in Agriculture: Iran', *Library of Congress*, 1 May 2015, http://www.loc.gov/law/help/water-law/iran.php.
45. Vida Nassehi-Benham, 'Change and the Iranian Family', *Current Anthropology* 26 no. 5 (December 1985): 557.
46. Nassehi-Benham, 'Change and the Iranian Family', 558.

BIBLIOGRAPHY

Archival Volumes

Development Plans of the GCC States, 1962–1995 (Cambridge, UK: Cambridge Archive Editions, 1994).

Gazetteer of Arabian Tribes, ed. R. Trench (Cambridge, UK: Cambridge Archive Editions, 1996).

Lorimer, John Gordon, *Gazetteer of the Persian Gulf, Oman, and Central Arabia, Volume II* (Calcutta, India: Superintendent Government Printing, 1908).

_____, *Gazetteer of the Persian Gulf, Oman and Central Arabia* (Cambridge, UK: Cambridge Archive Editions, 1986).

_____, *Gazetteer of the Persian Gulf* (online: General Books LLC, 2012).

Persian Gulf Administration Reports, ed. Penelope Tuson (Cambridge, UK: Cambridge Archive Editions, 1989).

Political Diaries of the Arab World: Persian Gulf 1904–1965, ed. Robert Jarman (Cambridge, UK: Cambridge Archive Editions, 1998).

Political Diaries of the Persian Gulf (Cambridge, UK: Cambridge University Press, 1990).

Qatar Digital Library.

Records of Kuwait, 1899–1961, ed. Alan Rush (Cambridge, UK: Cambridge University Press 1989).

Records of Kuwait, 1961–1965, ed. Anita Burdett (Cambridge, UK: Cambridge Archive Editions, 1997).

Records of Kuwait, 1966–1971, ed. Anita Burdett (Cambridge, UK: Cambridge University Press, 2003).

Records of Oman, 1867–1960, ed. R. Bailey (Cambridge, UK: Cambridge Archive Editions, 1992).

Records of Oman, 1961–1965, ed. A. Burdett (Cambridge, UK: Cambridge Archive Editions, 1997).

Books

Abrahamian, Ervand, *A History of Modern Iran* (Cambridge, UK: Cambridge University Press, 2008).

Adeel, Z. (ed.), *Sustainable Management of Marginal Drylands: Applications of Indigenous Knowledge for Coastal Drylands – Proceedings of a Joint UNU-UNESCO-ICARDO International Workshop, Alexandria, Egypt, 21–25 September 2002* (Tokyo, Japan: United Nations University, 2002).

Allen, Calvin H., and W. Lynn Rigsbee II, *Oman Under Qaboos: From Coup to Constitution, 1970–1996* (New York, NY: Routledge, 2013).

Anderson, Lisa, *The State and Social Transformation in Tunisia and Libya (1830–1980)* (Princeton, NJ: Princeton University Press, 1986).

Azoulay, Rivka, *Kuwait and al-Sabah: Tribal Politics and Power in an Oil State* (London, UK: I. B. Tauris, 2020).

al-Azri, Khalid M., *Social and Gender Inequality in Oman: The Power of Religious and Political Tradition* (New York, NY: Routledge, 2013).

Bates, Robert H., *Essays on the Political Economy of Rural Africa* (Cambridge, UK: Cambridge University Press, 1983).

Bradbury, Mark, *Becoming Somaliland* (London, UK: Progressio, 2008).

Bradley, John R., *Saudi Arabia Exposed: Inside a Kingdom in Crisis* (New York, NY: Palgrave Macmillan, 2005).

Bratton, Michael, and Nicholas van de Valle, *Democratic Experiments in Africa: Regime Transitions in Comparative Perspective* (Cambridge, UK: Cambridge University Press, 1997).

Carsten, Janet, *After Kinship* (Cambridge, UK: Cambridge University Press, 2004).

____, *The Heart of the Hearth: The Process of Kinship in a Malay Fishing Community* (Oxford, UK: Clarendon Press, 1997).

Chandra, Kanchan (ed.), *Constructivist Theories of Ethnic Politics* (New York, NY: Oxford University Press: 2012).

Chaudhry, Kiren Aziz, *The Price of Wealth: Economies and Institutions in the Middle East* (Ithaca, NY: Cornell University Press, 1997).

Cronin, Stephanie, *Armies and State Building in the Modern Middle East: Politics, Nationalism, and Military Reform* (New York, NY: I. B. Taurus, 2014).

____, *Tribal Politics in Iran: Rural Conflict and the New State, 1921–1941* (New York, NY: Routledge, 2007).

Crystal, Jill, *Kuwait: The Transformation of an Oil State* (New York, NY: Routledge, 1992).

____, *Oil and Politics in the Gulf: Rulers and Merchants in Kuwait and Qatar* (Cambridge, UK: Cambridge University Press, 1990).

Daniel, Elton L., *The History of Iran* (Westport, CT: Greenwood Press, 2001).

Darden, Keith, *Resisting Occupation in Eurasia: Mass Schooling and the Creation of Durable National Loyalties* (Cambridge, UK: Cambridge University Press, forthcoming).

Dickson, H. R. P., *Kuwait and Her Neighbours* (London, UK: George Allen & Unwin, 1956).

Edgar, Adrienne Lynn, *Tribal Nation: The Making of Soviet Turkmenistan* (Princeton, NJ: Princeton University Press, 2004).

Eickelman, Dale F., *The Middle East: An Anthropological Approach* (Hoboken, NJ: Prentice Hall, 1989).

Evans-Pritchard, E. E., *The Nuer: A Description of the Modes of Livelihood and Political Institutions of a Nilotic People* (Oxford, UK: Oxford University Press, 1940).

Fitzgerald, Nina J., *Somalia: Issues, History, and Bibliography* (Huntington, NY: Nova Science Publishers, 2002).

Freer, Courtney, *Rentier Islam: The Influence of the Muslim Brotherhood in Gulf Monarchies* (Oxford, UK: Oxford University Press, 2018).

Fromherz, Allen J., *Qatar: A Modern History* (New York: I. B. Tauris, 2012).

____, *Qatar: A Modern History, Updated Edition* (Washington, DC: Georgetown University Press, 2017).

Fukuyama, Francis, *The Origins of Political Order: From Prehuman Times to the French Revolution* (New York, NY: Farrar, Straus and Giroux, 2011).

de Gaury, Gerald, *Review of the 'Anizah Tribe*, ed. Bruce Ingham (Lebanon: Kutub Limited, 2005).

Gause III, Gregory F., *Oil Monarchies: Domestic and Security Challenges in the Arab Gulf States* (New York, NY: Council on Foreign Relations Press, 1994).

Gellner, Ernst, *Muslim Society* (Cambridge, UK: Cambridge University Press, 1981).

____, *Nations and Nationalism* (Ithaca, NY: Cornell University Press, 1983).

al-Ghanim, Selwa, *The Reign of Mubarak al-Sabah: Shaikh of Kuwait 1896–1915* (New York, NY: I. B. Tauris, 1998).

Gulliver, P. H., *Neighbours and Networks: The Idiom of Kinship in Social Action Among the Ndendeuli of Tanzania* (Berkeley, CA: University of California Press, 1971).

Hale, Henry E., *Patronal Politics: Eurasian Regime Dynamics in Comparative Perspective* (Cambridge, UK: Cambridge University Press, 2014).

Herb, Michael, *All in the Family: Absolutism, Revolution, and Democracy in the Middle Eastern Monarchies* (Albany, NY: State University of New York Press, 1999).

Herbst, Jeffrey, *States and Power in Africa: Comparative Lessons in Authority and Control* (Princeton, NJ: Princeton University Press, 2000).

Hertog, Steffan, Giacomo Luciani and Marc Valeri, *Business Politics in the Middle East* (London, UK: C. Hurst & Co., 2013).

Hsu, Francis L. K., *Kinship and Culture* (New Brunswick, NJ: Aldine Transaction, 1971).

Hutchinson, John, and Anthony Smith (eds), *Ethnicity* (New York, NY: Oxford University Press, 1996).

Ibn Khaldoun, *al-Muqaddimah: An Introduction to History – Abridged Edition*, trans. Franz Rosenthal (Princeton, NJ: Princeton University Press, 2015)

Inkeles, Alex, *Exploring Individual Modernity* (New York, NY: Columbia University Press, 1983).

Inkeles, Alex, and David Horton Smith, *Becoming Modern: Individual Change in Six Developing Countries* (Cambridge, MA: Harvard University Press, 1974).

Jones, Jeremy, and Nicholas Ridout, *A History of Modern Oman* (Cambridge, UK: Cambridge University Press, 2015).

Kamrava, Mehran, *Qatar: Small State, Big Politics* (Ithaca, NY: Cornell University Press, 2015).

Khoury, Philip S., and Joseph Kostiner, *Tribes and State Formation in the Middle East* (Los Angeles, CA: University of California Press, 1990).

Lancaster, William, and Fidelity Lancaster, *Honour is in Contentment: Life Before Oil in Ras al-Khaimah (UAE) and some Neighbouring Regions* (Berlin, Germany: de Gruyter, 2011).

Landen, Robert Geran, *Oman Since 1856: Disruptive Modernization in a Traditional Arab Society* (Princeton, NJ: Princeton University Press, 1967).

Layne, Linda, *The Dialogics of Tribal and National Identities in Jordan* (Princeton, NJ: Princeton University Press, 1994).

Lewis, I. M., *Blood and Bone: The Call of Kinship in Somali Society* (Lawrenceville, NJ: Red Sea Press, 1994).

Lienhardt, Peter, *Shaikhdoms of Eastern Arabia* (New York, NY: Springer Publishing, 2001).

Limbert, Mandana E., *In the Time of Oil: Piety, Social Memory, and Social Life in an Omani Town* (Stanford, CA: Stanford University Press, 2010).

Majd, Mohammad Gholi, *Great Britain and Reza Shah: The Plunder of Iran, 1921–1941* (Gainesville, FL: University Press of Florida, 2001).

Manickavasagan, A, Mohammed M. Essa and E. Sukumar (eds), *Dates: Production, Processing, Food, and Medicinal Values* (New York, NY: CRC Press, 2012).

Metz, Helen Chapin (ed.), *Qatar: A Country Study* (Washington, DC: Library of Congress Federal Research Division, 1993).

_____ (ed.), *Somalia: A Country Study* (Washington, DC: Government Press Office for the Library of Congress, 1992).

Mockaitis, Thomas R., *British Counterinsurgency in the Post-Imperial Era* (New York, NY: Manchester University Press, 1995).

al-Nakib, Farah, *Kuwait Transformed: A History of Oil and Urban Life* (Stanford, CA: Stanford University Press, 2016).

North, Douglass C., *Institutions, Institutional Change and Economic Performance* (Cambridge, UK: Cambridge University Press, 1990).

Omani Ministry of Education and The World Bank, *Education in Oman: The Drive for Equality, Volume 2* (Muscat, Oman: Omani Ministry of Education and The World Bank, 2013).

Parolin, Gianluca Paolo, *Citizenship in the Arab World: Kin, Religion and Nation-state* (Amsterdam, The Netherlands: Amsterdam University Press, 2009).

Peterson, John, *Historical Muscat: An Illustrated Guide and Gazetteer* (Leiden, The Netherlands: Brill, 2006).

Posner, Daniel, *Institutions and Ethnic Politics in Africa* (Cambridge, UK: Cambridge University Press, 2005).

Rabi, Uzi, *The Emergence of States in a Tribal Society: Oman Under Sa'id bin Taymur 1932–1970* (Brighton, UK: Sussex Academic Press, 2006).

_____ (ed.), *Tribes and States in a Changing Middle East* (Oxford, UK: Oxford University Press, 2016).

Rahman, Habibur, *The Emergence of Qatar* (London, UK: Kegan Paul International, 2005).

Rakaan bin Hathleen: Poet, Cavalier, and Sheikh of the Ajman (Kuwait: Rabian Publishing and Distribution Company, 2003) (Arabic).

al-Rasheed, Madawi, *A History of Saudi Arabia* (Cambridge, UK: Cambridge University Press, 2010).

Rizzo, Helen Mary, *Islam, Democracy, and the Status of Women: The Case of Kuwait* (New York, NY: Routledge, 2005).

Rubin, Barry, *Crises in the Contemporary Persian Gulf* (New York, NY: Frank Cass Publishers, 2002).

Rush, Alan, *Al-Sabah: History and Genealogy of Kuwait's Ruling Family, 1752–1987* (Atlantic Highlands, NJ: Ithaca Press, 1987).

al-Sa'eed, Mat'ab bin Othman, *Urbanized Nejdi Family Lineages in Kuwait* (Kuwait: Maktaba Afaq, 2011) (Arabic).

Samatar, Abdi Ismail, *The State and Rural Transformation in Northern Somalia, 1884–1986* (Madison, WI: University of Wisconsin Press, 1989).

Samin, Nadav, *Of Sand or Soil: Genealogy and Tribal Belonging in Saudi Arabia* (Princeton, NJ: Princeton University Press, 2015).

Schatz, Edward, *Modern Clan Politics: The Power of 'Blood' in Kazakhstan and Beyond* (Seattle, WA: University of Washington Press, 2004).

Schneider, David, *American Kinship: A Cultural Account* (Chicago, IL: University of Chicago Press, 1968).

_____, *A Critique of the Study of Kinship* (Ann Arbor, MI: University of Michigan Press, 1984).

al-Shamlaan, Seif Marzouq, *Min Tarikh al-Kuwait* (Kuwait: Thaat al-Silasil Publications, 1986) (Arabic).

al-Sharifi, Ibrahim Jarallah bin Dakhna, *The Golden Encyclopedia of Individuals of the Tribes and Families of the Arabian Peninsula* (Ann Arbor, MI: University of Michigan Press: 1998) (Arabic).

Teebi, Ahmad S. (ed.), *Genetic Disorders Among Arab Populations* (Oxford, UK: Oxford University Press, 1997).

Tetreault, Mary Ann, *The Kuwait Petroleum Corporation and the Economics of the New World Order* (Westport, CT: Quantum Books, 1995).

al-Thafir, 'Attiya bin Kareem, *Qabilat al-Thafir: Dirasa Tarikhia L'Ghuiya Muqarina* (Kuwait: Mutab'a Muassasa Dar Al-Siyasa, 1995) (Arabic).

Tilly, Charles, *Coercion, Capital, and European States: A.D. 990–1992* (Malden, MA: Blackwell Publishing, 1992).

Valeri, Marc, *Oman: Politics and Society in the Qaboos State* (New York, NY: Columbia University Press, 2009).

Weber, Eugen, *Peasants into Frenchmen: The Modernization of Rural France, 1970–1914* (Stanford, CA: Stanford University Press, 1976).

Weber, Max, *Economy and Society: An Outline of Interpretive Sociology*, eds Guenther Roth and Claus Wittich (Berkeley, CA: University of California Press, 1978).

____, *Politics as a Vocation*, trans. H. H. Gerth and C. Wright Mills (Philadelphia, PA: Fortress Press, 1972).

Wilkinson, John C., *The Imamate Tradition of Oman* (Cambridge, UK: Cambridge University Press, 1987).

____, *Water and Tribal Settlement in South-east Arabia: A Study of the Aflaj of Oman* (Oxford, UK: Clarendon Press, 1977).

Wittfogel, Karl A., *Oriental Despotism: A Comparative Study of Total Power* (New Haven, CT: Yale University Press, 1957).

Wynbrandt, James, *A Brief History of Saudi Arabia* (New York, NY: Infobase Publishing, 2010).

Zahlan, Rosemary Said, *The Creation of Qatar* (Lanham, MD: Rowman and Littlefield Publishers, 1979).

Articles and Dissertations

Aldous, Joan, 'Urbanization, the Extended Family, and Kinship Ties in West Africa', *Social Forces* 41 no. 1 (October 1962): 6–12.

Antoun, Richard T., 'Civil Society, Tribal Process, and Change in Jordan: An Anthropological View', *International Journal of Middle East Studies* 32 no. 4 (November 2000): 441–63.

Armer, Michael, and Robert Youtz, 'Formal Education and Individual Modernity in an African Society', *American Journal of Sociology* 76 no. 4 (January 1971): 604–26.

Asmi, Rehunama, 'Finding a Place to Sit: How Qatari Women Combine Cultural and Kinship Capital in the Home Majlis', *Anthropology of the Middle East* 11 no. 2 (Winter 2016): 18–38.

Axelrod, Robert, and Robert O. Keohane, 'Achieving Cooperation under Anarchy: Strategies and Institutions', *World Politics* 38 no. 1 (October 1985): 226–54.

Balali, Mohammad Reza, Jozef Keulartz and Michiel Korthals, 'Reflexive Water Management in Arid Regions: The Case of Iran', *Environmental Values* 18 no. 1 (February 2009): 91–112.

Baldwin, Kate, *When Politicians Cede Control of Resources: Land, Chiefs and Coalition-building in Africa*, Afrobarometer Working Papers, Working Paper No. 130 (2011).

Bill, James A., 'Modernization and Reform from Above: The Case of Iran', *Journal of Politics* 32 no. 1 (February 1970): 19–40.

Bonine, Michael E., 'From *Qanat* to *Kort*: Traditional Irrigation Terminology and Practices in Central Iran', *Iran* 20 (1982): 145–59.

Boone, Catherine, 'Rural Interests and the Making of Modern African States', *African Economic History* 23 (1995): 1–36.

Brinks, Daniel M., 'Informal Institutions and the Rule of Law: The Judicial Response to State Killings in Buenos Aires and Sao Paulo in the 1990s', *Comparative Politics* 36 no. 1 (October 2003): 1–19.

Chandra, Kanchan, 'What is Ethnic Identity and Does it Matter?', *Annual Review of Political Science* 9 (June 2006): 397–424.

Charrad, Mounira M., 'Central and Local Patrimonialism: State-Building in Kin-Based Societies', *Annals of the American Academic of Political and Social Science* 636 (July 2011): 49–68.

Charrad, Mounira M., and Julia Adams, 'Introduction: Patrimonialism Part and Present', *Annals of the American Academy of Political and Social Science* 636 (July 2011): 6–15.

Cole, Donald P., 'Where Have the Bedouin Gone?', *Anthropological Quarterly* 76 no. 2 (Spring 2003): 235–67.

Collins, Kathleen, 'Clans, Pacts, and Politics in Central Asia', *Journal of Democracy* 13 no. 3 (July 2002): 137–52.

____, 'The Logic of Clan Politics', *World Politics* 56 no. 2 (January 2004): 224–61.

Collins, Randal, 'Patrimonial Alliances and Failures of State Penetration', *Annals of the American Academy of Political and Social Science* 636 (July 2011): 16–31.

Cooke, Miriam, *Tribal Modern: Branding New Nations in the Arab Gulf* (Los Angeles, CA: UCLA Press, 2014).

Darden, Keith, and Anna Grzymala-Busse, 'The Great Divide: Literacy, Nationalism, and the Communist Collapse', *World Politics* 59 no. 1 (October 2006): 83–115.

English, Paul Ward, '*Qanats* and Lifeworlds in Iranian Plateau Villages', *Yale F&ES Bulletin* 103 (1998): 187–205.

Freer, Courtney, and Andrew Leber, 'Defining the "Tribal Advantage" in Kuwaiti Politics', *Middle East Law and Governance* (forthcoming).

Geddes, Barbara, 'How the Cases You Choose Affect the Answers You Get: Selection Bias in Comparative Politics', *Political Analysis* 2 no. 1 (1990): 131–50.

Ghabra, Shafeeq, 'Kuwait and the Dynamics of Socio-Economic Change', *Middle East Journal* 51 no. 3 (Summer 1997): 358–72.

Gonnelli, Michele, 'Clan and State Politics in Somalia: Between Local Governance and Federalism, International Actors and Pirates', *International Commentary* 9 no. 34 (December 2013): 8–10.

Grandmaison, Collette Le Cour, 'Spatial Organization, Tribal Groupings, and Kinship in Ibra', *Journal of Oman Studies* 3 no. 2 (1977): 95–106.

Greif, Avner, and David D. Latin, 'A Theory of Endogenous Institutional Change', *American Political Science Review* 98 no. 4 (November 2004): 633–52.

al-Haddad, Mohammed Suleiman, 'The Effect of Detribalization and Sedentarization on the Socio-Economic Structure of the Tribes of the Arabian Peninsula: Ajman Tribe as a Case Study', PhD dissertation, University of Kansas, 1981.

al-Haj, Majid, 'Kinship and Modernization in Developing Societies: The Emergence of Instrumentalized Kinship', *Journal of Comparative Family Studies* 26 no. 3 (Autumn 1995): 311–28.

Hamzeh, A. Nizar, 'Qatar: The Duality of the Legal System', *Middle Eastern Studies* 30 no. 1 (January 1994): 79–90.

Harkness, Geoff, and Rana Khaled, 'Modern Traditionalism: Consanguineous Marriage in Qatar', *Journal of Marriage and Family* 74 (June 2014): 587–603.

Hashim, Alice, 'Conflicting Identities in Somalia', *Peace Review* 9 no. 4 (1997): 527–31.

Hassan, Mehmood Ul, Asad Sarwar Qureshi and Nader Heydari, 'A Proposed Framework for Irrigation Management Transfer in Iran: Lessons from Asia and Iran', *International Water Management Institute Working Paper* 118 (2007).

Hendrix, Cullen S., 'Measuring State Capacity: Theoretical and Empirical Implications for the Study of Civil Conflict', *Journal of Peace Research* 47 no. 3 (May 2010): 273–85.

Hirschfeld, Lawrence A., 'Kinship and Cognition: Genealogy and the Meaning of Kinship Terms', *Current Anthropology* 27 no. 3 (June 1986): 217–42.

Holsinger, Donald B., 'The Elementary School as Modernizer: A Brazilian Study', *International Journal of Comparative Sociology* 14 no. 3–4 (1973): 180–202

Inkeles, Alex, 'Industrial Man: The Relation of Status to Experience, Perception, and Value', *American Journal of Sociology* 66 no. 1 (July 1960): 1–31.

al-Kalbani, M. S., and M. F. Price, 'Sustainable *aflaj* Water Management in Al Jabal Al Akhdar, Sultanate of Oman', *Water Resources Management* 8 (2015): 28.

Kechechian, Joseph A., 'A Vision of Oman: State of the Sultanate Speeches by Qaboos Bin Said, 1970–2006', *Middle East Policy Council* 15 no. 4 (Winter 2008): 112–33.

Khalaf, Sulayman N., 'Settlement of Violence in Bedouin Society', *Ethnology* 29 no. 3 (July 1990): 225–42.

Kobaisi, Abdulla Juma, 'The Development of Education in Qatar, 1950–1977 with an Analysis of some Educational Problems', PhD Dissertation, University of Durham, UK, 1979.

Krasner, Stephen D., and Thomas Risse, 'External Actors, State-Building, and Service Provision in Areas of Limited Statehood: Introduction', *Governance* 27 no. 4 (October 2014): 545–67.

Lightfoot, Dale, 'The Origin and Diffusion of *Qanats* in Arabia: New Evidence from the Northern and Southern Peninsula', *The Geographical Journal* 166 no. 3 (2000): 215–26.

Lund, Christian, and Catherine Boone, 'Introduction: Land Politics in Africa – Constituting Authority Over Territory, Property and Persons', *Africa* 83 no. 1 (February 2013): 1–13.

al-Maliki, Abdallah Yousef, 'Public Administration in the State of Qatar: Origin, Development, Problems, and Current Directions', PhD dissertation, Golden Gate University, 1989.

al-Marshoudi, Ahmed Salem, 'Water Institutional Arrangements of Falaj Al Daris in the Sultanate of Oman', *International Journal of Social Sciences and Management* 5 no. 1 (2018): 31–42.

Marx, Emmanuel, "The Tribe as a Unit of Subsistence: Nomadic Pastoralism in the Middle East', *American Anthropologist* 79 no. 2 (June 1977): 343–63.

Minale, Gedamu Kalewongel, 'How did Somaliland Emerge as a Stable and Peaceful Polity?', *International Commentary* 9 no. 34 (December 2013): 29–33.

Mitchell, Jocelyn Sage, and Justin J. Gengler, 'What Money Can't Buy: Wealth, Inequality, and Economic Satisfaction in the Rentier State', *Political Research Quarterly* 72 no. 1 (2019): 75–89.

Moritz, Jessie, 'Reformers and the Rentier State: Re-Evaluating the Co-optation Mechanism in Rentier State Theory', *Journal of Arabian Studies* 8 (2018): 46–64.

Mylonas, Harris, and Keith Darden, 'Threats to Territorial Integrity, National Mass Schooling and Linguistic Commonality', *Comparative Political Studies* 49 no. 11 (September 2016): 1446–79.

Nagy, Sharon, 'Social and Spatial Process: An Ethnographic Study of Housing in Qatar', PhD dissertation, University of Pennsylvania, 1997.

al-Nakib, Farah, 'Revisiting Hadhar and Badu in Kuwait: Citizenship, Housing, and the Construction of a Dichotomy', *International Journal of Middle Eastern Studies* 46 (2014): 5–30.

al-Nakib, Rania, 'Human Rights, Education for Democratic Citizenship and International Organizations: Findings from a Kuwaiti UNESCO ASPnet School', *Cambridge Journal of Education* 42 no. 1 (March 2012): 97–112.

al-Naqeeb, Khaldoun, 'Political Tribalism and Legitimacy in the Arab Peninsula', presentation at the Council on Foreign Relations, New York, NY, January 1992.

Nash, Harriet, and Dionisius A. Agius, 'Use of the Stars in Agriculture in Oman', *Journal of Semitic Studies* 56 no. 1 (2011): 167–82.

Nassehi-Benham, Vida, 'Change and the Iranian Family', *Current Anthropology* 26 no. 5 (December 1985): 557–62.

Norman, W. R., W. H. Shayya, A. S. al-Ghafri and I. R. McCann, '*Aflaj* Irrigation and On-Farm Water Management in Northern Oman', *Irrigation and Drainage Systems* 12 (1998): 35–48.

Peterson, J. E., "Oman: al-Ghafiriyah and al-Hinawiyah Tribal Confederations," *Arabian Peninsula Background Note*, No. APBN-001, 2003.

____, 'Oman's Diverse Society: Northern Oman', *Middle East Journal* 58 no. 1 (Winter 2004): 32–51.

____, 'Tribes and Politics in Eastern Arabia', *Middle East Journal* 31 no. 3 (Summer 1977): 297–312.

'Promoting QNV 2030's Vision of a Good Society: Towards a Social Policy for Qatar', *Social Affairs Department, General Secretariat for Development Planning*, May 2009.

Remmington, Grace, 'Transforming Tradition: The *Aflaj* and Changing Role of Traditional Knowledge Systems for Collective Water Management', *Journal of Arid Environments* 151 (2018): 134–40.

Salih, Kamal Eldin Osman, 'Kuwait Primary (Tribal) Elections 1975–2008: An Evaluative Study', *British Journal of Middle Eastern Studies* 38 no. 2 (2011): 141–67.

Sartori, Giovanni, 'Concept Misinformation in Comparative Politics', *American Political Science Review* 64 no. 4 (1970): 1033–53.

Seawright, Jason, and John Gerring, 'Case Selection Techniques in Case Study Research: A Menu of Qualitative and Quantitative Options', *Political Research Quarterly* 61 no. 2 (June 2008): 294–308.

al-Shawi, Ali A. Hadi, 'Political Influences of Tribes in the State of Qatar: Impact of Tribal Loyalty on Political Participation', PhD dissertation, Mississippi State University, 2002.

Alshawi, A. Hadi, and Andrew Gardner, 'Tribalism, Identity, and Citizenship in Contemporary Qatar', *Anthropology of the Middle East* 8 no. 2 (Winter 2013): 46–59.

Shils, Edward, 'Primordial, Personal, Sacred and Civil Ties', *British Journal of Sociology* 8 no. 2 (June 1957): 130–45.

Slezkine, Yuri, 'The USSR as a Communal Apartment, or How a Socialist State Promoted Ethnic Particularism', *Slavic Review* 53 no. 2 (Summer 1994): 414–52.

Swagman, Charles F., 'Tribe and Politics: An Example from Highland Yemen', *Journal of Anthropological Research* 44 no. 3 (Autumn 1988): 251–61.

Takriti, Abdel Razzaq, 'The 1970 Coup in Oman Reconsidered', *Journal of Arabian Studies: Arabia, the Gulf, and the Red Sea* 3 no. 2 (2013): 155–73.

Thelen, Kathleen, 'Historical Institutionalism in Comparative Politics', *Annual Review of Political Science* 2 (1999): 369–404.

Ulrichsen, Kristian Coates, 'Politics and Opposition in Kuwait: Continuity and Change', *Journal of Arabian Studies* 4 no. 2 (2014): 214–30.

Weiner, Scott, and Dillon Tatum, 'Rethinking Identity in Political Science', *Political Studies Review* 19 no. 3 (2021): 464–81.

Wlezien, Christopher, 'On the Salience of Political Issues: The Problem with "Most Important Problem"', *Electoral Studies* 24 (2005): 555–79.

Worral, James, 'Oman: The "Forgotten" Corner of the Arab Spring', *Middle East Policy Council* 19 no. 3 (Fall 2012): 98–115.

Online Media

'A Brief History', *Kuwait University*, http://www.kuniv.edu/ku/AboutKU/BriefHistory/index.htm.

Aboudi, Sami, 'Kuwait Protests Challenge Ruling Family', *Reuters*, 24 October 2012, https://www.reuters.com/article/us-kuwait-politics/kuwait-protests-challenge-ruling-family-idUSBRE89N0MS20121024.

'Administrative Court of Justice Rules it Lacks Jurisdiction', *altowayyah.blogpost.com*, 16 February 2008, https://altowayyah.blogspot.com/2008/02/blog-post.html.

Agence France-Presse, 'Saudi FM Says Embassy to Reopen in Qatar Within Days', *Voice of America*, 16 January 2021, https://www.voanews.com/middle-east/saudi-fm-says-embassy-reopen-qatar-within-days.

Alkhonaini, Abdullah, 'Kuwait Goes to the Polls: Discussing the 2020 Parliamentary Elections', Online Speaker Panel, *London School of Economics*, 8 December 2020, https://www.lse.ac.uk/middle-east-centre/events/2020/kuwait-goes-to-the-polls.

'An Historic Glimpse', *Ministry of Electricity and Water, State of Kuwait*, 2014, http://www.mew.gov.kw/?com=content&id=73# (Arabic).

Beaugrand, Claire, 'Biduns in the Face of Radicalization in Kuwait', *Arab Gulf States Institute in Washington*, 18 August 2015, http://www.agsiw.org/biduns-in-the-face-of-radicalization-in-kuwait/.

'Car Bomber Fails in Attempt to Kill Leader of Kuwait', *New York Times*, 26 May 1985, http://www.nytimes.com/1985/05/26/world/car-bomber-fails-in-attempt-to-kill-leader-of-kuwait.html.

Champion, Marc, 'Qatar's Departure from OPEC Suggests Gulf Rights is Here to Stay', *Bloomberg*, 3 December 2018, https://www.bloomberg.com/news/articles/2018-12-03/qatar-s-departure-from-opec-suggests-gulf-rift-is-here-to-stay.

Dahle, Stephanie, 'Weddings in Oman: Traditional and Modern', *Forbes*, 22 February 2011, http://www.forbes.com/sites/stephaniedahle/2011/02/22/weddings-in-oman-traditional-and-modern/#4efb04a53ef3.

'Decree for Establishing the Supreme Petroleum Council (26 August, 1974)', *Ministry of Oil, State of Kuwait*, http://www.moo.gov.kw/About-Us/Ministry-Decrees/Decree-for-Establishing-the-Supreme-Petroleum-Coun.aspx.

'Decision of the Emir of the State of Qatar Number 62 in the Year 2004 Renewing the Membership of Some Members of the Shura Council and Appointment of New Members to the Council', *Al-Meezan Qatar Legal Portal*, 15 February 2005, http://www.almeezan.qa/LawView.aspx?LawID=5565&language=ar&opt (Arabic).

Diwan, Kristin Smith, 'The Politics of Transgression in Kuwait', *Foreign Policy*, 19 April 2013, http://foreignpolicy.com/2013/04/19/the-politics-of-transgression-in-kuwait/.

Exarhu, Elsa, 'The Majlis Culture in Qatar', *Qatar Tribune*, 12 October 2016, http://qatar-tribune.com/news-details/id/28164.

'Fines, Jail for Illegal Marriages in Oman', *Times of Oman*, 16 July 2018, https://timesofoman.com/article/138251/Oman/340-marriage-law-violations-recorded-in-Oman-last-year.

'Forty Nine Couples Enter Wedlock at Group Wedding Held in Al Khaboura', *Times of Oman*, 22 June 2013, http://timesofoman.com/article/19113/Oman?page=-43.

Hamid, Shadi, 'There aren't Protests in Qatar – So Why Did the Emir Just Announce Elections?', *The Atlantic*, 1 November 2011, https://www.theatlantic.com/international/archive/2011/11/there-arent-protests-in-qatar-so-why-did-the-emir-just-announce-elections/247661/.

Al Haremi, Tariq Ziad, 'Ministry Approves Five Omani Dishdasha Designs', *Times of Oman*, 15 January 2017, https://timesofoman.com/article/100598.

'Head of al-Murrah Tribe Confirms Qatar Revokes Family's Citizenship', *al-Arabiya*, 14 September 2017, http://english.alarabiya.net/en/features/2017/09/14/Head-of-al-Marri-tribe-confirms-Qatar-revokes-family-s-citizenship.html.

'History', *Kahramaa*, https://www.km.com.qa/AboutUs/Pages/History.aspx (accessed 31 July 2018).

'History', *Sultanate of Oman Ministry of Housing*, https://eservices.housing.gov.om/eng/Pages/History.aspx (accessed 23 July 2018).

'Human Rights Violations in Qatar: Al-Ghufran Family', *Arab Federation for Human Rights*, February 2018, http://arabfhr.org/wp-content/uploads/2018/03/Qatar-Ghufran-Feb-2018-Final.pdf.

'I'm Qatari, and I want to be able to decide for myself who I marry', *Doha News*, 8 November 2016, https://dohanews.co/im-qatari-want-able-decide-marry/.

'Introduction to OPWP', *OmanPRP.com*, http://www.omanpwp.com/About.aspx#1opwp.

Izzak, B., 'Cabinet Sworn in with 7 Ruling Family Members', *Kuwait Times*, 4 August 2013, http://news.kuwaittimes.net/cabinet-sworn-in-with-7-ruling-family-members/.

_____, 'Lawmakers Reject Proposed Measures to Reduce Welfare – New Anti-Corruption Law to be Approved on Jan 12', *Kuwait Times*, 27 December 2015, http://news.kuwaittimes.net/website/lawmakers-reject-proposed-measures-to-reduce-welfare/.

'Judicial System of Kuwait', *Abdul Razzaq Abdullah & Partners*, http://www.arazzaqlaw.com/judicial-system-of-kuwait/.

Khan, Maryam, 'From Access to Success: The Story of Oman's School Education System', *Muscat Daily*, 18 November 2013, https://www.muscatdaily.com/Archive/Oman/From-access-to-success-The-story-of-Oman-s-school-education-system-2pri.

Kirkpatrick, David D., and Sheera Frankel, 'Hacking in Qatar Highlights a Shift Toward Espionage-for-Hire', *New York Times*, 8 June 2017, https://www.nytimes.com/2017/06/08/world/middleeast/qatar-cyberattack-espionage-for-hire.html.

'Kuwait', *CIA World Factbook*, https://www.cia.gov/library/publications/the-world-factbook/geos/ku.html (accessed 6 October 2014).

'Kuwait', *FAO Corporate Document Repository*, http://www.fao.org/docrep/W4356E/w4356e0g.htm (accessed 8 January 2015).

'Kuwait', *Freedom House*, 2009, https://freedomhouse.org/report/freedom-world/2009/kuwait.

'Kuwait: National Assembly Announces Vacancy of Two Convicted MPs' Seats', *Asharq al-Awsat*, 31 January 2019, https://aawsat.com/english/home/article/1570261/kuwait-national-assembly-announces-vacancy-two-convicted-mps-seats.

'Kuwaiti Ruler Grants $4 Bln, Free Food to Citizens', *al-Arabiya*, 17 January 2011, https://english.alarabiya.net/articles/2011/01/17/133805.html.

'Law No. 2 of 1961 on the Qatari Nationality (repealed)', *Qatar Legal Portal*, http://www.almeezan.qa/LawView.aspx?opt&LawID=2578&language=en (accessed 26 July 2018).

'Legislation on Use of Water in Agriculture: Iran', *Library of Congress*, 1 May 2015, http://www.loc.gov/law/help/water-law/iran.php.

'Maj. General Siad Barre', *Harvard Divinity School Religious Literacy Project*, https://rlp.hds.harvard.edu/faq/maj-general-siad-barre.

'Majlis, a Cultural and Social Space', *UNESCO Intangible Cultural Heritage*, 2015, https://ich.unesco.org/en/RL/majlis-a-cultural-and-social-space-01076.

McGinley, Shane, 'Qatar Sets up Corruption Watchdog for State Agencies', *Arabian Business*, 30 November 2011, https://www.arabianbusiness.com/qatar-sets-up-corruption-watchdog-for-state-agencies-432769.html.

Miller, Judith, 'War in the Gulf: The Royal Family; Kuwait's Joy Tempered by Rift Over Absolutism', *New York Times*, 28 February 1991, http://www.nytimes.com/1991/02/28/world/war-in-the-gulf-the-royal-family-kuwait-s-joy-tempered-by-rift-over-absolutism.html.

Mirgani, Suzi, 'Strengthening the Family in Qatar: Challenges and Required Actions', *Georgetown University Qatar Center for International and Regional Studies*, May 2015, https://cirs.georgetown.edu/community-outreach/strengthening-family-qatar-challenges-and-required-actions.

'MOCI Warns Against Altering Traditional Omani Attire', *Muscat Daily*, 3 July 2016, http://www.muscatdaily.com/Archive/Oman/MoCI-warns-against-altering-traditional-Omani-attire-4r4b.

al-Mokhaizim, Sara, 'Kuwait Marks over 100 Years of Introducing "Electricity"', *Arab Times*, 6 April 2018, http://www.arabtimesonline.com/news/kuwait-marks-over-100-yrs-of-introducing-electricity/.

al-Mubailesh, Khalid, 'Kuwaiti Families in the Old Neighborhoods and Quarters', *KuwaitPast.com*, 2007 (Arabic).

'Muhammed bin Saud [1744–1765]'," *GlobalSecurity.org*, http://www.globalscurity.org/military/world/gulf/muhammad-bin-saud.htm.

al-Naimi, Nayla, 'The Morphology of Urban Qatari Homes', *Building Doha*, 7 February 2017, http://sites.northwestern.edu/buildingdoha/2017/02/07/morphology-of-urban-qatari-homes/.

Nasrallah, Tawfiq, 'Oman to Phase Out Water and Electricity Subsidies in 5 Years', *Gulf News*, 21 December 2020, https://gulfnews.com/world/gulf/oman/oman-to-phase-out-water-and-electricity-subsidies-in-5-years-1.1608504634277.

'Nationality Law, 1959', *Refworld*, http://www.refworld.org/docid/3ae6b4ef1c.html.

Noorudeen, Mohd, 'Wasta is Very Much a Part of Qatari Culture', *Qatar Living*, May 2017, https://www.qatarliving.com/life-qatar/posts/wasta-part-culture-qatar.

'Oman', *UNESCO*, 2016, http://en.unesco.org/countries/oman.

'Oman: Omani Citizenship Law (Repealed)', *Gulf Labour Markets, Migration, and Population (GLMM) Programme*, http://gulfmigration.eu/oman-omani-citizenship-law-repealed/ (accessed 25 July 2018).

'Oman Police Kill Two Protestors', *Reuters*, 27 February 2011, http://www.reuters.com/article/us-oman-protests-idUSTRE71Q0U420110227.

'Public Prosecution Issues Statement concerning Tribal Fora or Gatherings and this is the Text', *Atheer.com*, 8 May 2018, https://ath.re/2I7Z4Vm (Arabic).

al-Qalesh, Ruqaya, 'Kuwaitis Practiced Pearl Diving for Livelihood, Bearing Risks, Hardships', *Kuwait News Agency*, 24 August 2013, https://www.kuna.net.kw/ArticleDetails.aspx?id=2329735&language=en.

'Qatar', *Institute on Statelessness and Inclusion, Rights Realization Centre & Global Campaign for Equal Nationality Rights*, 4 October 2019, http://www.institutesi.org/UPR33_Qatar.pdf.

'Qatar Appoints Four Women to Shura Council', *Al-Jazeera*, 9 November 2017, https://www.aljazeera.com/news/2017/11/qatar-appoints-women-shura-council-171109165044169.html.

'Qatar General Electricity & Water Corporation: Adapting Infrastructure for Changing Demands', *IndustryME*, 20 February 2016, https://industry-me.com/features/infrastructure/qatar-general-electricity-water-corporation-adapting-infrastructure-for-changing-demands/.

'Qatari Tribe Accuses Authorities of Systematic Repression', *Gulf News*, 18 September 2017, https://gulfnews.com/news/gulf/qatar/qatar-crisis/qatari-tribe-accuses-authorities-of-systematic-repression-1.2092012.

Reidel, Bruce, 'After Qaboos, Who Will be Oman's Next Sultan?', *al-Monitor*, 25 January 2015, http://www.al-monitor.com/pulse/originals/2015/01/oman-abdullah-qaboos-succession-power-yemen.html.

'Report on Violations of the Minority Rights of the Al Tuwaiya People in Oman', *UN Office of the High Commissioner on Human Rights*, 2011, http://lib.ohchr.org/HRBodies/UPR/Documents/Session10/OM/TDF_TamkeenDevelopmentFoundation_eng.pdf.

'Royal Decree No 38/2014: Promulgating the Omani Citizenship Law', *Official Gazette*, no. 1066, http://www.refworld.org/pdfid/58dcfe444.pdf.

Scott, Victoria, 'Managing Water Supply a Key Challenge Facing Qatar, Expert Says', *Doha News*, 26 November 2013, http://dohanews.co/managing-water-supply-a-key-challenge-facing-qatar-expert-says/.

al Shaibany, Saleh, 'Oman's Historic Homes Under Threat', *The National*, 11 January 2010, http://www.thenational.ae/news/world/middle-east/omans-historic-homes-under-threat.

_____, 'Sultan Qaboos Fires Oman's Police Chief', *The National*, 15 March 2011, http://www.thenational.ae/news/world/middle-east/sultan-qaboos-fires-omans-police-chief.

'Smooth Qatar Handover Rooted in Turbulent Past of "Father Emir"', *Reuters*, 3 July 2013, https://www.voanews.com/a/smooth-qatar-handover-rooted-in-turbulent-past-of-father-emir/1694301.html.

'Sultan's Decree No. 116/2011: Promulgates Municipal Councils Law', *Muscat Municipal Council*, 2011, https://www.mmc.gov.om/Pages.aspx?PAID=3&MID=13&PGID=8.

Teller, Matthew, 'The Pearl Fishers of Arabia', *BBC News*, 15 November 2014, https://www.bbc.com/news/blogs-magazine-monitor-30042226.

Al Thani, Khalid, 'The Development of Qatar Over the Past Few Decades', *The Peninsula*, 16 November 2017, https://www.thepeninsulaqatar.com/article/16/11/2017/The-development-of-Qatar-over-the-past-few-decades.

'The Bedoons of Kuwait: Citizens Without Citizenship', *Human Rights Watch*, August 1995, https://www.hrw.org/reports/1995/Kuwait.htm.

Toumi, Habib, 'Kuwait's Highest Court Upholds Two-Year Jail for Al Barrak', *Gulf News*, 18 May 2015, http://gulfnews.com/news/gulf/kuwait/kuwait-s-highest-court-upholds-two-year-jail-for-al-barrak-1.1513094.

'Tribal Families in Qatar', *Harvard Divinity School Religious Liberty Project*, https://rlp.hds.harvard.edu/faq/tribal-families-qatar.

'Tribal Leaders Re-Affirm Allegiance to HH Amir, Reject Violence', *Kuwait News Agency (KUNA)*, 21 October 2012, https://www.kuna.net.kw/ArticleDetails.aspx?id=2269731&Language=en.

Ulrichsen, Kristian Coates, 'Kuwait; Political Crisis at Critical Juncture', *BBC*, 23 October 2012, http://www.bbc.com/news/world-middle-east-20026581.

____, 'Qatar and the Arab Spring: Policy Drivers and Regional Implications', *Carnegie Endowment for International Peace*, 24 September 2014, https://carnegieendowment.org/2014/09/24/qatar-and-arab-spring-policy-drivers-and-regional-implications-pub-56723.

Vaidya, Sunil K., 'Conserving Water', *Gulf News*, 11 November 2006, http://gulfnews.com/news/gulf/oman/conserving-water-1.265209.

'Water and Desalination', *Hukoomi – Qatar e-Government*, http://portal.www.gov.qa/wps/portal/topics/Environment+and+Natural+Resources/Water+and+Desalination.

Weiner, Scott, 'The Muscat Commute: A Young Generation's Journey Between Tradition and Modernity', *Arab Gulf States Institute in Washington*, 18 June 2015, http://www.agsiw.org/the-muscat-commute-a-young-generations-journey-between-tradition-and-modernity/.

INDEX

Printed and bound by CPI Group (UK) Ltd, Croydon, CR0 4YY

06/04/2025

01841386-0002